"Despite significant differences betv
philosophy, the nonjudgmental cultiv.
jectivity known in existential therapy as the *phenomenological method* is strikingly
similar to the traditional practices of meditation and mindfulness intrinsic to the
teachings of Zen Buddhism and, as this volume emphasizes in particular, the
Taoism of Lao-Tzi and, later, Chuang-Tzu (Zhuangzi). Tragically, psychotherapy
today has become enamored with a hypermedicalized, materialistic, heavily
pharmacological, strictly symptom-focused, intervention-driven, manualized
approach designed to rapidly dampen down what renowned existential therapist
Rollo May referred to as the *daimonic*. Most therapists these days are taught to
see their role (and themselves) as being little more than technicians, tasked with
reducing, "treating" or "curing" the confusion and suffering of those seeking
their assistance by rotely applying predetermined techniques. In ways not unlike
Alan Watts' *Psychotherapy East and West*, this diverse collection of essays, expertly
edited by Dr. Yang, demonstrates the inherent philosophical intersection existing
between ancient Taoism and the improvisational practice of contemporary existential therapy, offering an alternative view of how clinicians can more creatively
and effectively encourage clients or patients to find their own way in life. While
there is certainly value in Western treatment methods, the philosophically
informed clinical wisdom of existential therapy, like the profound spiritual wisdom of Taoism, provides a timely, much-needed corrective counterbalance to
the alarmingly lopsided and dangerous trend in psychotherapy today."

—**Stephen A. Diamond, PhD**, author, *Anger, Madness,
and the Daimonic: The Psychological Genesis of Violence, Evil, and Creativity*

"This remarkable book applies the wisdom of Zhuangzi, one of the two Taoist
Sages, to contemporary psychotherapy, especially existentially-oriented approaches.
The result is an original synthesis that spans time and place to provide novel per-
spectives that will enrich the therapeutic encounter and enhance its effectiveness."

—**Stanley Krippner, PhD**, professor of psychology, Saybrook University

"In today's rapidly interconnected world, it is essential that scholars try to understand and learn from each other's cultures. In *Existential Psychology and the Way
of the Tao: Meditations on the Writings of Zhuangzi*, psychologist Mark Yang has
done just that. As a dual resident of both China and the United States, Dr. Yang
is able to relate Western existential psychology to Taoist concepts, and translate
this understanding into clear clinical applications. His respect for ancient indigenous philosophies aligned with Western psychology makes a valuable contribu-
tion to the international practice of psychology."

—**Ilene A. Serlin, PhD, BC-DMT**, fellow, past-president, Society for
Humanistic Studies of the American Psychological Association; associated
distinguished professor of integral and transpersonal psychology,
California Institute of Integral Studies; editorial board, *The Humanistic
Psychologist* and the *Journal of Humanistic Psychology*

EXISTENTIAL PSYCHOLOGY AND THE WAY OF THE TAO

In ancient China, a revered Taoist sage named Zhuangzi told many parables. In *Existential Psychology and the Way of the Tao*, a selection of these parables will be featured. Following each parable, an eminent existential psychologist will share a personal and scholarly reflection on the meaning and relevance of the parable for psychotherapy and contemporary life. The major tenets of Zhuangzi's philosophy are featured. Taoist concepts of emptiness, stillness, Wu Wei (i.e., intentional non-intentionality), epistemology, dreams and the nature of reality, character building in the midst of pain, meaning and the centrality of relationships, authenticity, self-care, the freedom that can come from one's willingness to confront death, spiritual freedom, and gradations of therapeutic care are topics highlighted in this book.

Mark C. Yang, a licensed clinical psychologist, is co-editor of *Existential Psychology East-West* Vol. 1 (2009), and has published professional articles on the practice and training of humanistic and existential psychologists in international settings. Dr. Yang is co-founder and director of the International Institute of Existential-Humanistic Psychology, whose mission is to promote humanistic-existential psychology and provide clinical training to mental health professionals in Asia.

EXISTENTIAL PSYCHOLOGY AND THE WAY OF THE TAO

Meditations on the Writings of Zhuangzi

Edited by Mark C. Yang, PsyD

Routledge
Taylor & Francis Group

NEW YORK AND LONDON

First published 2017
by Routledge
711 Third Avenue, New York, NY 10017

and by Routledge
2 Park Square, Milton Park, Abingdon, Oxon, OX14 4RN

Routledge is an imprint of the Taylor & Francis Group, an informa business

Library of Congress Cataloging-in-Publication Data
Names: Yang, Mark C., editor.
Title: Existential psychology and the way of the Tao : meditations on the
    writings of Zhuangzi / edited by Mark C. Yang, PsyD.
Description: New York, NY : Routledge, 2017.
Identifiers: LCCN 2016045130 | ISBN 9781138686991 (hbk) |
    ISBN 9781138687004 (pbk) | ISBN 9781315542485 (ebk)
Subjects: LCSH: Zhuangzi. | Taoism—Psychology. | Existential psychology.
Classification: LCC BF175.4.R44 E95 2017 DDC 299.5/1482—dc23
LC record available at https://lccn.loc.gov/2016045130

ISBN: 978-1-138-68699-1 (hbk)
ISBN: 978-1-138-68700-4 (pbk)
ISBN: 978-1-315-54248-5 (ebk)

Typeset in Bembo
by Apex CoVantage, LLC

CONTENTS

FOREWORD

Back when I was a fledgling psychotherapist, I sometimes felt like a useless tree. All about me I'd see suffering but I had no answer for it. I just stood there, "covered with knots and gnarls," but without any "sap" or "wood" for people to use, without any substance for people to use, or so I thought. I felt this sense of helplessness at the state hospital at which I did my internship, at the psychiatric emergency center at which I began practicing psychotherapy, and at the family mental health clinic at which I began working with parents and children. And then one day I came upon this slim volume called the *Tao Te Ching*, and my outlook transformed. I spent many a day absorbing that book and feeding off its encouraging message. What it basically said to me was that we are all like useless trees at times, we all feel small and without power, but what at first looks powerless may indeed be more powerful than the most flourishing oak, to continue the analogy. For while the oak seems to have great strength, copious nutrients, and plentiful wood, it can also get quickly hacked—and if its sole purpose is to be a towering bundle of riches for greedy consumers, it surely will not endure. It may provide quick fixes and fleeting highs, but it probably will not provide what that "useless tree," with its gnarls and knots, can provide— which is comfort and shade, respite for the weary, and long-lasting support.

While the metaphor of the useless tree was a later interpretation of the *Tao Te Ching* by Zhuangzi, the hero of the present volume, it cleaves very close to what I absorbed and was profoundly grateful for in my reading of Lao Tzi's original rendering. For in that little book, I learned that to be small and humble can clear the way for expansive new insights and effective actions—precisely by *not* acting in the conventional sense. I learned in short that being a useless tree was in a striking sense not useless at all; that providing shade and comfort, or what I would now term "presence" to my clients, was not useless at all, and that simply "being with" both myself and my clients at times of great trial was perhaps the most powerful form of "use" that has yet been discovered. Paradoxically, "being with" our fragility can lead to our awareness of the "more" of who we are, or as I have put it elsewhere, the "awesomeness" of who we are; and that the combination of the two constitutes our vitality.

In this volume, Mark C. Yang and his colleagues have done a remarkable service in their explication of these principles. Over the course of fourteen chapters, they unpack the power of Zhuangzi's wisdom, as well as awe-based wisdom across the millennia. They also show how arduously we in the West have attempted to counter that wisdom, but to little avail—and the latest psychotherapy outcome research is a sterling example of that contention. No matter how hard we in the calculative world have attempted to highlight technical "action" as therapeutically effective, we are continually tossed back to Zhuangzi's wisdom. And what we have begrudgingly learned is that it is not chiefly the technique (or program) that heals, but the "shade and comfort of the tree," the therapist's presence, that provides the underlying sustenance. This book is a wonderful retrieval of that ancient insight.

Kirk Schneider, Ph.D.
Adjunct Faculty, Saybrook University and
Teachers College, Columbia University
Founding Member, Existential-Humanistic Institute

CONTRIBUTORS

Richard Bargdill, Ph.D., received his Ph.D. in clinical psychology from the Existential Psychology program at Duquesne University in Pittsburgh, PA. His dissertation was on people's experiences of habitual boredom. He currently teaches at the Virginia Commonwealth University after spending a decade at Saint Francis University in Loretto, PA. He is the author of *An Artist's Thought Book: Intriguing Thoughts about the Artistic Process.* He is also editor and co-editor of two upcoming books: *A History of Psychology's Good Life* and *Introduction to Humanistic Psychology: A Supplemental Text.* In addition, he has served as secretary, membership chair, and member-at-large for The Society for Humanistic Psychology, which is Division 32 of the American Psychological Association. Finally, he has won awards for his very short poems and for some of his visual artwork. His sculpture titled "I'm a tree chopped down everyday" was awarded first place at the official state art show in Pennsylvania. Recently, he had both a painting and a poem appear in *Stay Awhile: Poetic Narratives on Multiculturalism and Diversity.*

Rodger Broomé is an assistant professor at Utah Valley University teaching in the emergency services. He is a retired fire battalion chief and fire marshal who was responsible for fire code enforcement, community safety and development, and administrating the fire investigations team. He began his public safety career as a police officer where he served as a patrol officer for seven years. As a police officer, he worked as a field training officer, medic on the SWAT team, and lead arson investigator. His education includes undergraduate degrees in criminal justice, fire science, and psychology. Afterwards, he graduated from Saybrook University in San Francisco, California, with a master's and a doctorate degree in psychology. His research interests are in public safety and emergency worker psychology. Researched topics include: police firearms training, police vehicle pursuits, police shootings, firefighters' building collapse survival, firefighter psychomotor training methods, and police dispatcher stress. He has been a volunteer member of the Utah Critical Incident Stress Management program since 2005 and is currently a mental health consultant to the Provo City Police, Utah. He still volunteers as a police patrol officer on a part-time basis.

Trent Claypool is an American Licensed Clinical Psychologist in the state of Colorado. He is a co-founder and the Director of Marketing of the International Institute of Existential-Humanistic Psychology (http://www.iiehp.org). He also works full time as a staff psychologist at the University of Colorado at Colorado Springs, where he provides psychotherapy, psychological testing, and clinical supervision; he also operates his own private practice. He has served as the CE Chair for the Society for Humanistic Psychology, Division 32 of the American Psychological Association. His clinical specialties include treatment of eating disorders, treatment of traumatic stress, and evaluation of learning disorders. He was born in Wyoming and currently resides in Colorado Springs, Colorado with his wife and daughter.

Erik Craig is a licensed psychologist in private practice in Santa Fe, New Mexico. He has been studying, teaching, and practicing humanistic and existential psychology and psychotherapy for well over forty years, having studied intensively for many years each with such influential existential thinkers and practitioners as Medard Boss, Clark Moustakas, and Paul Stern. He has held lengthy full-time graduate faculty positions in psychology at Assumption College, University of New Mexico, and Pacifica Graduate Institute. Most recently he spent ten years studying Tao Psychotherapy with its founder, Rhee Dongshick in Korea. His primary interest is in developing phenomenological, hermeneutic grounds for understanding critical issues in psychological theory, research, and practice with the hope of achieving a comprehensive approach to existential depth psychology and psychotherapy. As an internationally regarded independent scholar, practitioner, lecturer, and workshop leader in the fields of humanistic psychology, existential analysis, and psychotherapy, as well as the analysis of dreams in personal and professional life, he has taught, trained, and lectured worldwide. He has authored nearly fifty articles and is editor of two special groundbreaking issues of *The Humanistic Psychologist* entitled "Psychotherapy for Freedom: The Daseinsanalytic Way in Psychology and Psychoanalysis" (1988) and "Depth, Death and Dialogue: New Inquiries in Existential Depth Psychotherapy" (2008). Erik is currently president of the New Mexico Psychoanalytic Society, as well as a past president of APA's Society for Humanistic Psychology and the International Association for the Study of Dreams. In 2015 he received the Rollo May Heritage Award from APA's Society for Humanistic Psychology for independent and outstanding pursuit of new frontiers in humanistic psychology. You may contact Erik at 113 Camino Escondido, #3, Santa Fe, NM 87501 or at DrErikCraig@aol.com.

Jason Dias is a novelist in Colorado Springs, Colorado. He was born in the United States but grew up in England, returning to America as a young man. In addition to writing, he teaches psychology to the underserved at his local community college as well as to graduate students at Saybrook University. He enjoys traveling to teach and learn more about existential psychology. His author page can be found at http://www.amazon.com/Jason-Dias/e/B00K2EQQIY/ref=ntt_athr_dp_pel_1

Todd DuBose is a full professor at The Chicago School of Professional Psychology, where he is the Course Stream Coordinator for the Existential-Humanistic orientation. He is also a licensed clinical psychologist in private practice. He holds degrees in philosophy, religion, and psychology, and is interested in the integration of contemporary Continental philosophy of religion and human science psychology. Specifically, his specialization is in existential-hermeneutical-phenomenological care for persons experiencing hopelessness or meaninglessness within life situations that are unwanted, unchangeable, irreversible, incurable, or unrelenting. He has various multi-disciplinary, peer-reviewed publications and supervises, consults, and presents at local, national, and international venues, such as in the Czech Republic, Great Britain, Canada, Hungary, Belgium, Greece, and China. He appreciates the gift of dialogue and friendship across countries, seas, and cultures, especially the lifelong project of discovering what it means to be a human be-ing in our shared existence.

David N. Elkins is a licensed clinical psychologist and a professor emeritus of psychology in the Graduate School of Education and Psychology at Pepperdine University, where he taught for thirty years. He is a fellow of the American Psychological Association (APA) and has served twice as president of Division 32, Society for Humanistic Psychology of APA. He was selected by Division 32 to receive the Mike Arons/Mark Stern award for lifetime service to the division. He is on the board of editors of three professional journals and has served as a board member of the Association for Humanistic Psychology (AHP). Dr. Elkins has authored many journal articles and three books. In 2009, he published *Humanistic Psychology: A Clinical Manifesto: A Critique of Clinical Psychology and the Need for Progressive Alternatives (University of the Rockies Press)*. His most recent book is titled *The Human Elements of Psychotherapy: A Nonmedical Model of Emotional Healing* (in press, APA, 2015). Dr. Elkins has also published two feature articles in *Psychology Today* magazine and has been interviewed on National Public Radio. He lives in Carefree, Arizona with his wife, Sara, and their little Yorkie dog named Peanuts.

Louis Hoffman is an executive faculty member and director of the Existential, Humanistic, and Transpersonal Psychology Specialization at Saybrook University in San Francisco. He is a past-president of the Society of Humanistic Psychology, a division of the American Psychological Association, and author of seven books, including *Existential Psychology East-West*. He serves on the editorial board of several journals, including *The Humanistic Psychologist*, *The Journal of Humanistic Psychology*, *PsycCRITIQUES: APA Review of Books*, and *Janus Head*. An avid writer, he has published numerous book chapters and journal articles on a range of topics including existential and humanistic therapy, international psychology, diversity issues in psychology, poetry and therapy, and philosophical issues in psychology. As a licensed psychologist, Dr. Hoffman has many years of clinical experience providing therapy, supervision, and psychological assessments. Dr. Hoffman is active conducting trainings, giving conference presentations and lectures, and teaching courses in various countries around the world.

Li Yun, who was born in June, 1992, was obtaining her master's degree at the City University of Macau at the time of the book's publication. Her main research interests include moral psychology, criminal psychology, and forensic psychology. Her previous publications include "The Role of Top-down Attentional Control Setting in Attentional Capture" in *The Journal of Psychology*.

Michael Moats describes himself (first and foremost) as a father, a husband, and a friend, and he understands the value of relationships in life and in the therapy room. His passion as a clinical psychologist lies in working with clients who are learning to redefine their lives and create new meaning, especially those dealing with grief and loss in its many forms (i.e., death, divorce, job loss, recent move, natural disaster, war.) He was raised in a rural area, in which family and community were an important part of his cultural heritage. However, racism was also a part of this community. Struggle, challenge, curiosity, and death were all experiences that would set him on a path that he did not understand until later in his life. Time and time again, it has been relationships that have proven to be the most valuable and useful cornerstone in providing his life-changing encounters. It is only through these relationships that he has found his greatest accomplishments, including seeing the person beyond the class, color, belief, or whatever other domain society tends to use to create separation versus flavor. Along with teaching cultural diversity at the college level, his research interests include a qualitative, cross-cultural study (China and the United States) that investigated meaning making and the lessons learned through loss, as well as continuing to dialogue internationally to contribute to a more rounded perspective within the global psychological community. Additionally, he is a co-founder of the International Institute of Existential-Humanistic Psychology and a published poet and author of various book chapters and articles.

Jennifer Tam is a licensed psychologist in private practice in New York. She has been a passionate advocate for the use of the experiential and creative modalities in enhancing people's ability to tell and re-tell personal stories of depth through her work as a drama therapist and clinical psychologist. She received her MA in drama therapy at New York University, and PsyD in clinical psychology at Alliant International University. She has received training in existential-humanistic psychology from the International Institute of Existential-Humanistic Psychology. She focuses her clinical work upon creating a safe and creative space to access the potential within human hearts.

Wu Fei is a professor at Xuhui Institute of Education in Shanghai, China. She is also a licensed psychotherapist by training and a licensing examiner for the Chinese National Board of Psychology. Her research interests involve the integration of Chinese traditional culture and indigenous psychological approaches with the practice of existential-humanistic psychology. She has also developed and lectured courses in teachers' psychological adjustment and personal growth.

Doreen Xuekang Deng is a training therapist in the China-American Psychoanalytic Alliance (CAPA) program at the time of the publication of this book. She began her second career as a mental health professional in 2012. She graduated from Beijing University in 1992 with a BA in international politics. She went on to study for and graduated with an MBA in 2003. She is a member of the translation team for CAPA and translated *Standing in the Spaces: Essays on Clinical Process Trauma and Dissociation* (awaiting publication) by Philip M. Bromberg, as well as *Confucius on Psychological Peace and Joy* by Meili Pinto (not yet published).

Mark C. Yang is a licensed clinical psychologist and co-founder and director of the International Institute of Existential-Humanistic Psychology (http://www.iiehp.org), whose mission is to promote humanistic-existential psychology and provide counseling skills training to mental health professionals in Asia. He is also an adjunct professor, the Director of the Existential-Humanistic Programs in Asia, and the Co-Director of the International Psychology Certificate Program at Saybrook University (www.saybrook.edu). He is actively involved in the training and supervision of psychology students from the humanistic-existential perspective throughout Asia. His professional interests include existential psychology, individual and group psychotherapy, grief and bereavement counseling, legal and ethical issues in clinical practice, and cross-cultural psychology. He was born in Taiwan and immigrated with his family to the United States when he was nine years old.

Yang Shaogang is a professor of psychology and the Director of the Institute of Mental Health Education at the South China Business College, Guangdong

University of Foreign Studies. He is a fellow member of the Division of Social Psychology and the Division of Family Education at the Chinese Psychological Association and the Chinese Educational Association, respectively. He is also actively involved in a number of local psychological and educational societies in Guangdong Province. He has published various research articles and written and translated numerous books focusing on the areas of moral development and humanistic-existential psychology. For more than thirty years, he has dedicated his life to teaching in the areas of general psychology, educational psychology, moral education psychology, history of Western psychology, cognitive psychology, social psychology, organizational behavior, and professional English of psychology.

Zhen Shiyan graduated from the Department of Psychology at East China Normal University. He is an editor at Anhui People's Publishing House, a part-time clinical psychologist, and a council member of the Anhui Psychological Counseling Association. His professional interests include Chinese culture, existential psychology, counseling, and psychotherapy. He is a big fan of Rollo May and Carl Rogers, and thus popularizing existential-humanistic psychology in China. He is co-editor of the Chinese editions of *The Paradoxical Self, Rediscovery of Awe, Existential-Integrative Psychotherapy*, and *The Handbook of Humanistic Psychology* by Kirk Schneider. He is also co-translator of the Chinese edition of *Existential-Humanistic Therapy, Career Counseling, and Reality Therapy*. He is a movie buff and recently completed a Chinese book about movies and psychology titled *The Application of Movies in Psychotherapy*.

Lihua Yang is a Chinese licensed clinical psychologist and a research assistant in Tongji University. His professional interests include existential psychology, Chinese culture, psychoanalysis, and self-psychology. He is the translator of the Chinese edition of *Getting Control of Your Anger, Triumph over Shyness, and Our Inner Conflicts*.

PREFACE

My studies in existential psychology have led me back to my own Chinese roots to study the timeless teachings of the Chinese existential and Taoist sages, Lao Tzi and Zhuangzi. Their teachings have deepened my understanding of existence and helped me to offer more incisive and illuminating explanations and descriptions of the beauty of the existential approach within psychology. For me, existential psychology is not just a psychological school of thought but a way of life. Yet I and countless others have consistently struggled to articulate and teach this approach to our students and colleagues. One reason for this difficulty I believe is that existential psychology, much like the teachings of Taoist sages, is often mysterious, paradoxical, and difficult to explain in words. As Lao Tzi said, "A way that can be walked is not The Way. A name that can be named is not The Name" (Lao Tzi, 2003, p. 14). So often, the existential approach is criticized and discounted because it cannot be easily explained. And because it cannot be easily learned and adapted, many will say that it is not practical or relevant. Some will go as far as saying that it's useless. This is why I chose to title the opening chapter of this book The Useless Tree. Zhuangzi's parable of the Large Gourd and the Useless Stink Tree[1] gives a penetrating and unapologetic explication of the existential approach. In his terse and challenging way, Zhuangzi confronts those who call something useless simply because they cannot see its usefulness: "Useless? You should worry!" Or in another translation, "Being useless, how could it ever come to grief" (Zhuangzi, 1998, p. 9). After reading this book, it is my hope that you'll come to a better appreciation of the usefulness of being "useless"!

Editing this book has been a labor of love for me. The sharing of the journey in the creation of this book with each author is an important part of what is meaningful to me about this book project. I am fortunate to know each of the contributors personally and seeing their thoughts come alive and their voices come through as they meditated on the writings of Zhuangzi has been both exciting and fulfilling. The Talmud urges us to plant a tree, have a child, and/ or write a book in order to leave something of lasting value behind. Bridging the cultures of the East and West, it is immensely satisfying for me to work on this collective project that is at the same time a collection of such unique voices and perspectives. The Tao embodies both the collective and individual. There are indeed a myriad of ways of embodying the wondrous Tao!

I wish all readers joy and enlightenment as you encounter the wondrous stories of Zhuangzi and the meditations of contemporary existential psychologists. I believe you will discover for yourself that Zhuangzi has an amazing ability to get to the heart of existential issues and to illumine the practice of existential psychotherapy.

Mark C. Yang
September 2015

Note

1 The titles to many of Zhuangzi's parables in this book were created by the editor of this book or borrowed from other writers for easy identification. With the exception of "The Autumn Floods," the title of the seventeenth chapter of the book *Zhuangzi*, these parables are embedded within various chapters of the book *Zhuangzi* and do not have titles of their own.

ACKNOWLEDGMENTS

I would like to acknowledge the following artists for graciously contributing their artful interpretations of Zhuangzi's various parables found in each chapter of the book. A special thanks goes to Dr. Rich Bargdill who recruited all of the artists listed here below:

Dr. Richard Bargdill (Chapter 1)
Julia Brown (Chapter 2)
Anna Chiara (Chapter 3)
Trish Vernazza (Chapter 4)
Natalia Mello (Chapter 5)
Yvette Lyons (Chapter 6)
Nesreen Frost (Chapter 7)
Leah Pritchard (Chapter 8)
Jyl Anais Ion (Chapter 9)
Gina Belton (Chapter 10)
Robin Good (Chapter 11)
Lisa Vallejos (Chapter 12)
Mona Elsayed (Chapter 13)
Jimmy Hernandez (Chapter 14)

OVERVIEW OF THE BOOK

As you can see from the table of contents, the book is organized into four sections according to their themes. The last section of this book is focused on "The Autumn Floods," Chapter 17 in the book of *Zhuangzi,* which is considered by many to be an excellent summary of many of Zhuangzi's most important ideas. Given its prominence, a majority portion of this seminal chapter from *Zhuangzi* is included at the beginning of this section for the reader's ease of reference. In addition, I've also included a short introduction to each of the chapters below in case you wanted a quick overview of the book.

Background on Zhuangzi

Scholars believe that the core of Zhuangzi's writings was originally composed in the latter half of the fourth century B.C.E., but the text as a whole was not completed until the end of the second century B.C.E. (Zhuangzi, 1998). This period was known as the Warring States Period, also called the period of the Contending Kingdoms (475–221 B.C.). In spite of the political disruptions and the social chaos of this period, intellectually this was by far the most exciting and lively era in the whole of Chinese history. This period can be compared to the classical period of the Hellenistic society. Nomadic philosophers wandered through the land vying for the favor of any ruler who might be willing to put their ideas into practice. These times of feuding ideologies are not dissimilar to our current debates about empirically based practices. The different sages vying for the attention of the masters of states are similar to the various schools and sub-schools within psychology battling for acceptance and validation within the overall profession. The debates in Zhuangzi's times were hotly contested and these sages were not above making fun of each other at the other's expense.

This accounts for the biting nature of some of these stories. Think about it. Who can claim to *encompass the beauty of heaven and earth exclusively* (an arrogant and foolish claim on the part of the Earl of the Yellow River in the chapter on the Autumn Floods) or to corner the market on the efficacy of psychotherapy? But this is exactly the spirit of some of the arguments coming from those who would limit the definitions of what is considered "empirically based practices." Instead, we will do well to be reminded by Rodger Broomé in his chapter "Humanity's Search for Meaning in Existence: A Taoist Epistemology" (Chapter 4) that "while it is the work of scientist and philosophers to seek knowledge and understanding of the world, we should do so humbly knowing that Truth as it stands is beyond our horizons of thought." From the words of the ancient Taoist sages:

> Then there was great disorder under heaven and the worthies and the sages no longer illuminated it. The Way and virtue were no longer unified and, for the most part, all under heaven narcissistically held to one aspect of them. This may be compared to the ears, eyes, nose, and mouth. They all have that which they illumine but they are not interchangeable. Likewise, the various experts of the hundred schools all have their strong points and those moments when they are useful. Nevertheless, they are neither comprehensive nor inclusive but scholars whose views are partial. When they judge the beauty of heaven and earth, analyze the principles of the myriad things, examine the wholeness of the ancients, few can encompass the beauty of heaven and earth or declare the features of spiritual intelligence. For this reason, the Way of internal sagehood and external kingship has become obscure and unillumined, constrained and unexpressed. But all men under heaven, because of their individual desires in these matters, devise their own theories. How sad that the hundred schools go along with their own ways without turning back so that they will of necessity never join together! The students of later generations have unfortunately not seen the simplicity of heaven and earth. The techniques of the Way as they were so greatly embodied by the men of antiquity are being sundered by all under heaven.
>
> *(Zhuangzi, 1998, p. 335)*

Additional Background on Zhuangzi

Besides Lao Tzi (circa 571–471 B.C.), many consider the Chinese ancient Taoist literary scholar Zhuangzi (circa 369–286 B.C.) to be the other founder of Chinese Taoism. In the long developmental history of Chinese Taoist philosophy and culture, Zhuangzi is known for his spiritual strength of character, which can be observed in his deep respect for nature and the broad perspective he maintains in the search for spiritual freedom. His collected works entitled *Zhuangzi,* originally composed of fifty-three chapters during the Han Dynasty (202 B.C.–A.D. 220), now contains only thirty-three chapters. This book, with its features of free spirit and gorgeous and colorful characteristics, was regarded as a brilliant, wonderful work among scholars during the Pre-Chin Period (2100–221 B.C.), which spanned Xia (2100–1600 B.C.), Shang (1600–1046 B.C.), and Zhou (1046–256 B.C.) dynasties encapsulating the two glorious eras of Chinese history: The Spring and Autumn (722–481 B.C.) and Warring States Period (475–221 B.C.). The book *Zhuangzi* consists of three parts: Inner Chapters (1–7), Outer Chapters (8–22), and Miscellaneous Chapters (23–33). It is generally acknowledged that the inner chapters were written by Zhuangzi himself and reflected his true inner world, whereas the outer chapters were written by his closest disciples with Zhuangzi's direct blessing. Though very comparable, numerous scholars note that the disciples' writings lacked the fine and ingenious quality that is evident throughout Zhuangzi's original writing. The miscellaneous chapters were written either by his disciples or other Taoist scholars. Though there were deviations from Zhuangzi's original writings, they were minor and sufficiently distinct from the other schools of thought as to merit inclusion in the book *Zhuangzi*, for they make their own significant contributions.[1]

Notes Regarding Translation

As you read the English translations of Zhuangzi's writings derived from multiple authors/translators, please keep in mind that Zhuangzi's collection of parables was written in classical Chinese, which is poetic, terse, and extremely difficult to translate. In the words of Victor Mair, "to render faithfully an extraordinary text like this into a living language such as English or Mandarin requires a stupendous act of transformation, not merely a mechanical translation" (Zhuangzi, 1998, p. xviii). Furthermore, I have chosen to adopt the Pinyin as opposed to the Wade-Giles system of Romanization of Zhuangzi's name. This is because Pinyin is currently the most widely used Romanization of the Chinese language. In the Wade-Giles system of Romanization, Zhuangzi would be translated as Chuang Tzu.

This book includes chapters written in English by authors from the United States, China, and Hong Kong. There were Chinese authors writing in English, which is not their native tongue; and chapters written in Chinese that were translated into English. Having been involved in the training of Asian students for the past decade, I have found a good translator to be rare and extremely valuable. The success of a workshop is entirely in their hands. Good translation is difficult work. It was basically an impossible task to find someone with the combination of the necessary language skills (both strong English and Chinese), psychological knowledge including clinical experience, and a sufficient understanding of Taoism. Being unsuccessful in locating a person with such a unique skill set, I employed a team approach in which I proofread and edited the translator's work to make sure that the English translations of the Chinese text were comprehensible and not overly taxing to read. In doing so, instead of making the translated chapters read like academic English, we did our best to honor the original voice of the Chinese authors as much as possible. I sincerely hope that adding the Chinese chapters in this book helped to bring the East that much closer to the West.

Chapter Introductions

Chapters 1–3: Emptiness, Stillness, and Wu Wei

The first chapter of this book titled "The Useless Tree and the Empty Gourd" is written by the editor himself. This lengthier chapter introduces the parables of The Empty Gourd and The Useless Tree to the readers. Through both parables, the author teaches readers about the utility of uselessness, emptiness, stillness, and non-action. How can a twisted and gnarled stink tree prove to be useful? Zhuangzi suggests that such utilities are best found in the land of waste and desolation, where only the "twisted and deformed" can survive to provide shelter and sanctuary to those struggling in the wasteland.

Jason Dias wrote about the fundamental concept of Wu Wei in his chapter with the same title. In his idiosyncratic way, he teaches us about how to become natural and effortless at being and not-doing in therapy. He helps us to apply Zhuangzi's understanding of stillness, non-intention, and non-action to the practice of existential psychotherapy. Like the sage himself, Dias seamlessly weaves Zhuangzi's parables into his writings while illustrating the moral of the parables with a number of excellent case examples. He reminds us paradoxically that being/becoming ourselves is both the starting and end points of our paths to becoming an effective healer. The readings in existential psychology that he recommends are not so much to teach methods but to open ourselves up to certain stances and attitudes. One of these attitudes is to balance rather than resolve the many paradoxes that we encounter in Taoism: "Paradoxes do not require solution. The solution to a paradox is to grow large enough to contain the various meanings suggested by the problem." Finally, Dias's area of expertise in family therapy is evident in the unique perspective he offers on how to appreciate the Taoist principles underlying some fundamental concepts in family systems.

In Michael Moats's chapter titled "Steadiness in the Midst of Chaos," he explicates how our fear of ubiquitous water is related to our fear of the unknown. We are capable of using almost anything to distance ourselves from the unknown. Through the morals of two of Zhuangzi's parables, Moats explains how we ironically become slaves of and hasten our own demise when we actively run away from our fears. Instead, aligning himself with the teaching of Zhuangzi, Moats encourages us to dive into the water/unknown, for it is only through engagement and struggle that resilience and understanding can be attained. Moats includes an illustrative case where the client initially struggled with and then eventually learned to swim in the dark waters of uncertainty. Finally, Moats offers us an excellent personal example of learning the skill of archery through the concept of Wu Wei, where one achieves action through inaction and intentionality without intention, and how this is related to the process of psychotherapy.

Chapters 4–5: Knowledge and Epistemology

Rodger Broomé presents us with an insightful chapter regarding epistemology, which is well represented by the two questions he was posed with as an undergraduate student in philosophy: "What do you mean?" and "How do you know?" He begins his chapter by challenging his readers to re-examine the relationships between science and philosophy, and knowledge and understanding. He follows this with an excellent illustrative example in regards to speech and language acquisition. I bet you never thought about language being "both the midwife of our ideas while also being the product of our thoughts?" Furthermore, through Zhuangzi's writings about how one searches for the Tao (the parable of How Knowledge Went North, Chapter 22 of *Zhuangzi*), Broomé reminds us that "knowledge and understanding are always on their way toward *Truth* but without having the ability to ever capture it." This shows his deep understanding of the opening statements of Chapter 1 of the *Tao Te Ching*, "The Tao that can be spoken is not the eternal Tao." Broomé's scholarly interest lies within phenomenology and his chapter does an excellent job of relating the work of Edmund Husserl, the father of phenomenology, to Zhuangzi's writings. For example, Broomé introduces readers to the method of imaginative variation within descriptive phenomenology research and relates this important concept to the practice of psychotherapy and how imaginative variation is central to knowing about the Tao. Finally, Broomé ties all of this together by giving us an example of how he helped a law enforcement colleague let go of disturbing thoughts regarding a sexual molestation case that he had investigated. Through the case example, Broomé showed his readers how he engaged in the Wu Wei spirit of non-doing and non-action and helped his colleague to arrive at his own meaningful answers.

Trent Claypool's chapter "Knowledge and Psychotherapy: Lessons from Zhuangzi's Parable 'When Knowledge Went North'" reminds the reader that knowledge must not be equated with competence. Through Zhuangzi's parable of When Knowledge Went North, he distinguishes between blind knowing and wise knowing. He warns the reader of the dangers of the over-reliance upon knowledge and believing that one is "knowledgeable" about the client at the exclusion of client attunement and feedback. Instead, through the teachings of Zhuangzi, Claypool urges us to operate with a humble naïveté about the matters of our clients and adopt an attitude of non-action and not knowing. He distinguishes between three types of practitioners in the known. The first is the expert technician who knows and is always in command of the session. The second is the one who does not know, but pretends to know. In their efforts at pretense, integrity and humanity become lost. Finally, there is the wise practitioner who does not know and does not pretend to know. Because they adopt an attitude of not knowing and non-action, the wise practitioner stays attuned to the client and what is essential in therapy takes place naturally, without premeditation. Claypool ends his chapter with a case example of how maintaining a stance of not-knowing in regards to his client allowed him to help her work through instances of sexual abuse from her past.

Chapters 6–11: Miscellaneous Chapters

Erik Craig's chapter "On the Power of Butterflies: Dreaming, Waking, and the Therapeutical Potential of Nocturnal Beings" tackles the tricky epistemological question of determining the nature of reality. Craig, a contemporary expert on the existential-phenomenological understanding of dreams, describes dreams as an inconvenient reality, a gadfly of the soul. Here Craig mirrors Zhuangzi's playfulness, going so far as to identify the sage as a gadfly, a fox, and a trickster. This in itself will likely pique your interest in savoring this chapter based upon Zhuangzi's famous passage in which he questions whether he is a man dreaming about himself as a butterfly or a butterfly dreaming about himself as a man! In this illuminating chapter, Craig addresses three basic questions with respect to the phenomenon of dreaming and its relation to waking existence: "Are dreams real? What is the difference between our experiences of dreaming and waking, and how are they each related to our lives as a whole? And what is the existential and therapeutic potential of dreaming?" Craig then goes on to argue eloquently that dreaming and waking modes of being are equiprimordial (existing together as equally fundamental) and arise coequally from our one and only existence. He then offers us a transdisciplinary reflection regarding the differences between our waking and dreaming modes of existence. He instructs that paradoxically, while our dreaming worlds are more delimited and preselected, it also brings to our attention that which is most affectively salient or alive. Finally, he offers a persuasive explanation for the personal and therapeutic value of dreaming.

In Richard Bargdill's chapter titled "Master Hui's Grave: To Sharpen Your Character, Rub it up against Something Abrasive," we learn about how death can enlighten us about significant things in our life. He also shares with us how strong friendships, even rivalries, are important in bringing out the best in us. The chapter includes lessons about how our greatest achievements are likely to come from our most difficult journeys, how maturity includes coming to terms with our limitations, and how virtues are developed from the daily discipline of self-reflection and will often require us to rub up against something abrasive.

These are the reminisces of Zhuangzi as he passes by the grave of his longtime rival and friend Master Hui.

In Louis Hoffman's chapter titled "Releasing the Jade, Grasping Meaning," the author introduces us to the power of symbols and myths. He helps the readers to understand how Zhuangzi's parable of The Flight of Lin Hui can be viewed as a myth which gives significance to our existence and helps us make meaning in a senseless world. Hoffman goes on to show us how the rich symbol of the jade in the parable can be understood as representing power and prestige, which also can be conceived of as meaning systems. The critical question then becomes whether all that the jade represents will prove to be a system of meaning that will ultimately sustain. The symbol of the jade is contrasted with that of a child, which epitomizes the centrality of relationships. The parable challenges the reader to examine one's bond with the jade symbol versus one's bond with one's child and friends. One bond is made perfect in calamity while the other dissolved. Hoffman relates this juxtaposition with how the Western world has decentered the centrality of the family and relationships, replacing it with the supreme valuation of the individual and personal happiness. He reminds us that the moral of Zhuangzi's parable is to return us to the centrality of sustaining relationships in our lives. To this end, Hoffman shows us his understanding of what Zhuangzi means when he compares the tastelessness of wise friendships with the sweetness of friendship with fools. He points out that water, while being tasteless, is essential for sustenance while sweet beverages, while enjoyable, can be destructive when overly indulged.

One of the most personal chapters in this book can be attributed to David Elkins, as he shares with readers his personal lifelong lessons regarding authenticity. Through Zhuangzi's parable of a turtle who chooses to live a simple life of "dragging its tail in the mud" rather than sacrifice himself to the altar of fame and veneration, Elkins provides some genuine reflections regarding the question of authenticity and fame and fortune. Elkins organized his chapter around a powerful quote regarding authenticity by the German philosopher Fredrick Nietzsche. Like Nietzsche, he warns us that "all hell will [likely] break loose" if we pursue an authentic existence. Elkins illustrates this warning through numerous examples in his personal life—the most powerful of which is that of his wife, who developed a rare life-threatening autoimmune disease. Through this confrontation with mortality, Elkins shared how he's learned to live in a more authentic fashion. In the end, Elkins offers the readers both inspiration and painful enlightenment as he boldly challenges our romantic notions regarding authenticity.

Jennifer Tam's chapter "Plough Deeply: Cultivating Authentic Living" is another chapter in which the author shares deeply from her own lived experience. Through her own personal odyssey, Tam described how the beginning of her carefree wondering, a main theme within Zhuangzi's writings, was initiated by a strong desire for change; a desire fueled by a courageous and painful confrontation with herself. Through her story, Tam illustrates Zhuangzi's paradoxical principles of gaining through losing, productivity without being productive, and arriving to a better destination without planning or intention. It is evident through her journey that Tam learned many important lessons regarding Zhuangzi's writings about the Tao. One of these lessons was the need for us to plough deeply in cultivating what is nurturing to our souls. Tam shares that ploughing deeply involves turning inward towards our authentic selves and aligning ourselves with the Tao, or the ways of nature. In her own words, "This involves the willingness to delve deeply into whatever is in front of us, the courage to experience the unknown, and the readiness to launch into deep inner journeys. These are the pathways to authentic living." Finally, Tam illustrates such lessons with additional examples of her life including a personal experience with panic attacks, a bold decision to share herself deeply with her classmates, and an awakening trip of confrontation with death and existence through a Malaysian rain forest.

If you want to learn about the usefulness of uselessness, read Zhen Shiyan's chapter about freedom before death. He begins the chapter with an honest examination of the rationale behind his procrastination and how it's related to his doubts about Zhuangzi's teachings. He contrasts Ernest Becker's writings about the Denial of Death and the hero complex and Irvin Yalom's defense against death with Zhuangzi's teachings about how to overcome death anxiety. Through descriptions of Zhuangzi's own eventual death and the death of his wife and friend, Zhen explicates how Zhuangzi rejected a dualistic view of life and death. Instead, Zhuangzi's viewed life and death as natural rhythms of nature and not something worthy of our fears. Zhuangzi goes on further to state that there is pleasure to be found in death, something akin to returning home or a well-deserved rest after a life of labor. Such is the attitude of freedom that Zhuangzi espouses according to Zhen. And following the writings of many existentialists, Zhen shared additional parables by Zhuangzi that teach about how the contemplation of death gives us the wisdom and courage to live authentic lives. Finally, Zhen ends his chapter by explaining Zhuangzi's paradoxical philosophy of the usefulness of uselessness as expressed through two additional parables. Thus, this chapter makes important contributions in explaining the title of this book.

Chapters 12–14: "The Autumn Floods" (Chapter 17 of Zhuangzi)

In the chapter titled "Along the Way to Spiritual Freedom: From Rivers to Seas and Heaven to Tao," Professor Yang Shaogang shares with us how Zhuangzi employs the natural occurrence of the annual Autumn Floods to teach us about spiritual freedom. He argues that spiritual freedom is to be found in the recognition of how wide-ranging and expansive the world is and our humble place within it. Yang helps us to understand how an Earl of the Yellow Sea awakened to existence when he grasped and accepted his limitation upon encountering the vastness and wisdom of the Overlord of the Northern Sea. Just as the Overlord enlightened the Earl, as existential therapists, we are to similarly guide our clients to paradoxically embrace their limitations in order to transcend them in their journeys toward spiritual freedom. How do we accomplish this? Through non-interference, according to Zhuangzi. Non-interference, writes Yang, is about aligning ourselves with the wondrous Tao, the natural order of things. "Having encountered the wonderful Tao, one can know clearly that every single thing in the universe has its own value of existence ontologically, and possesses all its magical effect in accordance with the Tao of existence." If we can accept the fact that the world is uncertain and life incomplete, yet nevertheless everything in the universe still has its own reason for existence, then we can, like the annual Autumn Floods, flow from the river to the sea, from earth to heaven, and finally to the realm of the Tao.

Wu Fei opens her chapter on the Autumn Floods by giving the reader a brief introduction to the setting of this important chapter and how the imagery of water is utilized extensively in Chinese wisdom literature. She breaks up her chapter into four sections. The first section is the lengthiest and discusses how the broadening of one's perspective begins with the knowledge of self and the understanding of one's limitations. She supports her observations with numerous examples of Chinese idioms, and this is decidedly a strength of this chapter. In section two, through the discourse between the River and the Sea, Wu discusses the relativity of existence and the dialectic of things. She teaches that the dimensions of things are not only relative but interdependent; of how thing are often both simultaneously opposing and unitary. She calls this "dialectic unity" and illustrates this beautifully with a number of Chinese idioms, including how dialectic unity is at play in the construction of Chinese characters. Section three is devoted to the theme of having a proper respect for nature and the importance of allowing things to flow naturally. Examples are provided of how the respect for destiny and natural law in Zhuangzi's Taoist thought is foundational to the practice of existential-humanistic psychotherapy. The final section of Wu's chapter presents on the concept of freedom, which is a central tenet to Zhuangzi's writings. She describes how Zhuangzi's inner state of joy and freedom is outwardly manifested in the simple carefree life that he lived. Wu ends the chapter by describing the various ways Zhuangzi may serve as a model for us on how to live a carefree life devoted to freedom and transcendence.

Todd DuBose presents us with a richly philosophic chapter discussing the convergence between Taoism and Western existential-hermeneutical-phenomenological practices of care. He identifies the central theme of Zhuangzi's chapter on the Autumn Floods as relative gradations, which implies the equalization of all things, recognizing "that all sentient being is relative to goal, situation, and function." He explicates for us how Zhuangzi's understanding of vastness and smallness is used to invite humility and displace the centricity from which we view nature and our own beloved paradigms. We are reminded that nature and life do not exist solely for us and does not evolve around us. The same principle of relative gradations is applied to the concept of usefulness, which is the title of this book and the theme of the introductory chapter. DuBose enlightens us that "difference neither means deficient nor exemplary, but simply 'is.'" The implications of relative gradations is translated to the existential-hermeneutical-phenomenological concepts of relative contextualization, radical validation, hermeneutical reframe, compassionate equalization, and horizontalization when applied to therapeutic care. These are highly specialized terms, yet DuBose provides excellent definitions, explanations, and clinical examples of how these Taoist themes and Western existential-hermeneutical-phenomenological concepts are applied in the practice of therapeutic care. Finally, DuBose offers insightful critique and challenges in regards to the implications of radical gradation for the practice of therapeutic care. His critique involves a brief discussion of nihilism and an absolutist position as related to relative gradation. He introduces us to his concept of "radical validation" in challenging us to understand while not colluding, and staying open while not privileging one way of being over another, when practicing therapeutic care. DuBose's critique also challenges the traditions of case presentations, clinical assessments, and empirical, evidence-based best practice in light of relative gradation.

Note

1 This paragraph introducing the background of Zhuangzi the Sage and the book by the same title was written by Professor Yang Shaogang, who also contributed a chapter in this book titled "Along the Way to Spiritual Freedom: From Rivers to Seas and Heaven to Tao."

References

Lao Tzi. (2003). *Tao Te Ching: The definitive edition.* (J. Star, Trans.). New York, NY: Penguin Group.
Zhuangzi. (1998). *Wandering on the way: Early Taoist tales and parables of Chuang Tzu.* (V. Mair, Trans.). Honolulu, HI: University of Hawaii Press.

PART I

Emptiness, Stillness, and Wu Wei

1

THE USELESS TREE AND
THE EMPTY GOURD

Mark C. Yang

FIGURE 1.1 Created by Dr. Richard Bargdill

The image and metaphor of the useless tree was of such importance for Zhuangzi that he wrote two different parables with it as the main symbol. Here are both parables:

The Useless Tree (*Zhuangzi*, Chapter 1)

Master Hui said to Master Chuang, "The King of Wei presented me with the seeds of a large gourd. I planted them and they grew to bear a fruit that could hold five bushels. I filled the gourd with liquid but its walls were not strong enough for me to pick it up. I split the gourd into ladles but their curvature was so slight they wouldn't hold anything. Although the gourd was admittedly of huge capacity, I smashed it to bits because it was useless."

"Sir," said Master Chuang, "It's you who were obtuse about utilizing its bigness. There was a man of Sung who was good at making an ointment for chapped hands. For generations, the family occupation had been to wash silk floss. A stranger who heard about the ointment offered him a hundred pieces of gold for the formula. The man of Sung gathered his clan together and said to them, 'We have been washing silk floss for generations and have earned no more than a few pieces of gold. Now we'll make a hundred pieces of gold in one morning if we sell the technique. Please let me give it to the stranger.' After the stranger obtained the formula, he persuaded the King of Ngwa of its usefulness. Viet embarked on hostilities against Ngwa, so the King of Ngwa appointed the stranger to the command of his fleet. That winter, he fought a naval battle with the forces of Viet and totally defeated them (because his sailor's hands didn't get chapped). The king set aside a portion of land and enfeoffed[1] him there.

"The ability to prevent chapped hands was the same, but one person gained a fief with it while the other couldn't even free himself from washing floss. This is because the uses to which the ointment was put were different. Now you, sir, had a five-bushel gourd. Why didn't you think of tying it on your waist as a big buoy so that you could go floating on the lakes and rivers instead of worrying that it couldn't hold anything because of its shallow curvature? This shows, sir, that you still have brambles for brains!"

Master Hui said to Master Chuang, "I have a big tree people call Stinky Quassia. Its great trunk is so gnarled and knotted that it cannot be measured with an inked line. Its small branches are so twisted and turned that neither compass nor L-Square can be applied to them. It stands next to the road, but carpenters pay no attention to it. Now sir, your words are just like my tree—big, useless, and heeded by no one."

"Sir," said Master Chuang, "are you the only one who hasn't observed a wild cat or a weasel? Crouching down, it lies in wait for its prey. It leaps about east and west, avoiding neither high nor low, until it gets caught in a snare or dies in a net. Then there is the yak, big as the cloud suspended in the sky. It's big, all right, but it can't catch mice. Now you, sir, have a big tree and are bothered by its uselessness. Why don't you plant it in the Never-never Land with its wide open spaces? There you can roam in non-action by its side and sleep carefreely beneath it. Your Stinky Quassia's life will not be cut short by axes, nor will anything else harm it. Being useless, how could it ever come to grief?"

(Zhuangzi, 1998, pp. 7–9)

The Useless Tree II (*Zhuangzi*, Chapter 4)

A carpenter named Shih, who was on his way to Ch'i, came to Bent Shaft. There he saw a chestnut-leaved oak that served as the local shrine. The tree was so big that several thousand head of cattle could take a shade beneath it and it was a hundred spans in circumference. It was so tall that it surveyed the surrounding hills; only above eighty feet were there any branches shooting out from the trunk. It had ten or more limbs from each of which you could make a boat. Those who came to gaze upon it were as numerous as the crowds in a market. The master carpenter paid no attention to it, but kept walking without slowing his pace a bit. After his disciples had had their fill of gazing upon the great tree, they caught up with carpenter Shih and said, "Since we have taken up our axes to follow you, master, we have never seen such marvelous timber as this. Why sir, were you unwilling to look at it, but kept on walking without even slowing down?"

"Enough! Don't talk about it! It's defective wood. A boat made from it would sink. A coffin made from it would rot right away. An implement made from it would break right away. A door made from it would exude resin. A pillar made from it would soon be grub-infested. This tree is worthless. There's nothing you can make from it. That's why it could grow to be so old."

After the carpenter had returned to his own country, the shrine oak appeared to him in a dream saying, "With what tree will you compare me? Will you compare me with those that have fine-grained wood? As for the hawthorn, the pear, the orange, the pomelo, and other fruitiferous trees, once their fruits are ripe, they are torn off, and the trees are thereby abused. The big branches are broken and the smaller branches are snapped. These are trees that make their own lives miserable because of their abilities. Therefore, they cannot finish out the years allotted to them because of the assaults of the worldly. It's the same with all things. But I have sought for a long time to be useless. Now, on the verge of death, I have finally learned what use-lessness really means and that it is of great use to me. If, after all, I had been useful, would I have been able to grow so big? Furthermore, you and I are both things, so why the deuce should you appraise another thing? You're a defective person on the verge of death. What do you know about 'defective wood?'"

When carpenter Shih awoke, he told the dream to his disciples. "If the oak's intention is to be useless, then why does it serve as the local shrine?" they asked.

"Silence! Don't say another word! The oak is merely assuming the guise of a shrine to ward off the curses of those who do not understand it. If it were not a shrine, it would still face the threat of being cut down. Moreover, what the oak is preserving is different from the masses of other trees. If we attempt to understand it on the basis of conventional morality, won't we be far from the point?"

Sir Motley of Southune made an excursion to the Hillock of Shang. There he saw an unusual tree so big that a thousand four-horse chariots would be shaded by its leaves.

"Goodness! What tree is this?" asked Sir Motley. "It must have unusual timber." Looking upward at the smaller branches, however, he saw that they were all twisted and unfit to be beams. Looking downward at the massive trunk, he saw that it was so gnarled as to be unfit for making coffins. If you lick one of its leaves, your mouth will develop ulcerous sores. If you smell its foliage, you fall into a drunken delirium that lasts for three days.

"This tree is truly worthless," said Sir Motley, "and that is why it has grown so large. Ah! The spiritual man is also worthless like this."

In the state of Sung, there is a placed called Chingshih where catalpas, arborvitae, and mulberry trees thrive. Those that are more than a hand's breadth or two around are chopped down by people who are looking for tether posts for their monkeys. Those that are three or four spans in cir-cumference are chopped down by people who are looking for lofty ridgepoles. Those that are seven or eight spans in circumference are chopped down by the families of aristocrats or wealthy merchants who are looking for coffin planks. Therefore, they do not live out the years allotted to them by heaven but die midway under the ax. This is the trouble brought about by having worth. Conversely, in carrying out an exorcistic sacrifice, one cannot present oxen with white foreheads, suckling pigs with upturned snouts, or people with hemorrhoids to the gods of the river. All of this is known by the magus-priests, who consider these creatures to be inauspi-cious. For the same reasons, the spiritual person considers them to be greatly auspicious.

(Zhuangzi, 1998, pp. 37–39)

*Permission to republish material has been granted by University of Hawai'i Press. Zhuangzi, (1998). *Wandering on the Way: Early Taoist Tales and Parables of Chuang Tzu.* (V. Mair, Trans.). Honolulu, HI: University of Hawaii Press.

Tale of the Large Gourd

With the allegorical tale of the Large Gourd, Zhuangzi is warning us of systems and institutions that grow too big, and perhaps too fast, with walls that are not strong enough to carry what it's meant to carry. This theme is addressed in the parable of The Sage and the Thief, Chapter 10 in the book *Zhuangzi*. Zhuangzi warns of the dangers of over-reliance upon systems and dogma and becoming enamored with the size of such systems and institutions. It would be foolish for us to equate utility with size. The important thing is to determine if the walls of the gourd are sufficiently proportionate to its size if we are to carry water, the source of life, or anything of substance within. Growing too big, too fast will render the gourd useless for carrying things of substance. The question becomes, the systems and institutions may be large, but are they carrying anything of substance? Do not mistake size for substance!

Utility of the Gourd

Instead, wisdom lies in recognizing the appropriate utility of the gourd. In regards to this, Zhuangzi shares the story of the secret ointment for preventing chapped hands. The secret lies not only in the ancient ointment formula but also in how the ointment is to be used. In psychotherapeutic practice, we should learn our techniques well, but it's much more important that the techniques be properly applied at the right time. For "the ability to prevent chapped hands was the same, but one person gained a fief with it while the other couldn't even free himself from washing floss" (Zhuangzi, 1998, p. 8). Here, Zhuangzi is reminding us that it is not only about the technique or the formula but how and when it is used. The proper use can set us free. With one's sights set on temporary gain (a hundred pieces of gold), we will forever be stuck with minimal gain. Indeed Wampold (2010), in his meta-analysis of psychotherapeutic research in the past few decades, found that it is much more the within-group difference (difference amongst the therapists) rather than the between-group difference (difference between therapeutic orientations) that accounts for the efficacy of treatment. This suggests that how the therapy is practiced is much more important than which therapeutic orientation is employed. Similarly, James Bugental (1992) warned us about the limitation of therapeutic techniques as well:

> Over the years I have acquired many aids to that search. And I have left beside the road many of those I acquired. Standardized tests, projective techniques, hypnosis, empty chair enactments, role-playing, guided fantasies,

psychoactive substances—all useful, some occasionally used by me still, all limiting even as they were facilitative. They offered, each in its own way, intriguing, even valuable, glimpses of the people with whom I worked. Ultimately though, they made those persons into objects—objects of my study, objects of investigation, objects of the techniques themselves.

I have come to believe that all of these aids to the quest for the true subjectivity are still photographs of wild animals—or at their best, like seeing those animals in a zoo. They show the quarry but without the animating spirit, the action which is its most central, most meaningful characteristics.

(p. 120)

This is a lesson not only to be learned in psychology, but perhaps much more so in the competitive world of business. Which businessman would not crave a fief compared to one hundred pieces of gold? So many businessmen look for that secret formula, leading them to earn more than just a few pieces of gold. And some have succeeded. However, wise are the ones who are able to transform that formula into a revolution. This was accomplished by Steve Jobs and his team who took Toshiba's "formula" of the 1.8 inch diameter portable hard disk and transformed it in ways unimaginable prior to his creation. In one aspect, the iPod was essentially a portable hard disk that Toshiba didn't know what to do with. Interestingly, already on the market was the Nomad Jukebox from Singapore-based Creative Inc. This jukebox-on-the-go was based on the 2.5 inch portable hard disk made by Fujitsu. However, Jobs and his team saw something different. They created a "fief" around this hard disk and built a culture, a revolution, a way of life around a simple hard disk. Now many of us are thinking, why didn't I think of it? So Zhuangzi reminds us that it's about perspective. Whereas many see a large, hollow, useless gourd with weak walls to be smashed, the wise will "go with the flow" and recognize that its inherent utility lies in its emptiness where others see waste and uselessness.

Jobs understood the ways of the Tao and was famous for his Zen approach to design. Below are additional quotes from the iPod creation team members that substantiate Jobs's surrendering himself to the ways of the Tao:

"Steve made some very interesting observations very early on about how this was about navigating content," I've told *The New York Times*. "It was about being very focused and not trying to do too much with the device—which would have been its complication and, therefore, its demise. The enabling features aren't obvious and evident, because the key was getting rid of stuff."

I've told the *Times* that the key to the iPod wasn't sudden flashes of genius, but the design *process*. His design group collaborated closely with manufacturers and engineers, constantly tweaking and refining the design.

"It's not serial," he told the *Times*. "It's not one person passing something on to the next."

"Apple's designers spend 10 percent of their time doing traditional industrial design: coming up with ideas, drawing, making models, brainstorming," he said. "They spend 90 percent of their time working with manufacturing, figuring out how to implement their ideas."

"Most people make the mistake of thinking design is what it looks like," Jobs told the *Times*. "That's not what we think design is. It's not just what it looks like and feels like. Design is how it works."

(Kahney, 2006)

Note the team's focus. The emphasis is upon process, not sudden flashes of genius. The design process was holistic, not serial and reductionistic. It was also a lot of hard work, upholding Benjamin Franklin's famous quote about invention being 10% inspiration and 90% perspiration. Finally, Jobs's gift was his ability to paradoxically balance simplicity with creativity, by doing more with less. Experienced therapists will recognize all of these Taoist principles to be the central tenets of the practice of existential psychotherapy.

Emptiness

It is also worth pointing out that the utility and purpose of the gourd lies in its emptiness. Zhuangzi reminds us again that it is in emptiness that we find utility. Consider Verse 11 of the *Tao Te Ching*, which teaches us about the importance of recognizing the value of emptiness and paying attention to silence:

> *Wu* is nothingness, emptiness, non-existence
> Thirty spokes of a wheel all join at a common hub
>   yet only the hole at the center
>   allows the wheel to spin
>
> Clay is molded to form a cup
>   yet only the space within
>   allows the cup to hold water.
>
> Walls are joined to make a room
>   yet only by cutting out a door and a window
>   can one enter the room and live there.
>
> Thus, when a thing has existence alone
>   it is mere dead-weight
> Only when it has *wu*, does it have life.
>
> (Lao Tzi, 2003, p. 24)

Paradoxically, it is often during the pregnant silences, the empty spaces, in therapy when the most significant movement takes place. This theme is explored more in depth in the chapter titled "Wu Wei" (Chapter 2) written by Jason Dias. Similarly, Rollo May reminds us of the "significance of the pause," which is the title of one of his chapters in his book *Freedom and Destiny* (May, 1981). It is when clients are droning on endlessly about themselves that they are most distant from themselves, reflecting Zhuangzi's teaching that one is perhaps most useless when one appears to be very productive.

Conversely, it is during the pause when the clients and therapists are still and not talking that the most significant movement is taking place. Similarly, James Bugental (1999) instructs us to help clients talk out of themselves instead of talking about themselves—to speak subjectively out of their beings rather than objectively reporting about themselves. We must learn to distinguish this important difference. Similarly, during the process of group therapy, "people's speech and actions are figural events. They give the group form and content. The silences and empty spaces, on the other hand, reveal the group's essential mood, the context for everything that happens. That is the group field" (Heider, 1986, p. 21). Zhuangzi teaches us that we must empty ourselves and learn about the uselessness of noise and the usefulness of emptiness, stillness, and silence. Interestingly, Western ideals place more values on action and substance. "He is a man of substance, a man of action"; whereas Eastern ideals place more significance on emptiness and the non-material. Trent Claypool, in his chapter "Knowledge and Psychotherapy: Lessons from Zhuangzi's Parable 'When Knowledge Went North'" (Chapter 5), explores the same theme when he writes of the practitioner who overcompensates for his insecurities by propping himself up with his numerous accomplishments and qualifications. On the outside, this practitioner looks to be very knowledgeable and an expert technician when in fact, according to Zhuangzi, this is the person who is least in the known. Such are the principles behind Wu Wei, a fundamental concept within Taoism. Readers will find more writings on this central concept of Wu Wei in the chapters written by Jason Dias and Michael Moats (Chapters 2 and 3).

According to Zhuangzi, the most suitable utility for the emptiness of the gourd is for us to take advantage of its buoyancy to go floating down lakes and rivers. The themes of floating, wandering, going with the flow are the central thesis in Zhuangzi's writing. Emptiness or the emptying of our selves allows us to immerse and submit ourselves to life, to destiny, and follow the flow of life symbolized by lakes and rivers. Wu Fei, too, in her chapter on the Autumn Floods (Chapter 13), writes about how the imagery of water is utilized extensively in Chinese wisdom literature. There is much wisdom to be found in water, in nature, if we will simply follow the flow and engage in non-action. Wu Fei and Zhen Shiyan, in his chapter on freedom and death (Chapter 11), also write about the wisdom of having a proper respect for nature and allowing things to flow naturally. They both point out that to wander, to follow the flow, living in a carefree manner which typifies the concept of freedom, is the highest form of wisdom according to Zhuangzi. Likewise, Professor Yang, writing on the same chapter of "The Autumn Floods" (Chapter 12), points out that the Earl of the Yellow River gained wisdom and awakened to his own limited existence in the context of the vast universe when he "flowed down" the river and encountered the vastness of the seas.

In response to being chastised for failing to recognize the utility of the large gourd, Master Hui strikes back and criticizes Zhuangzi's teaching as being "big, useless, and heeded by no one"—critiques often leveled at existential psychology with its abstract, grand, and impractical ideas. A multitude of responses to such critique is the impetus and inspiration for this book. Zhuangzi's response was at once bold and unapologetic. He gives no ground and instead offers a pointed warning to Master Hui in the end.

Parable of the Useless Tree

Characteristics—Twisted and Gnarled

Let's begin by looking at the characteristics of the useless tree. We see that Master Hui disparages the tree as being useless, stinky, gnarled, knotted, twisted, and turned. It is inelegant, impractical, not linear, and cannot be measured. But as we learn from the second parable of the useless tree, it is precisely these repulsive attributes that are responsible for keeping the useless tree alive. These useless attributes are the foundations of its spiritual value. Its defectiveness is its secret to survival. Zhuangzi urges us to reflect upon defectiveness with a different attitude and ponder it not through conventional morality but rather a perspective of "relative gradation" where all things are equal; where things are not just perceived as useful or useless, beautiful or gnarled, but are innately *both* "useful" and "useless" according to their proper function. These viewpoints are discussed at length in the chapter on the Autumn Floods written by Todd DuBose (Chapter 14). Thus, it is only through our spiritual eyes can we "see" the beauty of deformity. Paradoxically, the useless tree's beauty, elegance, usefulness, and practicality lie within its "revolting" attributes! This is the beauty of *zhi-mian* (直面, direct confrontation), the Chinese term originating from the modern Chinese writer Lu Xun and adopted for an indigenous Chinese approach to existential psychotherapy by Wang Xuefu (Wang, 2011).

Has it not always been so? From early on in history, the best and most gifted healers have all been wounded or even defective in their own way. This was well recognized by Carl Jung and Henri Nouwen who wrote a book with the title, *The Wounded Healer* (Nouwen, 1979). Shamans, who practiced psychotherapy well before the word was invented, were often deformed in some way. They lived on the margins of their tribes. They were set apart because of their differences, their deformities, which were often revolting in their appearance. Yet the tribesmen recognized the beauty, wisdom, and usefulness of these enigmatic gifts bestowed upon the shamans because of their deformities. So Zhuangzi teaches us that we must see with different eyes, or "radical validation" according to Todd DuBose in his chapter on the Autumn Floods. Similarly Richard Bargdill in his chapter "Master Hui's Grave: To Sharpen Your Character, Rub It Up Against Something Abrasive" (Chapter 7), reminds us that our greatest achievements come from our most difficult journeys and often this involves the pain of coming to terms with our limitations. Zhuangzi reflected upon this when he passed by the grave of his chief rival Master Hui. He reminisced about Master Hui being his chopping block, one who challenged him to be more than he could be. Indeed the path to resilience lies in despair; wisdom is birthed in stench; practicality in uselessness; and beauty through deformity. Spiritually, true beauty lies in courage: the courage to dwell in emptiness and provide shelter in the wastelands. Zhuangzi shares with us that:

> To travel on water yet not flee from crocodiles and dragons is the courage of the fisherman; to travel on land yet not flee from rhinoceroses and tigers is the courage of the hunter; to have naked blades cross before him yet view death as calmly as life is the courage of the ardent warrior; to know that adversity is due to destiny and that success is due to the times yet face great difficulty without fear is the courage of the sage.
>
> *(Zhuangzi, 1998, p. 160)*

Or the reminder from Rainer Maria Rilke (n.d.):

> Do not assume that he who seeks to comfort you now, lives untroubled among the simple and quiet words that sometimes do you good. His life may also have much sadness and difficulty, that remains far beyond yours. Were it otherwise, he would never have been able to find these words.

Characteristics—Not Easily Measured

The other characteristic of the tree is that it is not linear and thus not easily measured. Neither compass nor ruler can be applied to them. Unable to be measured, Master Hui argues that the tree and its twisted and gnarled branches are thus useless. This is similar to our current emphasis and reliance upon evidenced-based practices which are epistemologically based upon empiricism. Empiricism asserts that knowledge comes only or primarily from sensory experience. Empiricism emphasizes the role of experience and evidence, especially sensory perception, in the formation of ideas, over the notion of ideas or traditions (Baird & Kaufmann, 2008). However, Zhuangzi's tale warns us about the danger of reducing sensory experience and evidence to that which is tangibly measurable. We are reminded to heed the warning of Albert Einstein, who knew a little something about what is useful or not. It was rumored that Einstein hung a sign in his Princeton office stating that "not everything that counts can be counted and not everything that can be counted counts" (Einstein, n.d.). Furthermore, in the children's book *Little Prince*, Antoine de Saint Exupéry (2000), through the voice of a very wise fox, lets us in on a secret: "Here is my secret. It is very simple. It is only with the heart that one can see. One sees clearly only with the heart. Anything essential is invisible to the eye" (Chapter 21, para. 50). The author goes further to remind us that, "Grown-ups never understand anything by themselves, and it is exhausting for children to have to provide explanations over and over again" (Chapter 1, para. 7). Similarly, Rodger Broomé, in his chapter on Taoist epistemology (Chapter 4), reminds us once again that "knowledge and understanding are always on their way toward *Truth* but without having the ability to ever capture it." And Todd DuBose warned us about the possible oppressiveness of rank-ordered scales of measurement when "we compare each other's ways of being as somehow better or worse than ourselves, while ignoring the uniqueness of each way of being in the world as valuable and meaningful." Whatever indexical category we employ in measurement must be relative to its function. Zhuangzi shares these same sentiments when it comes to his debate with Master Hui. Particularly when it comes to his warning at the end of the story.

Simple Truth—Returning to Self

The location of this large, useless tree is also instructive: "It stands next to the road, but carpenters pay no attention to it" (Zhuangzi, 1998, pp. 8–9). The tree is accessible to all; right in front of our eyes. Yet carpenters, who know their woods, pay no attention to it. It is big, but it is useless and heeded by none. Such is the secret to its longevity. As suggested by the children's story above, wisdom indeed arises from the mouth of babes (Psalm 8:2; Matthew 21:16, King James Version of the Bible). This wisdom is available to us all. It's just that we are blind or pay them no heed. Like the emptiness of the large gourd, it is a matter of perspective. This is why existentialists, out of the humanistic tradition, remind clients to return to themselves to seek for what they have forgotten. As Jason Dias reminds us in his chapter on Wu Wei (Chapter 2), being ourselves is paradoxically both the beginning and end-point of training. And we remind ourselves to return to the wisdom of the philosophers and the intuition and insights of the artists who point us back to the essential elements of life and reveal to us new ways of appreciating such simple truths. Thus, what we disregard as useless returns to us again as that which is critical for our living.

But this returning to ourselves can carry a heavy price. Aligning himself with the work of the German philosopher Fredrick Nietzsche, David Elkins, in his chapter on authenticity and the tale of the turtle (Chapter 9), reminds us that "all hell will [likely] break loose" if we choose to pursue an authentic existence. We are reminded again that the useless tree is not elegant and straightforward. Stinky, twisted, and gnarled are not pleasing to the eye. It is a path that is ignored by most.

Stillness and Non-Action

Zhuangzi goes on using two metaphors to juxtapose usefulness with uselessness. Through the wildcat or weasel, Zhuangzi teaches us about the paradox of action through inaction. He teaches us that "from the sage's emptiness, stillness arises. From stillness, action. From action, attainment" (Merton, 2010, p. 80).

From their stillness comes their non-action, which is also action. This is the way of the Tao. How is it possible for a weasel to catch prey by simply crouching, lying in wait? Free lunch indeed! But herein again, it's about perspective. An amateur, one who is not familiar with psychotherapy, will comment that the technique of reflective listening is simple parroting. Simple, useless, and unproductive! The client is jumping here and there, high and low, and the therapist does nothing but follow. The amateur sees idleness rather than stillness; randomness rather than depth; languor rather than anticipation; scattered rather than focused; unlearned rather than mastery; novice rather than *shifu* (a master/expert).

Zhuangzi teaches us further about the still, silent ways of the weasel and wildcat; lessons for all therapists regarding the important work of listening. Note that the wildcat is crouching in anticipation. It would be foolish to understand the wildcat as being inactive, unproductive, doing nothing. In crouching, the wildcat is being receptive in anticipation, not unlike that of a competitive diver poised for his or her dive. Rollo May (1975) noticed the same sort of receptivity and anticipation in the work of artists:

> The receptivity of the artist must never be confused with passivity or laziness. Receptivity is the artist's holding him or herself alive and open to hear what being may speak. Such receptivity requires a nimbleness, a fine-honed sensitivity in order to let one's self be the vehicle of whatever vision may emerge. It is the opposite of the authoritarian demands impelled by "will power." . . . It requires a high degree of attention, as when a diver is poised on the end of the springboard, not jumping but holding his or her muscles in sensitive balance for the right second. It is an active listening, keyed to hear the answer, alert to see whatever can be glimpsed when the vision or the words do come. It is a waiting for the birthing process to begin to move in its own organic time. It is necessary that the artist have this sense of timing, that he or she respect these periods of receptivity as part of the mystery of creativity and creation.
>
> *(pp. 80–81)*

So just as the weasel and wildcat in crouching stalks its prey, we as therapists stalk the inner authentic selves of our clients. But it is a stalking through "non-action." It is staying with the client in anticipation. As midwives, we facilitate and await the births of our client's authentic selves. It is waiting as Vladimir and Estragon wait for Godot:

> We find ourselves caring despite the apparent meaninglessness of the situation. Godot does not come, but in the waiting there is care and hope. It matters that we wait and that we, like the characters in the drama, wait in human relationship—we share with each other the ragged coat, the shoes, the piece of turnip. Waiting is caring, and caring is waiting.
>
> *(May, 1969, p. 305)*

In that waiting, we practice what Zhuangzi called the "fasting of the mind," which involves listening to emptiness. It requires the emptying of ourselves. Zhuangzi (1998) teaches:

> Listen not with your ears but with your mind. Listen not with your mind but with your primal breath. The ears are limited to listening, the mind is limited to tallying. The primal breath, however, awaits things emptily. It is only through the Way that one can gather emptiness, and emptiness is the fasting of the mind . . . Observe the void—the empty emits a pure light. Good fortune lies in stopping when it is time to stop. If you do not stop, this is called "galloping while sitting." Let your senses communicate within and rid yourself of the machinations of the mind. Then even ghosts and spirits will take shelter with you, not to mention men. This is how the myriad things are transformed.
>
> *(pp. 32–33 [excerpts])*

*Permission to reproduce granted by University of Hawaii Press. Zhuangzi, (1998). *Wandering on the Way: Early Taoist Tales and Parables of Chuang Tzu.* (V. Mair, Trans.). Honolulu, HI: University of Hawaii Press.

In addition, verses 15 and 43 of the *Tao Te Ching* (see below) teach the same principles of action through non-action, achieving results without action. This is the Taoist concept of Wu Wei. Lao Tzi, the author of the *Tao Te Ching*, teaches us about receptiveness in stillness. It is in our stillness, our serenity that clients find sanctuary, shelter, and the mirror for their inner selves. It is by stilling our own souls that we help clients to still theirs. And again this stillness involves emptying ourselves of our desire to cure our clients. We cannot cure our clients. Clients cure themselves. The Reverend R. Inman (2009) agrees: "A great teacher never strives to explain her vision; she simply invites you to stand beside her and see for yourself." And Alexandra Trenfor (2014) concurs: "The best teachers are those who show you where to look, but don't tell you what to see." For we are more catalysts rather than active agents of change in our clients' lives. It is the clients themselves who must be the active agents. In Zhuangzi's parable, it is the prey which jumps into the trap on its own. Yet, the weasel and wildcat crouch in anticipation. How often have we learned the lesson of the wisdom of remaining unmoving till the right action arises by itself?

Carl Rogers taught us that, paradoxically, "acceptance is the beginning of change." This is another aspect of non-action as illustrated in Chapter 43 of the *Tao Te Ching*. Jim Bugental (1999) advocates the same thing in regards to aligning with our clients' resistance. Gentle yielding often overcomes rigid resistances. Similar to principles in aikido, if we are able to empty ourselves through yielding, we offer clients nothing to resist or defend against. Zhuangzi understood this concept of offering no resistance when he told the following tale:

> If a man is crossing a river
> And an empty boat collides with his own skiff,
> Even though he be a bad-tempered man
> He will not become very angry.
> But if he sees a man in the boat,
> He will shout at him to steer clear.
> If the shout is not heard, he will shout again,
> And yet again, and begin cursing.
> And all because there is somebody in the boat.
> Yet if the boat were empty,
> He would not be shouting, and not angry.
>
> If you can empty your own boat
> Crossing the river of the world,
> No one will oppose you,
> No one will seek to harm you.
> (Merton, 2010, p. 114)

The prey "leaps about east and west, avoiding neither high nor low, until it gets caught in a snare." This is the way of the Master.

Tao Te Ching, *Verse 15*

> The masters of this ancient path
>   are mysterious and profound
> Their inner state baffles all inquiry
> Their depths go beyond all knowing
> Thus, despite every effort,
>   we can only tell of their outer signs—
> Deliberate, as if treading over the stones of a winter brook

Watchful, as if meeting danger on all sides
Reverent, as if receiving an honored guest
Selfless, like a melting block of ice
Pure, like an uncarved block of wood
Accepting, like an open valley

Through the course of Nature
   muddy water becomes clear
Through the unfolding of life
   man reaches perfection
Through sustained activity
   that supreme rest is naturally found

Those who have Tao want nothing else
Though seemingly empty
   they are ever full
Though seemingly old
   they are beyond the reach of birth and death
                (Lao Tzi, 2003, p. 28)

Tao Te Ching, *Verse 43*

The most yielding thing in the world
   will overcome the most rigid
The most empty thing in the world
   will overcome the most full
From this comes a lesson—
   Stillness benefits more than action
   Silence benefits more than words.

Rare indeed are those who are still
Rare indeed are those who are silent
And so I say:
   Rare indeed are those
   who obtain the bounty of this world.
              (Lao Tzi, 2003, p. 56)

Dangers of Systems and Institutions—Dogma

Contrast the way of the wildcat with the mighty yak. The yak is indeed powerful as the conglomerate and not to be trifled with. Its might is well suited for a number of important tasks. Yet, it cannot catch mice. What does the yak symbolize? In existential psychology, the limitation of the yak may represent the shortcomings of science and the medical model. Science and modern medicine have made great advances in the areas of healthcare. We have all benefitted from such advances and are living longer lives as a result. But has the yak of science and technology improved the quality of our lives as well? The medical field is indeed as powerful as the mighty yak. Psychology has also benefitted tremendously from the scientific revolution. However, when it comes to the care of the soul, science is limited in what it can offer. It struggles to define and capture the essence of such important concepts as soul, love, compassion, and even empathy—concepts central to the essence and healing of one's being. Furthermore, when it goes too far in asserting power and influence, lives are damaged in the process. This is what has happened with the pharmaceutical industries when it comes to psychopharmacology. Zhuangzi's tale "The Sage and the Thief," Chapter 10 of the book *Zhuangzi*, warns us against the dangers of systems and dogma and alerts us to the dangers of loosing the mighty yak where it does not belong! No wonder Nietzsche wrote, "I mistrust all systematisers and I avoid them. The will to system is a lack of integrity" (Nietzsche, 1954, p. 470). For the sake of brevity, only the relevant passages from Zhuangzi's parable will be included:

> In guarding against thieves who ransack coffers, search through bags, and break open cupboards, people are sure to bind them with ropes and cords, secure them with clasps and hasps. This is what common opinion calls being wise. But if a giant thief comes, he will put the cupboard on his back, pick up the coffer, carry the bag on a pole over his shoulder, and run away with them, fearing only that the ropes and cords, the clasps and hasps may not be secure enough. This being so, is not he whom I just referred to as wise merely collecting things for the great thief?
>
> Let me try to explain. Is not he whom common opinion calls ultimately wise collecting things for the great thief? Is not the so-called ultimate sage a guardian for the great thief? How do we know this is so? . . . By shrewdly surmising that valuables are stored in a room, the robber shows his sageness. By entering first, he shows his bravery. By going out last, he shows his righteousness. By knowing whether the robbery may be attempted or not, he shows his wisdom. By dividing the spoils equally, he shows his humanness. There is no one under heaven who is not possessed of these five qualities that can become a great robber.
>
> If the sage does not die, there will be no end to great robbers. The more emphasis is placed on the sage in governing all under heaven, the greater the gain for Robber Footpad. If bushels and pecks are devised for measuring, then he will steal by the bushel and the peck. If weights and steelyards are devised for weighing, then he will steal by the weight and the steelyard. If tallies and seals are devised for verifying, then he will steal

by the tally and the seal. If humanness and righteousness are devised for reforming the world, he will steal by humanness and righteousness.

How do we know that this is so?
He who steals a belt buckle is executed;
He who steals a state becomes a feudal lord.
It is within the gates of the feudal lords
That humanness and righteousness are preserved.
(Zhuangzi, 1998, pp. 84–86 [excerpts])

*Permission to republish granted by University of Hawaii Press. Zhuangzi, (1998). *Wandering on the Way: Early Taoist Tales and Parables of Chuang Tzu.* (V. Mair, Trans.). Honolulu, HI: University of Hawaii Press.

Uselessness and Location of the Tree

So what is the utility of a useless tree? "Everybody knows the utility of usefulness, but nobody knows the utility of uselessness" (Zhuangzi, 1998, p. 41). Zhuangzi suggests that we plant the useless tree in emptiness, in the wastelands where it can provide rest and shelter in a land of desolation. Paradoxically, the utility of the useless tree lies in its "uselessness" and that is the secret to its ability to survive in the wastelands. Being big and "useless," it provides a most important function in the land of desolation. It provides shade, rest, and sanctuary. Shading from the harshness of life. Sanctuary, comfort, and compassion in the midst of emptiness and pain. All of this harkens back to the tale of another tree called The Giving Tree, the classic children's story by Shel Silverstein (2014). At the end of the story, after the boy has sold all of her apples (for money), chopped off her branches (for a house), and even her trunk (for a boat), this "useless" stump provides the last of the boy/man's need at the end of his life. And what is this need but simple companionship in the form of "a quiet place to sit and rest"? This final stage of giving, and the entire story, ends with the sentence, "And the tree was happy."

The wastelands are infertile. Yet the useless tree survives in its midst. It adapts to the land of desolation. Zhuangzi warns us not to take the useless tree for granted. It is to be reckoned with. It outlasts many a useful trees of greater worth. The usefulness of the useless tree will last the ages because it is not direct and linear. Its elegance and beauty lies in its crookedness. It requires one to perceive beyond the obvious and contemplate its uselessness in order to appreciate its beauty and utility. This is the spiritual practice Zhuangzi inspires us to in the following two parables below:

In the state of Sung, there is a place called Chingshih where catalpas, arborvitae, and mulberry trees thrive. Those that are more than a hand's breadth or two around are chopped down by people who are looking for tether posts for their monkeys. Those that are three or four spans in circumference are chopped down by people who are looking for lofty ridgepoles. Those that are seven or eight spans in circumference are chopped down by the families of aristocrats or wealthy merchants who are looking for coffin planks. Therefore, they do not live out the years allotted to them by heaven but die midway under the ax. This is the trouble brought about by having worth. Conversely, in carrying out an exorcistic sacrifice, one cannot present oxen with white foreheads, suckling pigs with upturned snouts, or people with hemorrhoids to the gods of the river. All of this is known by the magus-priests, who consider these creatures to be inauspicious. For the same reasons, the spiritual person considers them to be greatly auspicious.

(Zhuangzi, 1998, p. 39)

★Permission to republish granted by University of Hawaii Press. Zhuangzi, (1998). *Wandering on the Way: Early Taoist Tales and Parables of Chuang Tzu.* (V. Mair, Trans.). Honolulu, HI: University of Hawaii Press.

The mountain trees plunder themselves, the grease over a fire fries itself, cinnamon can be eaten, therefore the trees that yield it are chopped down. Varnish can be used, therefore the trees that produce it are hacked. Everybody knows the utility of usefulness, but nobody knows the utility of uselessness.

(Zhuangzi, 1998, p. 41)

The spiritual auspiciousness of the useless tree lies in its ability to survive in the wastelands, where it can provide shade and rest to those who are roaming in despair and desolation. This is the role of the existential therapist. We provide shelter, sanctuary, and companionship to those who are roaming in emptiness. When confronted with the harshness of life, the existential givens, clients often lose their direction. There is not much that can be done (non-action) and no easy answers during such challenging times. In the midst of these hardships, it's all about survival. The question becomes, will our clients find our companionship during such times of despair? Zhuangzi suggests that if we know about stench, about being gnarled and knotted, twisted and turned, then we will likely comprehend non-action and the utility of being useless. We will know that there are no easy solutions that will take away the abyss. We will follow the teaching of Carl Jung (n.d.), who reminded us that:

"Knowing our own darkness is the best method for dealing with the darkness of other people"
"How can I be substantial if I do not cast a shadow? I must have a dark side also if I am to be whole?"

"Neurosis is always a substitute for legitimate suffering."

"The greatest and most important problems of life are all fundamentally insoluble. They can never be solved but only outgrown."

Companionship in the Wasteland

Companionship is the most powerful healing medicine of all. In the end, it is the relationship that heals. As the popular Chinese saying goes, "life impacting life." Martin Buber (1965) explains it as "healing through meeting." Indeed no relationship can eliminate isolation, for each of us is alone in existence. Yet, "[a] great relationship," says Buber (1965, p. 175), "breaches the barriers of a lofty solitude, subdues its strict law, and throws a bridge from self-being to self-being across the abyss of dread of the universe." Consistent with Zhuangzi's concept of Wu Wei, what matters is not what we as therapists must do but how we must be (Rogers, 1980). A major part of the healing occurs with the therapist simply *being with* the client. Jiddu Krishnamurti (n.d.), a spiritual leader in India who died in 1986, was once asked what is the most appropriate thing to say to a friend who is about to die. He answered: "Tell your friend that in his death, a part of you dies and goes with him. Wherever he goes, you also go. He will not be alone." Similarly, in the play *Let Me Down Easy* by Anna Deavere Smith, a character portrayed was a remarkable woman who cared for African children with AIDS. Little help was available at her shelter. Children died every day. When asked what she did to ease the dying children's terror, she answered with two phrases: "I never let them die alone in the dark, and I say to them, 'You will always be with me here in my heart'" (Yalom, 2008, p. 132).

This type of work is taking place in "wastelands" all over the world. In addition to providing palliative care for dying children, Lyn Gould, a retired nurse from the United Kingdom, started the Butterfly Home in Changsha, China[2] so that she can simply "love the children till the very end, no matter what!" These children are often abandoned by their families because of the lack of hope. The families have been in the wastelands and can no longer sustain. The parents abandon these children with crushing grief and guilt in their heart. But Lyn and the Butterfly Home are there to provide shade and shelter. The Butterfly Home is a wonderful example of The Useless Tree because they refuse to give up in the face of such hopelessness. Lyn believes in the need to provide shelter in the midst of such despair even if the children are facing imminent death. What's the use of providing care to children who will die? Lyn and Zhuangzi will answer, "useless, how could it ever come to grief." The Butterfly Home's work will persist, endure, and expand for more and more people are rallying to its mission. As Cicero (1965, p. 56) taught us, "to philosophize is to prepare for death." And Zhuangzi repeats, "Useless, you should worry!"

Notes

1 Enfeoffments were granted by the ruling families for pledging to protect Kings or
ɪ Emperors in times of war.
2 http://butterflych.org/

References

Baird, F., & Kaufmann, W. (2008). *From Plato to Derrida.* Upper Saddle River, NJ: Pearson Prentice Hall.
Buber, M. (1965). *Between man and man.* New York, NY: Macmillan.
Bugental, J. (1992). *The art of the psychotherapist: How to develop the skills that take psychotherapy to beyond science.* New York, NY: W. W. Norton & Co.
Bugental, J. (1999). *Psychotherapy isn't what you think.* Phoenix, AZ: Zeig & Tucker.
Cicero. (1965). Cited in M. Montaigne, *The complete essays of Montaigne.* (D. Frame, Trans.). Palo Alto, CA: Stanford University Press.
de Saint Exupéry, A. (2000). *The little prince.* [Kindle for Android, 4.3.0.204]. (R. Howard, Trans.). Retrieved from Amazon.com
Einstein, A. (n.d.). [List of Quotes from Albert Einstein]. Retrieved from http://thinkexist. com/quotation/not_everything_that_counts_can_be_counted-and_not/15536.html
Heider, J. (1986). *The Tao of leadership: Lao Tzu's Tao Te Ching adapted for a new age.* Lake Worth, FL: Humanistics Publishing Group.
Inman, R. (2009, January 5). *Positive Thinker's Journal.* [Online Journal of Positive Thoughts and Inspirational Quotes]. Retrieved from http://positivethinkersjournal.blogspot. com/2009/01/teacher.html
Jung, C. G. (n.d.). [List of Quotes from Carl Gustav Jung]. Retrieved from http:// izquotes.com/quote/97814; http://izquotes.com/quote/97808; http://izquotes.com/ quote/97826; http://quoteallthethings.com/post/103888742747/cg-jung-quote-2007989
Kahney, L. (2006, October 17). *Straight Dope on the iPod's Birth.* [Website Article]. Retrieved from http://www.wired.com/gadgets/mac/commentary/cultofmac/2006/10/71956? currentPage=all
Krishnamurti, J. (n.d.). [Webpage of Quotes]. Retrieved from http://www.goodreads. com/quotes/79061-tell-your-friend-that-in-his-death-a-part-of
Lao Tzi. (2003). *Tao Te Ching: The definitive edition.* (J. Star, Trans.). New York, NY: Penguin Group.
May, R. (1969). *Love and will.* New York, NY: W. W. Norton & Co.
May, R. (1975). *The courage to create.* New York, NY: W. W. Norton & Co.
May, R. (1981). *Freedom and destiny.* New York, NY: W. W. Norton & Co.
Merton, T. (2010). *The way of Chuang Tzu.* New York, NY: New Directions Publishing.
Nietzshe, F. (1954). Twilight of the idols. In W. Kaufmann (Ed.), *The portable Nietzsche* (pp. 463–564). New York, NY: The Viking Press.
Nouwen, H. (1979). *The wounded healer: Ministry in contemporary society.* New York, NY: Doubleday Publishing.
Rilke, R. M. (n.d.). [List of Quotes from Rainer Maria Rilke]. Retrieved from http://www. goodreads.com/quotes/119250-do-not-assume-that-he-who-seeks-to-comfort-you
Rogers, C. R. (1980). *A way of being.* New York, NY: Houghton Mifflin Harcourt Publishing.
Silverstein, S. (2014). *The giving tree.* New York: NY: Harper & Row.

Trenfor, A. K. (2014, February 5). Philosiblog. [Online Blog Article]. Retrieved from http://philosiblog.com/2014/02/05/the-best-teachers-are-those-who-show-you-where-to-look-but-dont-tell-you-what-to-see/

Wampold, B. E. (2010). *The basics of psychotherapy: An introduction to theory and practice (theories of psychotherapy)*. Washington, DC: American Psychological Association.

Wang, X. (2011). Zhi Mian and existential psychology. In *The humanistic psychologist* (Vol. 39.3, pp. 240–247). Philadelphia, PA: Taylor & Francis.

Yalom, I. (2008). *Staring at the sun*. San Francisco, CA: Jossey-Bass.

Zhuangzi. (1998). *Wandering on the Way: Early Taoist tales and parables of Chuang Tzu*. (V. Mair, Trans.). Honolulu, HI: University of Hawaii Press.

2

WU WEI (無爲/无为)

Jason Dias

FIGURE 2.1 Created by Julia Brown

A strange thing about writing for audiences without a language in common is that some concepts represented by the words in one language might need explication and investigation in the other. This presents us a strange problem, as Wu Wei is one such concept. The readers in English might be very interested in some investigation of what Wu Wei means, but the Chinese audience might only scratch their heads and yawn.

As an English language writer, though, what choice is there, really?

Another problem is this: Taoist psychology is already a thing here, and other people know a lot more about it than this humble writer. When I say what Wu Wei means to me, they will clamor and protest that I am getting it all wrong. So, some caveats to begin:

First, I am not writing about tao psychology. Indeed I am not qualified to do so. I am writing about the elements of Zhuangzi's stories that seem to me to speak to concepts of existential psychology.

Second, my understanding of Wu Wei is going to be idiosyncratic, and studiedly so. Luckily, Chinese language is flexible, offering an array of meanings for many words and allowing you to select the one that you need or want at the time.

Finally, for now: I don't want to say anything at all about Taoism. Again, I am not qualified.

Now, to Wu Wei.

The two most salient meanings of this concept for our purposes are intentional inaction and effortless action (the more usual meaning but perhaps more properly Wei Wu Wei).

> From emptiness comes the unconditioned.
> From this, the conditioned, the individual things.
> So from the sage's emptiness, stillness arises:
> From stillness, action. From action, attainment.
> From their stillness comes their non-action, which is also action
> For stillness is joy. Joy is free from care
> Fruitful in long years.
> Joy does all things without concern:
> For emptiness, stillness, tranquility, tastelessness,
> Silence, and non-action
> Are the root of all things.
>
> (Merton, 2010, pp. 80–81)

For us Westerners with our Western stereotypes, it is easy to picture this kind of non-action and silence as the old wise man, with white flowing beard, meditating by the roadside. This stereotype certainly arose from somewhere rather than nowhere and, as beginners, we might indeed strain with intentional inaction. Sometimes the best thing to do is nothing and when is that more clear than in the therapy room?

The beginning therapist is failing just as the beginning meditator is failing. They force their self to stillness, biting back their commentary and interpretations and advice, and try to listen. But they cannot hear the client, just as the beginner at meditation cannot hear their own thoughts. They are too busy not-doing. It takes most of us a long time for not-doing to become effortless and natural, for the listening to become the activity rather than the thing between activities.

I encountered this problem most vividly in graduate school. A friend noted my high-strung nature, always pacing in the back of class and unable to be still. My nickname in graduate school was Pacing Jason, which annoyed me because it does not quite rhyme. This friend, as such friends often do, suggested I try meditation.

I objected that I have tried meditation but I am incapable of the required stillness. It takes so much energy to remain still that I cannot do the further work of trying to watch thoughts, never mind quieting them.

She suggested a walking meditation, however. This would allow my body to do what it does naturally—move!—and free up my mind to do the work I wanted it to do. She also went on to explain that only some kinds of meditation are about the empty mind, and went on to show me some of them. Now meditation is a practice and a discipline and I am at heart a lazy man, but even so I have found the information valuable. Isaac Newton supposed that an object at rest must remain at rest unless acted upon by some force; and that an object in motion must remain in motion unless acted upon by some outside force. There might be an implication here that motion and stillness might be the same thing, and this seems especially true in the contexts of human life, thought, and therapy. This leads us to the next meaning of Wu Wei.

The second meaning is likely to be most valuable to us, and if we can come near to mastering it, it will very much help with the first. Here things move because they must move. Your non-actions are the same as actions, just natural products of being in tune with your self, place, and time. The non-action in question is probably best described by Bruce Lee:

> Wu Wei is the art of artlessness, the principle of no-principle. To state it in terms of gung fu, the genuine beginner knows nothing about the way of blocking and striking, and much less of his concern for himself. When the opponent tries to strike him, he instinctively blocks it. This is all he can do. But as soon as the training starts, he is taught how to defend and attack, and where to keep his mind, and many other technical skills—which make his mind "stop" at various junctures. For this reason whenever he tries to strike an opponent he feels unusually hampered. He has lost altogether his original sense of purity and freedom. But as the months and years go by, as his training acquires further maturity, his bodily attitude and his way of managing the techniques toward no-mindedness, will

resemble the state of mind he had at the very beginning of training, when he was altogether ignorant of gung fu.

(Lee & Little, 2001, p. 50)

Much less prosaically, imagine the relatively mundane act of riding a bicycle. When you are learning, it is very difficult and involves some skinned knees. Once you know how, thinking is not only not required but counterproductive. The cyclist who spends too much mental energy thinking about maintaining their balance risks losing it, going back to the beginning in a bad way.

It is not only Eastern mystics who understand the concept. Salvadore Minuchin was well known for advising we read his books and then forget all about them, that we practice to have the highest level of technique and then forget all about technique. The purpose of therapist training is not to become the highest level of technician in the room, but to become the right person to be of service to other people. Exactly as Lee and Little describe, we train ourselves to be the masters of our profession and then simply go and be with people. Once you have become that person, you no longer need to try to help them, you simply help them by being who you are.

"Be yourself" is popular advice these days. It seems silly, really—what other choices do you have other than to be yourself? In therapy, though, "be yourself" is the end point of training. The beginning point is to examine yourself, and the middle is to make yourself over into that helpful person, the expert technician. The end point, though, is "be yourself," once you have become the person you must be.

In other words:

> Before I had studied Chan (Zen) for thirty years, I saw mountains as mountains, and rivers as rivers. When I arrived at a more intimate knowledge, I came to the point where I saw that mountains are not mountains, and rivers are not rivers. But now that I have got its very substance I am at rest. For it's just that I see mountains once again as mountains, and rivers once again as rivers.
>
> *(Qingyuan Weixin, translated by Suzuki, D., Essays in Zen Buddhism, 1949)*

Carl Whitaker and Virginia Satir each said similar things. Once your work is done, your internal work is to become who you need to be; then really your only job is to be congruent (Satir) or disruptive (Whitaker), as best suits your nature.

This is a blessing and a curse of existential psychotherapies. The field has made great strides over the past ten years elucidating some methods for practice, some techniques. See, for example, Kirk Schneider's series of videos for the American Psychological Association, and his collaboration with Orah

Krug (2009). Even so, existential therapy tends to neglect the technique and focus more seriously on the person. There is no book to read and forget about (or few of them, anyway). The existentialist is thus more likely to come to their theoretical orientation relatively late in their training, full of the methods of other sorts of practice and ready to forget the methods, become the helper.

This training tends to involve reading a lot of very heavy material. Ernest Becker, Søren Kierkegaard, and Martin Heidegger probably round out the big three, but students might also find themselves reading into fiction such as Dostoevsky. For Americans, Rollo May is another chief writer and, more modern, Kirk Schneider. Beginners often report having been led here by the writings of Irvin Yalom, who is more accessible by far than the more dated and philosophic writers but also more elementary in his approach.

There are dozens of other writers, almost all equally weighty and held in high esteem by their readers, and right now probably some readers are making lists of authors that deserve mention and are definitely more important than those listed above. Adrian Van Kaam, Martin Buber, James Bugental, hundreds more. In terms of both accessibility and depth of knowledge and insight, one probably cannot do better than Louis Hoffman among modern writers.

Whomever one chooses to read, however, one might notice the purpose of the reading is to open one up to certain stances and attitudes much more than to teach methods by which to heal people. Existentialists tend to struggle with paradoxes, learning to hold two ideas at once in their minds. The biggest and foremost of these paradoxes is that we are both finite (destined to die) and worthwhile.

If that does not sound like a paradox, consider the work of Jeff Greenberg, Sander Koole, and Tom Pyszczynski (2004) (and, by now, hundreds if not thousands of others). Their theory, now known widely as terror management theory and backed by metric tons of empirical support, shows that death salience increases nationalism and xenophobia. The proposed mechanism, also with good support, is that encountering reminders of death causes us to feel more worthless. We seek affiliation with the in-group in order to improve our sense of self-esteem. Nationalism, religiosity, racism, sexism all result from encounters with death salience (to be sure, though, not exclusively from this source).

Our reading drags us kicking and screaming through the knowledge of our own mortality, back and forth like riding a bicycle for the first time. Eventually we become at least a little bit inured to the terror, a little more able to look it in the face.

A client of mine overcoming obsessive-compulsive disorder spoke of a dream in which something was outside her shower door. Cleanliness was one of her obsessions, so the fact that she was showering was no special surprise. In a variant, she was hanging clean, white sheets on the laundry line to dry. In each version, she became aware of the shape of a man seen vaguely through the marbled shower-door glass, or a shadow on the sheets. And the figure there became very frightening to her.

As we worked together, she was able to stay with the dream a little longer each time it happened. Eventually she was able to open the shower door to see who was there. The figure was a rotting, dirty person whom the client was able to describe in some vivid detail. Seeing him for the first time was too frightening an episode to sit through.

When she was ready, I asked her in therapy to imagine that person was here in the room with us, sitting just there, across from her in a chair. What might she want to ask this figure? She replied she would like to know why he kept coming to visit her.

The client's next job was to take the chair in which had sat the zombie, take his perspective. If he were here, how might he answer the question? She gamely slogged away with some answer or other I do not remember now and I did not think the intervention was very productive. I endeavored to try again another day, when she seemed more ready.

But the next week, the client came back with another dream of the dead figure. This time, the man reached out for her, and rather than scream or run or wake up she reached out and touched his hand. When she did so, the rotting man disappeared, and never really troubled her dreams again.

This is much of what is involved in existential training: balancing (rather than resolving) these sorts of paradoxes so that the mind does not have to labor over them, so that we can ride the bicycle without fear of falling off, so that we have our equilibrium in the therapy room. There is much of it in the work of Zhuangzi. For example, there is the story of the butcher who butchers the oxen without effort. Every slice of the knife sends flesh to the floor, parts joints like magic. The butcher does not even really notice the work:

> A good cook changes his knife once a year—because he cuts. A mediocre cook changes his knife once a month—because he hacks. I've had this knife of mine for nineteen years and I've cut up thousands of oxen with it, and yet the blade is as good as though it had just come from the grindstone. There are spaces between the joints, and the blade of the knife has really no thickness. If you insert what has no thickness into such spaces, then there's plenty of room—more than enough for the blade to play about in. That's why after nineteen years, the blade of my knife is still as good as when it first came from the grindstone.
>
> (Zhuangzi, 2013, Chapter 3, para. 5)

Here is another element of mastery: seeing the joints, the weaknesses in an argument, the path of least resistance, the flow, or any of a thousand other synonyms. This is effortless effort epitomized. The butcher works with so little effort that even the knife experiences the mastery. Knife and butcher both remain sharp.

In therapy, perhaps, this is knowing how to help the client with the least interference, the least expression of power. The knife is technique. There must be technique, but the edge of that technique must be invisibly small such that it fits into any space, meets no resistance. The technique never dulls because it never grinds against bones.

Carl Whitaker might have viewed therapy as an ox to a butcher. He is famous for his play and irreverence, sometimes rudeness to clients in the therapy room. This is usually explained as trust: he trusts in the relationship enough to be perfectly frank and often teasing. He did not practice therapy so much as show up in a room with a family and be Carl Whitaker. Every movement of his hips or shrug of his shoulder sent meat to the floor: his purpose was to keep the system unbalanced so it would have to change, to find a new balance. And he trusted that the family system would settle in a place that would be better than the current equilibrium.

Whitaker was not demonstrably a Taoist. His faith was not so much in families or in the eternal balance of the universe so much as in just good sense. The family was not in the room because their life was great, but because the way they were interacting was unacceptable in some way. So Whitaker messed with the balance and trusted where it settled next would be better, because the only options were better or the same. Worse was not a realistic choice.

Carl Whitaker is not generally listed among the rolls of existential therapists or thinkers, although his long-time colleague and co-author Augustus Napier was known for writing about the existential givens of family systems (for example, that they change). Even so, he in many ways exemplifies the present orientation of many existential thinkers and therapists, who prefer to work with what is in the moment rather than what is in the past or the present. Whitaker was so in tune with the present orientation he rarely if ever planned an activity. He thought about the case, then sat in the room and was himself authentically.

Whitaker's authentic self was often confrontational or abrasive or obnoxious. Doing therapy demonstrations on stage, he sat still mostly because he was wired to microphones. In the room, without microphone wires, he frequently moved to be closer to or farther away from people, to make or break up subsystems in the room: mother to child, child to child, mother to father. Joining and leaving systems created instability so that the systems could find a new level without him later. He did not do this in a planned out manner but only did what seemed natural in the therapy room.

In other words, he read the book and forgot about it.

This is the butcher. He does not even see the ox, does not look with his eyes. He looks with his mind and then makes the cuts that make sense, missing all the large bones. The thinking is done in advance, the rest is being. Zhuangzi could have been describing Carl Whitaker when he wrote:

> Confucius said, "Make your will one! Don't listen with your ears, listen with your mind. No, don't listen with your mind, but listen with your

spirit. Listening stops with the ears, the mind stops with recognition, but spirit is empty and waits for all things. The Way gathers in emptiness alone. Emptiness is the fasting of the mind."

(Zhuangzi, 2013, Chapter 4, para. 18)

We can see existential psychology as a type of psychodynamic therapy, meaning that one thing is transformed by the mind into another. In the original psychodynamic therapy, psychoanalysis, the problems we think we have often turn out to be relational problems with our parents, frequently centered around sex. In existential therapy, we are tempted to see the problems people report as echoes of some death anxiety they have transformed into a life problem because the death anxiety is too difficult to encounter, does not have a solution.

This does not always fit, even when it seems a useful way to think of problems. While the therapist might be tempted to intervene by making the death anxiety explicit, this might be wrong or might not resonate with the client even if correct (and if it does not resonate, how can we call it correct?). But the beginning existential therapist is prone to this mistake more than the practiced one. The solution to death anxiety might not be a confrontation with death but a confrontation with life, involvement with the daily practice of living.

Paradoxes do not require solution. The solution to a paradox is to grow large enough to contain the various meanings suggested by the problem, to stop insisting that only one thing be true at one time. Some stories might clarify:

> There was a man who was so disturbed by the sight of his own shadow and so displeased with his own footsteps that he determined to get rid of both. The method he hit upon was to run away from them.
>
> So he got up and ran. But every time he put his foot down there was another step, while his shadow kept up with him without the slightest difficulty.
>
> He attributed his failure to the fact that he was not running fast enough. So he ran faster and faster, without stopping until he finally dropped dead.
>
> He failed to realize that if he merely stepped into the shade, his shadow would vanish, and if he sat down and stayed still, there would be no more footsteps.
>
> *(Merton, 2010, p. 155)*

A story with a similar meaning occurs in Dias (2010):

> A student asked his master, "What happens to a person after death?"
>
> The master studied the student for a time until the student thought he was meant to learn from the silence of the master. But then the master spoke:
>
> "Go out of this place and walk on the north road. Go through the towns and villages you find there, go through the forests that exclude the

villages, go into the mountains. There you will find a bridge that has fallen. Walk across that bridge and you will know that which you seek."

The student packed a meager bag and set out that day. He walked through the villages he found, eschewing succor or companionship from the people there. He walked through the forests where no person could live, refusing the bounty of the trees and roots he found there. Many days later, he came to that bridge in the mountains and stood looking down into a dark chasm, wintery waters rushing past far beneath his feet.

Some time later the master found the student in the village outside the monastery, consorting with the villagers and eating what they offered.

"Did you discover what happens to a person after death?" asked the master.

"I no longer seek it," replied the student.

(p. 31)

In each case, the protagonist in the story is running from something. In the first case we can suppose it is death—what other footsteps and shadows are shared by all people? What else is so inevitable? In the second case we might suppose it is life or some aspect of life (such as toil or suffering or even ignorance). And the solution in each story is the same: to sit still and live rather than run away from or towards the fear object. Sitting in the shade and being still means to do what comes naturally: eat, laugh, love, work. In short, life is the cure for death and for death anxiety.

Erikson (1996) proposed this in 1959 with his idea of the final stage of life, the conflict between ego integrity and despair. If we resolve this crisis in favor of ego integrity, we have discovered our lives make sense. The choices we made mattered (even if they were merely choices about how to handle or cope with what happened to us). The story we tell ourselves about our lives is coherent, hangs together, has sufficient redemption sequences, leaves us without unfinished business. In the other case, though, our lives have not been the product of our devising but of capricious fates. All our hopes were ashes. Whatever we did, we could not produce a narrative with us as the hero.

In the former case, people are unlikely to be anxious about their passing. In the second, however, death is frightening, a specter that watches us shower or hang up laundry, waiting to soil us and our works with grave dirt. Here may be some of the mechanisms by which death salience transforms into lower self-esteem.

The same client who dreamed of the rotting man decided one day she was going to fly home to visit her dying parents. She was in her sixties, they in their eighties, and this would likely be their last meeting. This was to be her first flight on a plane since she was a child, and taking this on was a real challenge for her, a task of some epic proportions. Her obsessive-compulsive disorder took the form of a germ phobia generally, but really seemed to reflect a death anxiety, and she talked about this at length and of her own accord relating to this trip home.

But her reason for planning and taking the trip was plain. "I don't want to die knowing I could have done so much more," she said.

The trip to visit her parents was a success (and produced a lot of grist for the therapy mill). When it was done, she next planned a trip to go on a bird-watching tour. Her escape from her own home and from the clutches of the grave dirt she had piled up there was nearly complete.

Careful to align with the client's will, heeding the caution of the tiger keeper from Zhuangzi's story mentioned below, I very much encouraged these trips when the client mentioned them, but these were her ideas. I was careful to not judge her progress, to urge her outside, to press her to more involvement with life. This person decided for herself she should have these goals, and she decided them through investigating the paradox of death and self-value, confronting the rotting man in her dream.

Another sort of therapist would be delighted to suggest these trips to her, to help their clients create and clarify and measure goals. Indeed, some clients seem to demand or require this sort of treatment.

One thing that humanistic psychologists argue about incessantly is the extent to which it is appropriate to have goals for your clients, the extent to which those goals pollute the purity of the relationship.

Imagine two people. One person decides to follow the law, to be gracious, to give money to charity, to have empathy for the sick. Another person does all the same things but because someone else follows them around making sure they do all these things through coercion, judgment, or rewards. Which of these people is a good person?

This is a major question, one which Van Kaam (1966) tackles in more than a little detail. He advocates for the greatest possible care to avoid contaminating the will of the client with the intentions of the therapist. His books are greatly beloved but, sadly, out of print. A modern situation that might arouse him to write another (if only he were still alive) came up at my internship site.

Imagining we were arrogant enough to say we knew how to live correctly, it would be both impossible and unseemly to teach others how to live correctly. If it were possible, it would remain unseemly. In other words:

> If the Way could be presented, then everyone would present it to his lord. If the Way could be offered, then everyone would offer it to his parents. If the Way could be told, then everyone would tell it to his brothers. If the Way could be given, then everyone would give it to his descendants. However, the reason why one cannot do these things is that if there is no host for it within, it will not stay, and if there is no sign of it without, it will not proceed. If that which goes forth from within is not received without, the sage will not

let it go forth. If that which enters from without has no host to receive it within, the sage will not deposit it there.

(Zhuangzi, 1998, pp. 138–139)

*Reprinted with permission from University of Hawaii Press. Zhuangzi, (1998). *Wandering on the Way: Early Taoist Tales and Parables of Chuang Tzu.* (V. Mair, Trans.). University of Hawaii Press, Honolulu, HI.

This sort of thinking might tend to lead one away from goals, plans, and intentions.

A local consortium of psychologists devised a list of questions to ask clients to clarify the nature of our relationship and our progress towards goals. In particular, we were to ask the client to state their most significant problem for which they were seeking therapy, and then to rate how much that problem bothered them on a scale of one to 100. The expectation was obviously that the client rates their problem as less bothersome every week.

I used it because it was a condition of my internship. I never liked it. I was bothered particularly by the idea that the client has only one to three problems, and that those problems be quantifiable, and especially that those problems be construed as such, as symptoms to remit. Additionally, I was concerned that the client might not know what their problem really was, the actual reason they felt compelled to seek therapy. That reason might hide behind any number of stated goals, and we might work on those stated goals to the exclusion of discovering something much more important.

Here we have the woodworker making a bell stand. The woodcarver fasts before starting the work, and the longer he fasts, the more he is empty of intention. Here fasting is the emptying out. The utility of the vessel is in its emptiness, after all; you cannot fill a full cup. The woodworker empties out of intention and then goes into the woods to find wood for the stand. When he sees the stand, he cuts out all the wood that is not the stand. If he does not see the stand in a block of wood, he goes home.

The woodworker demonstrates non-attachment to outcome. I clearly come down on the side of non-intention. You can make the opposite case. Measuring outcomes might be necessary for your grants, insurance, or even to know you are doing a good job. How else do you know your therapy is effective? You might have limited resources and need to limit the effort spent on any one person in favor of helping many people, those who can and want to elucidate their goals clearly.

At the same time, though, measuring those outcomes injects an element of intention, and that intention interferes with the will of the person through a quite clear power dynamic. You have gone searching for the bell stand in the wood. If you do not find it, the choice is to relax into the form of what you have found, or to try to make over what you see into what you want it to be. But to teach the Way, you first have to imagine both that you know it and that it can be taught.

Approaching the client with any intention pollutes their will. Of course it is somewhere between difficult and impossible to have no intention towards the client. You want to help them (some contend you should want to help them; what good is therapy if you do not want to help clients?) But you are only a worker, not an artist. The job of the therapist is not to make this over into that, to create something that did not previously exist, but to guide the person into becoming the person they want to be. If that form is not inside them already it cannot be made.

Here is an essence of existential therapies: sitting with what is. Of course another complication is that there are as many ways to practice existentially as there are people practicing existentially. Additionally, it can take a good amount of time before we reach the point with our clients where they are comfortable with their discomfort. Some therapists in this modality use alternate modes of therapy to arrive at this place, such as cognitive behavioral interventions to develop coping skills. But, in the end, the meat and bones of the therapy can consist of learning to be with the feelings we have rather than the feelings we want.

In *The Meaning of Anxiety*, Rollo May (1950) writes for perhaps the first time in American psychology about the value of this particular emotion. Previously almost our entire attention to anxiety was in its relief, annihilation. It was this book that, at least for Americans, first really described anxiety as a partner. As more than a partner: as part of the person not best served by aggression.

Unlike the meat from the ox and unlike everything in the block of wood that is not a bell stand, anxiety cannot be simply cut away with sure strokes and effortless action. Anxiety is more like a tiger.

> And don't you know about the tiger keeper? He dares not give a live animal to his charges, for fear of stirring up their fury when they kill it, nor dares he give them a whole animal, for fear of stirring up their fury when they tear it apart. By gauging the times when the tigers are hungry or full, he can fathom their fury. Although the tigers are of a different species from man, they try to please their keeper because he goes along with them, whereas they kill those who go against them.
>
> *(Zhuangzi, 1998, pp. 36–37)*

★Reprinted with permission from University of Hawaii Press. Zhuangzi, (1998). *Wandering on the Way: Early Taoist Tales and Parables of Chuang Tzu.* (V. Mair, Trans.). University of Hawaii Press, Honolulu, HI.

Back to the dream of the rotting man, he only stopped bothering the dreamer when she stopped being bothered by him. She decided to treat him as a friend and an ally because, after all, he was her. The dreams we dream might be frightening, might contain some aversive feelings, might even contain monsters. But they are not projected into us from outside. They grow up inside of us, made of us. They are us. The rotting man was some aspect of the client's self she did not prefer to examine at first. Later, she was ready to welcome him in as part of the whole.

When she tried to run from him, he only came back the next night. What might have happened had the client tried to fight the rotting man? The only reasonable course of action was to look him in the face and extend a hand. Once he had said what he needed to say—what the client needed to tell herself—he was gone.

And so it is with anxiety and, indeed, with all the feelings we prefer not to have. Some of our more basic feelings have ready explication. I am hungry: my body says it is time to eat. Some are much more complicated to discern. What, for example, is the purpose of despair? And is it useful or even safe to sit with such a feeling, invite it in, try to find its value? Certainly many practitioners draw a line with emotions that can create or indicate risk to or from a client.

Another client came to therapy complaining that she could not get over a loss. She and a person she described as the love of her life had decided to part ways. They were no good together. They fought all the time, argued, disagreed on everything.

She had some history with therapy and expected I would try to help her get over it, help her contain the feelings and wall them off in some way. But I prefer to swim in the river we have, not to try to change the river.

> Confucius was seeing the sights at Lüliang, where the water falls from a height of thirty fathoms and races and boils along for forty li, so swift that no fish or other water creature can swim in it. He saw a man dive into the water, and supposing that the man was in some kind of trouble and intended to end his life, he ordered his disciples to line up on the bank and pull the man out. But after the man had gone a couple of hundred paces, he came out of the water and began strolling along the base of the embankment, his hair streaming down, singing a song. Confucius ran after him and said, "At first I thought you were a ghost, but now I see you're a man. May I ask if you have some special way of staying afloat in the water?"
>
> "I have no way. I began with what I was used to, grew up with my nature, and let things come to completion with fate. I go under with the swirls and come out with the eddies, following along the way the water goes and never thinking about myself. That's how I can stay afloat."
>
> (Zhuangzi, 2013, Chapter 19, para. 39)

I asked the client why she would ever want to get over the love of her life, and at first she was so surprised by the question she had no way to answer it or even understand it. I had to explain.

"If this person was really the love of your life, isn't it unreasonable to ask you, to ask yourself, to do something so unreasonable as to get over it? Doesn't that seem callous to you?"

And then she cried. It was the first time for me that it seemed so much happened in the first day of therapy. The client knew this was why all her previous efforts had failed her, why she still felt so much pain after this break-up that had happened two years before. She was not swimming in the currents, letting them pick her path. She was trying to push against the currents of her emotions, to swim upstream back to a place where she had never had this love, never been hurt by this love, never lost this love.

An uncomfortable truth for humans is that we are what we feel. What we think in language is just a thin scum floating on a very deep pond, and most of that pond is our feelings. The reason we can never simply get over our lost loves is because the love we feel is us, and the disappointment we feel is us, and the sadness and the grief we feel is us. The being that feels the feelings is not distinct from the feelings felt by the being.

Thus to try to annihilate grief is to try to annihilate part of the self, an important part that exists for a purpose. Think again of the person running from their shadow: it cannot be outrun, only accepted and made peace with. Grief informs us as to the depth of our love. Then this is accurate and reso-nates, why would one ever wish to be done with grief? When we accept grief as an expression of our love, why would one not both weep and rejoice at funerals?

This client made a lot of progress very quickly and not all that progress was permanent. In Zen Buddhism there is the concept of satori—and not being a Zen Buddhist I will likely err in this description. Satori can be understood as a glimpse behind reality, a sudden and inspiring new perspective that hints at enlightenment. Enlightenment is said to be the end result of all the years of study and practice, and satori the occasional peak experiences on the way there.

What my client experienced that first day was satori, not enlightenment; it was a way to value some of the pain, not a cure for the pain. She continued to hurt. She left therapy with me feeling quite good about life, with a new love she learned how to fight with productively and feelings she learned to respect more. And after a year or two she wanted more help I could not provide because I was out of the business of doing therapy.

This is sometimes the best we can do: to live better with our pain, to feel the same pain in a new way that is more satisfying, and gradually become the swimmer in experience. The Taoist and the Buddhist might suggest that the person really swimming in the experience has learned how to not experience suffering any longer. Give up attachment, give up grief. This is a disagreement I cannot overlook and the major reason I am neither a Taoist nor a Buddhist.

Perhaps if we had another year or two, if I could have been available on the occasional basis the client wished me to be available, I could have swam with her through her griefs and loves and other experiences. She was beautiful and sexual, passionate and brave. Such swimming held the promise of great currents, rapids, white water, and falls, things not to contain or resist but to be carried along by.

The therapist has the privilege of coming out on the far bank of their clients' experiences. The river is impermanent. For the client, though, such swimming is uninterrupted by banks and dry land. The feelings are not a river to navigate but a life to live in. They are their feelings just as we are ours. If we can swim alongside them for a short time and not fight the currents, we might do something worthwhile.

References

Dias, J. (2010). *Paintings in sand: Existential parables in a mythic voice.* Colorado Springs, CO: Dias Family Books.

Erikson, E., & Erikson, J. (1996). *The life cycle completed, extended version.* New York, NY: W. W. Norton & Co.

Greenberg, J., Koole, S., & Pyszczynski, T. (Eds.). (2004). *Handbook of experimental existential psychology.* New York, NY: The Guileford Press.

Lee, B., & Little, J. (2001). *Bruce Lee: An artist of life.* Rutland, VT: Tuttle.

May, R. (1950). *The meaning of anxiety.* New York, NY: Literary Licensing, LLC.

Merton, T. (2010). *The way of Chuang Tzu.* New York, NY: New Directions Publishing Corp.

Schneider, K., & Krug, O. (2009). *Existential-humanistic therapy.* Washington, DC: American Psychological Association.

Van Kaam, A. (1966). *The art of existential counseling: A new perspective in psychotherapy.* Wilkes-Barre: Dimension Books.

Weixin, Q. (1949). *Essays in Zen Buddhism.* (D. Suzuki, Trans.). New York, NY: Grove Press.

Zhuangzi. (1998). *Wandering on the way: Early Taoist tales and parables of Chuang Tzu.* (V. Mair, Trans.). Honolulu, HI: University of Hawaii Press.

Zhuangzi. (2013). *The complete works of Zhuangzi.* [Kindle for Android, 4.3.0.204]. (B. Watson, Trans.). Retrieved from Amazon.com

3

STEADINESS IN THE MIDST OF CHAOS

Michael Moats

FIGURE 3.1 Created by Anna Chiara

In the nineteenth chapter of the book *Zhuangzi:*

> Yen Yuan commented on Confucius, saying, "I was crossing the gorge at Chang Shan and the boatman guided the boat with real verve. I said to him, 'Can one study how to guide a boat?' He said, "Indeed. Someone who can swim well will have no trouble. If someone can dive under water, he may not have seen a boat before but he will know what to do." I asked him what this meant, but he could not say, so I am asking you: what do his words mean?
>
> "A good swimmer learns quickly," said Confucius, "because he knows how to ignore the water. Someone who can swim under the water may indeed have never seen a boat, but he regards the waters as though they were dry land, and the overturning of a boat as nothing more serious than a wagon turning over. So he too learns quickly. All forms of life can be overturning or sliding downwards right in front of his eyes, but he is not affected, nor does it disturb his inner calm, so there is nothing bad that can disturb him! In an archery competition, you shoot as skillfully as possible, hoping to win. If you compete to win decorated buckles, you are concerned with your aim. If you compete for gold, it can make you very nervous. Your skills are the same in all these cases, but because one of these is more significant than the others, this puts external pressure on you. To pay too much attention to such external things makes you thoughtless about the internal things."
>
> *(Zhuangzi, 2006, Chapter 19, para. 15–16)*

★Reproduced by permission of Penguin Books Ltd. Translated by Palmer, Martin with Breuilly, Elizabeth, Wai Ming, Chang, and Ramsay, Jay. *The Book of Chuang Tzu* (Arkana, 1996). Chapter 19, para. 15–16. Copyright © ICOREC, 1996.

Guiding the Boat

American comedian, Jerry Seinfeld, had a humorous observation on our relationship with water. He shared that we are made of water, bathe in water, play in water but will panic at the first raindrop that unexpectedly hits us. We freeze as if time had stopped. The idea that we, beings made primarily of water, are about to have water on us without our control changes everything. We run, we scatter, and we avoid. This irony is nonsensical without taking into consideration the deeper meaning, similar to that of Yen Yuan's encounter with the boatman.

How confusing this would be to the person only desiring to cross from one piece of land to another, while admiring the tool that facilitates his safe and dry journey. The very idea that the answer to gaining skill in guiding the boat comes from below the surface of the water had not entered his mind. He likely thought, "I am asking about the boat and you are telling me about water"? The man's focus is on the very object that keeps him from being submerged, similar to how people view happiness, peace, and comfort. The constant striving for happily maneuvering from one dry piece of comfortable land to the peacefulness of another without risking the dampness of the dark waters keeps the individual blindly dependent upon the external things of this world, or the overreliance on the rational self to avoid the emotional self.

Motivated by the need to maintain an illusion of peace, the passenger cannot see that his hidden, deeper motivation is that of his fear of loss: loss of his fantasy of control, loss of his *myth* (May, 1991) of happiness without suffering, or perhaps his sense of comfort. Tillich (2000) wrote, "The dangers connected with the change, the unknown character of the things to come, the darkness of the future make the average man a fanatical defender of the established order" (p. 66). In attempting to protect the fantasy, myth, or sense of comfort, the passenger, you and I, may seek out tools that help to seemingly maintain our highly coveted sense of peace. From the easily overlooked and often subconscious mental tools of denial and rationalization, to the more recognized pathological addictions of drugs, pornography, alcohol, and sex, people attempt to grasp at forms of external euphoria and thus enter into a dependency on a false sense of security. Even work can provide an oasis from one's unsatisfactory home life or low sense of self-worth by either avoiding the issues needing to be addressed or feeding on empty, external crumbs of external validation to keep the depths of unexplored emotions at bay. This theme is also touched upon in Zhuangzi's parable of Flight from the Shadow, in which a man "was so disturbed by the sight of his own shadow and so displeased with his own footsteps that he determined to get rid of both" (Merton, 2010, p. 155) by running away from them. His efforts to avoid them were so great that he lost sight of his options and dropped dead from exhaustion. We are capable of using just about anything to distance *ourselves* or escape our perceptions. But the unfortunate reality is that the greater lengths one takes to avoid one's fear, running from one's shadow or submersing into one's own waters, the more of an unknowing slave one becomes to what one fears, as well as hastily closing the gap between one's perceptual beast and oneself. There are physical dangers, or costs, in trying to escape one's emotional self.

Viktor Frankl (2006), a Holocaust survivor, shared a fable that speaks to how the power of fear and avoidance of loss, or symbolic death, can cause us to distort reality and react without clarity in an effort to *feel* as though we can *control* loss:

> A rich and mighty Persian once walked in his garden with one of his servants. The servant cried that he had just encountered Death, who had threatened him. He begged his master to give him his fastest horse so that he could make haste and flee to Teheran, which he could reach that same evening. The master consented and the servant galloped off on the horse. On returning to his house the master himself met Death, and questioned him, "Why did you terrify and threaten my servant?" "I did not threaten

him; I only showed surprise in still finding him here when I planned to meet him tonight in Teheran," said Death.

(p. 56)

Learning how to tolerate the discomfort of meeting Death, or facing potential loss (e.g., embarrassment, judgment, actual loss), and making changes that lead to breaking the *dependency* on the external things in life can sometimes be limited by our false sense of independent control. It is our need for that false sense of control that has us asking, "Can one study how to guide a boat?" In other words, can one safely gain knowledge on how to control this boat that keeps me from the water? Guiding a boat and navigating the waters are two different things. This is why Confucius states, "Someone who can swim under the water may indeed have never seen a boat, but he regards the waters as though they were dry land, and the overturning of a boat as nothing more serious than a wagon turning over" (Zhuangzi, 2006, Chapter 19, para. 15).

*Reproduced by permission of Penguin Books Ltd. Translated by Palmer, Martin with Breuilly, Elizabeth, Wai Ming, Chang, and Ramsay, Jay. *The Book of Chuang Tzu* (Arkana, 1996). Chapter 19, para. 15. Copyright © ICOREC, 1996.

Land is something we trust due to familiarity. There is security in what has been experienced with the support of the ground and the consistent law of gravity. However, although the water appears to be concrete and have form, the inability to grasp it and the unknowns it holds can create uncertainty and fear. By swimming in the water, one can become a student of the water, a student of self, gaining understanding of its currents and waves, building a sense of peace with what was once unknown, mysterious, and perhaps frightening. Only through engagement, through struggle, can resilience and understanding be attained (Moats, 2010). Confucius shares, "All forms of life can be overturning or sliding downwards" (Zhuangzi, 2006, Chapter 19, para. 16) but the individual who has swum beneath the waters will understand how to navigate the boat, to navigate life. He understands the difference between influence and control, which is reminiscent of the Serenity Prayer adopted by Alcoholics Anonymous: "God grant us the serenity to accept the things we cannot change, courage to change the things we can, and wisdom to know the difference" (Niebuhr, n.d.).

The Case of Samantha

Clinicians frequently encounter clients with limited ability to remain steadfast in the midst of chaos. One such client was Samantha, who had become so weary of facing the water that she had all but given up on even having the ferryman transport her across. She had an abusive family, relied on alcohol to ineffectively cope with what she did not want to feel or explore (her waters), and was giving up on life. Her ability to deny, to rationalize, and to escape through the use of alcohol were no longer able to hold back the waves of the sad realities she was trying to avoid. Rather than symbolically hold her head underwater as her family had done to her, which only instilled a greater distrust and fear, our therapy would provide an invitation to play in the shallows, until she was ready to wade deeper and eventually swim above and below the water line. In doing so, she had to face her fears and challenge old ways of thinking while tolerating the discomfort in creating a new way of being.

Samantha's prior way of being was leading her to increasing thoughts of suicide, which can be understood as a distorted attempt to feel in control of her life and a myth that she had learned to trust. She expressed that it was a miserable existence but one that was known and consistent, similar to the "wagon turning over" on dry land; she believed she knew how to deal with this. On the other hand, she also desired something different and initially wanted to learn how to guide the boat, attempting to skip over the significant need to first engage the water. The moment of change came when she recognized I would be by her side as she struggled to find her peace. Often she desired for me to hold her out of the water or to keep her afloat. Yet I would only offer encouragement and provide options while giving her a grounding point to help her stay oriented.

Samantha sometimes struggled and wanted to give up. But her persistence and willingness to tolerate the discomfort eventually transformed into resiliency, strength, and peace. She began to see that whereas she originally had been tolerating the discomfort with masking agents, without any progress, she is now able to change her suffering into meaning through the active swimming and struggling. Upon her termination from therapy, I shared a reflection I had written about her process and our time together, called *Adrift*:

> The warm blood in her heart, kept contained in her veins as to not draw the sharks that circle in the darkness, gives life to either, yet the duration differs. Floating alone at sea with the salt from her tears burning her eyes, she is weary and parched, numb to the jellyfish stings. The question replays in her mind with each passing wave, do I swim or do I drink?
>
> A colorful deviation bobs nearby. She ponders. An illusion? Maybe. A dream? Doubtful. For, it would mean that I am in a restful sleep. Do I bother to investigate? What the hell!
>
> This useless, old plank, weathered and cracked seems to carelessly drift around her. What is the likelihood? She grabs in desperation and attempts to push herself up on it, but it fails to lift her burdens from the water. Instead, she feels sharpness in her hand and recoils in confusion as her timbered optimism resurfaces. She hoped for buoyancy and, instead, got a splinter. Another let down? Damned to disappointment?
>
> In spite of the sting and anger she reaches again, refusing to let go. "I'm tired and . . . damn that splinter!" She looks to her hand. "Maybe

I can just inhale and let the waters take me . . . son of a bitch!" Nestled under the skin, she cannot seem to shake the pointed discomfort. "I actually thought this old board could save me"? The absurdity can no longer be ignored. How can this board float so at peace? Tossed by the waves it simply floats on. No fight. Her wry smile surfaces and shines brighter than the sun, and she begins to laugh.

Rolling to her back, she holds the plank close. Still aware of the water, she now feels the warmth of the sun on her face. Still wet, still alone, except for her wooden companion, yet something is different. She sees the clouds that will give her respite. She sees the gulls breaking free from gravity and finding nourishment from the depths that once consumed her. And, there is that damn splinter that will not go away.

A sea of water and nothing to drink. A painful splintering reminder that she is alive. What she wants could kill her, what causes discomfort interrupts the eddy in her mind. A current of determination creates peaceful freedom. "I don't know where I am going, but I know the sun rises in the East. If I die it will not be because of my decision. It will be because it was inevitable." And so, she swims.

This client was someone that Zhuangzi would say could navigate a boat through waters without ever having seen a boat because she first learned to swim in the waters. The symbolic waters offer gifts to those who are willing to swim through them and not simply bob in them or simply swim in an effort to get out of them. These gifts can be confidence in the self, embracing the understanding of influence (the relationship of one's power and limitations in relation to another power, such as a waterway or the wind) versus control (exerting power over something or someone), and that in spite of a situation we still can choose how to respond.

Archery

Following down the same path of being motivated by loss, Zhuangzi employs the analogy of an archery contest. Being an avid archer and hunter, the symbolism is both personal and powerful in how it highlights the intense concentration and mindful action that is required to hit the chosen target, regardless of the prize sought. With each additional measure of distance between the archer and the target, even the slightest deviation, shake, or misjudgment can have exponential negative effects on the shooter's success. Hours of practicing at different distances, in different environments, and with numerous shots that are less than perfect are required to continuously hone one's ability. Awareness of one's breath, the wind, the animal (if hunting), fatigue, anchor points, the target, and one's distractibility are all things that are being self-monitored while aiming and releasing the arrow. However, there is also a balance of knowing and not-knowing, of releasing the arrow through Wu Wei (無爲/无为), or inaction. Herrigel's (1999) account of learning to better himself with a bow demonstrates the need to relentlessly practice his release of the bow in a manner that is intentionally without intention, without mind and without choice, in which the arrow shoots itself.

With all that is required, any distraction beyond engaging the bow is likely to cause the very thing the archer is trying to avoid—failure. As the prize increases from "decorated buckles" to "gold," the amount of potential loss increases and can easily become distracting. "Your skills are the same in all these cases, but because one of these is more significant than the others, this puts external pressure on you." It is inner worth and inner sense of confidence that provides stability.

The archer is familiar with his bow, his arrows, and himself. He understands the impact of wind and distance on the flight of his arrows. These parameters do not change, whether it is practice or a competition. So he must maintain his reliance on what is under his influence, rather than being distracted by the pursuit for success. Frankl (2006) shares that the more one aims at success, like happiness, the more it eludes him because it must be a byproduct rather than something achieved. Therefore, much like the competitive archer competing for the prize, he must do what he knows to do rather than allow himself to be distracted by success or loss.

If the archer is capable of detaching from the prize and maintaining his mindful use of the skills he has attained by shooting thousands of arrows in practice, he increases his chances of winning; he does not guarantee it. Similar to Samantha proactively swimming in the sea, if the archer can place more value on the "inner things" than on the "external things," even if he ends up losing the competition, it was not because of his lack of effort; rather, it was because it was inevitable.

Conclusion

Through the use of the interaction of the water, boat, and passenger, as well as the bow, the archer, and the prize, Zhuangzi highlights the importance of creating personal freedom through a deeper understanding of one's self, emotions, fears, and abilities. He demonstrates the significance of working toward something instead of being motivated by the fear of loss. Understanding one's influence, instead of living with the illusion of having control, allows the synthesis of these lessons to create inner strength, in which the "overturning" of things in one's life does not "disturb his inner calm." Where the fear of loss perpetuates the loss trying to be avoided, the courage to embrace uncertainty decreases the fear of engagement through resiliency that the struggle builds. Strengthening of the self negates the need for dependency and increases the ability for interdependency.

References

Frankl, V. (2006). *Man's search for meaning*. Boston: Beacon Press.

Herrigel, E. (1999). *Zen in the art of archery*. (R. F. C. Hull, Trans.). New York: Vintage Book.

May, R. (1991). *The cry for myth*. New York: W. W. Norton & Co.

Merton, T. (2010). *The way of Chuang Tzu*. New York, NY: New Directions Publishing Corp.

Moats, M. (2010). *Learning through loss: A qualitative study investigating United States and Chinese meaning making through bereavement* (Doctoral dissertation, University of the Rockies). Available on ProQuest database.

Niebuhr, R. (n.d.). [Website Article on the Origin of the Serenity Prayer]. Retrieved from http://www.aahistory.com/prayer.html

Tillich, P. (2000). *The courage to be* (2nd ed.). New Haven, CT: Yale University Press.

Zhuangzi. (2006). *The book of Chuang Tzu*. [Kindle for Android, 4.3.0.204]. (M. Palmer, Trans.). Retrieved from Amazon.com

PART II

Knowledge and Epistemology

4

HUMANITY'S SEARCH FOR MEANING IN EXISTENCE

A Taoist Epistemology

Rodger Broomé

FIGURE 4.1 Created by Trish Vernazza

In order to guide his students to become more critical thinkers, a professor of psychology in my undergraduate studies, David Yells, guided us to always ask two questions when considering a knowledge claim. First, "what do you mean?" And second, "how do you know?" The purpose of these questions is to clarify a claim in the context of the way in which the claimant arrived at his or her conclusion (Yells, Clark, & Johns, 2003). This was meant to be advice to us for estimating the value of a claim and how *certain* we could be in its usefulness and how we might apply that knowledge.

Since the beginning of time, people have wanted to have more and more knowledge. Human beings have sought to master their world and protect themselves against life's tragedies and misfortunes. In primitive times and to a lesser degree today, people would lean on superstitions and rituals to feel a sense of control in their lives (Becker, 1975). Most importantly, we wanted to maximize our prosperity (sustainable subsistence) and minimize or thwart *evil* or the source of all suffering and even death. In ritualistic systems of religion and superstition, people *found* answers and largely depended upon keeping misfortune at bay by following traditional conventions of living; both symbolically and practically. Much of the symbolic ritual was aimed at appeasing good spirits and garnering their protection against bad ones (Becker, 1975). But this is and was always dubious because the system still failed us from time to time, and it is certainty that helps us reduce our existential anxiety (May, 1996).

In the West, science has largely conquered (socio-politically speaking) religion and superstition as a means of knowing about ourselves, our world, and the cosmos. Early on in Western philosophy, the great thinkers sought truth. They wanted to discover the truth about the human condition and the world. Science was the child of philosophy, particularly epistemology, which means the study of how we can know things, and the early scientists set out to discover the laws of nature. By understanding the laws of the cosmos, human beings believed that we could figure out how to manipulate aspects of nature for our benefit. In science, *certainty* became a primary value over truth (Dillon, 1998). In short, Western science is a knowledge-producing process by which observation and logic is used to construct knowledge toward a greater understanding of something. But knowledge is always incomplete, which means there is always some ambiguity within the realm of understanding. Therefore, knowledge seeks understanding while being the very building blocks of understanding. On the other hand, understanding is the ground upon which knowledge must be built, so some degree of understanding must exist prior to more knowledge being added to it in its construction. There is a never-ending circularity in the relationship between knowledge and understanding (Heidegger, 2008).

Language acquisition is a process that serves as a good example of the interplay between knowledge and understanding. Language is spoken and written, which means that it is both heard and read. Both the sounds we make and characters we write are complex systems of symbols. Fundamentally, children hear language first and so it is good to start there with understanding how we acquire language. Certain sounds and sound patterns become prominent. Soon they become associated with objects. Naming things comes first and then relating objects to other objects involves verbs. After a while, a person has a collection of sound patterns that relate to objects and activities. The point is, the language sounds and patterns are something that everyone is born into and taught. But children also make adorable language mistakes in grammar. These mistakes reveal little slices of their worldview about the things about which they are talking. As parents and teachers, we correct them and they acquire more refined knowledge of the language system. Furthermore, the correction can place a new perspective on the thing about which the child was speaking and a deeper understanding of the world via language is born.

Fluent language speakers become innovative. Slang and idiomatic uses of language are created by people wanting to put a fresh poetic on their expressions. Each generation creates some slang and some goes out of fashion. So while there is a stable system of formal language, there is also a creative and innovative dimension that is forever changing and playing within the infinite possibilities of arranging the sounds into new patterns. Even in regular conversation, people think about what they will say in a very general way then will begin to speak and formulate the actual words as they go. Consequently, we start with an understanding (idea) but formulate the expression into the particular words and sentences (script) according to the already-made structure of the language within the definitions and grammatical rules. As such, we surprise ourselves when we speak because we never know exactly what we are saying until we have said it (Landes, 2013).

At first, learning a second language is about learning sounds, words, and scripts. Learning phrases at first is total replication. The person thinks in his or her native language, translates it into the new language, and produces the speech in replication. But the speech is not phenomenologically expressive because the true expression begins in the native language. I remember the first time saying "谢谢" ("thank you") felt like an expression of gratitude. In my visit to China, I had learned to say it for the purpose of letting Chinese people know I was grateful. But after a half of a semester of college beginner Chinese back home, I began to say "谢谢" to my "老师" ("teacher") quite naturally in place of "thank you." It is my experience that short phrases that express emotion can be acquired much easier than practical sentences like asking for things or telling someone else something. Even young children can learn expletives very quickly, because they are expressions full of emotion. So it is evident that language reflects much of the way in which we know about and understand our world. There is an unstable-stability with which language is both replication and creation in a couple's dance that is not entirely complete until it has already been said. Language acquisition is never complete.

Even language experts are still learning more about language, but also because it is ever-being created and evolving through its use in society. Understanding our existence is also an unstable-stable process of continually unfolding knowledge acquisition that is integrated into one's understanding, but that also gives birth to new questions about life and living-it-toward finding truth.

The dialogic relationship between knowledge and understanding is paradoxically the expression and creation of meaning (Heidegger, 2008). As such, knowledge and understanding are always on their way toward *Truth* but without having the ability to ever capture it. This is because knowledge and understanding are both human products and our sense from life-experience is that Truth lies beyond what we can fully know and understand. However, it is still the work of scientists and philosophers to seek knowledge and understanding of the world, while ever so humble to Truth as it stands beyond our horizons of thought.

The Search for the Tao

Knowledge wandered north, looking for Tao (Zhuangzi, 1998, Chapter 22). In this first line, we can see that Knowledge seeks something beyond itself. Knowledge *knows* that it is incomplete and that there is something meaningful beyond its reach. Human beings are knowledgeable in the sense that we are the only beings on the face of the Earth that deal in meanings. Animals deal in significations, which is to say they simply use a sign to indicate something other than itself. But people deal in meanings through complex systems of symbols, both uttered and written, that we call language. Language is paradoxically both an expression of ideas while also being the fertile ground from which ideas can spring forth (Landes, 2013). Before we utter a word, there is a notion within us about what we might say, but it is not until we begin speaking or writing that our thoughts develop and are thus brought into existence. On the other hand, not one word could be uttered without there being a complex system of symbols (language) within which our thoughts could be born. Therefore, language is both the midwife of our ideas while also being the product of our thoughts. We have to know a language to use it, but languages originate from our minds due to our motivations to communicate our ideas to others. Our minds are powerful enough to deal with the idea of eternity, while recognizing our own finitude. Language gives us the ability to talk about eternity while being limited in its ability to fully explain it. Therefore, "The Tao that can be spoken is not the eternal Tao" (Lao Tzi, 2003, p. 5). Tao or Eternal Truth cannot be harnessed within knowledge and thus expressed in language. But that does not make seeking the Tao meaningless, useless, or foolish. There are many *hard problems* of existence that trouble us; make us feel lost in our worlds. But we can discover great and wonderful things in our pursuit of Eternal Truth, some of which we can discover within ourselves.

With every discovery, we find ourselves having reached one horizon only to find that there is another one in the distance. Life's journey in relationships, vocation, and hobbies is made up of a continual series of horizons pursued and achieved. Each journey allows for our discoveries and new knowledge through experience. "Discovery is really a mixture of instinct and method" (Husserl, 1970, p. 80). While Husserl was speaking in the context of philosophy and science, his reference to instinct really is addressing *that* which calls us toward a discovery. His reference to method is about the pathway we take toward that which calls us forth. "Knowledge wandered north to the banks of the Dark Water, where he climbed the hill of Obscure Prominence and happened to meet Dumb Non-action" (Zhuangzi, 1998, p. 210).

Knowledge thirsts for answers and the genuine philosopher or scientist understands that both pathways are self-correcting journeys. That is to say, philosophy and science provide answers until another replaces those answers. Integrity in science requires the scientist to seek accurate answers and understanding of that which he or she studies. For Husserl, the starting point is the observation and interrogation of experience as the starting point of inquiry. "Go back to the-things-themselves" is the rally cry of the phenomenologist to first look at how the world presents itself to consciousness in experience (Husserl, 2001). This is not to say that we should look inside ourselves for answers through introspection, like the psychoanalysts might suggest. Rather, it is to simply notice our present situation. It certainly is not a recommendation to seek the advice of the experts. In fact, phenomenology encourages us to suspend or let go of our already-attained knowledge so that we might see things with a fresh look. This is what Husserl (1983) called *bracketing*, which he adopted from mathematics. That is, we take our knowledge (presuppositions) and put them in brackets so that they can be brought into the equation at the proper time. If we do not suspend what we already know or think we know, all of our observations will still be influenced by those presuppositions. Not only in science and philosophy, but also in the counseling office, the taken-for-granted knowledge about things conceals the client's Way by dressing it up in theory and therapeutic procedures. Moreover, the client himself or herself is already clouded by his/her presuppositions about life's difficulties. For example, often times the expectations of others can be the source of the client's distress because he or she does not believe that the expectations can ever be fulfilled. May (2012) takes another perspective on the word *responsibility*, which is often used as another word for duty. He explains that *response-ability* is one's ability to respond to a current situation and in light of potential consequences. By divorcing the word from its common use as "duties," the presupposed way a person is feeling obligated to respond is bracketed so that new possibilities can be considered. In this way, the client can consider, "what are my options?"

Husserl's next methodological step is to use *imaginative variation* to open up the possibilities and identify what aspects of a situation are necessary or unchangeable (1983). Imaginative variation is a way of taking a thing in mind and modifying it so one can see what is essential and what is optional about it. We can do this with physical objects such as a table. What about a table is essential for it to be a table? We can imagine a table on a set of legs or on a pedestal. We can imagine a table high off of the ground or very close to it. We can imagine the table being made of wood, metal, plastic, etc. A table has to have a relatively flat surface, but we can see that a table with a slight slope does not change it from being a table into something else. Imaginative variation does get us to a place where we can say that a table has a relatively flat surface and is elevated off of the ground to some height. This mental exercise helps us consider options in a radical way so that we can begin to make some reasonable judgments about things. When considering psychosocial things such as relationships, love, hate, obligation, traditions, and other difficult life issues, we can use imaginative variation after having bracketed our presuppositions to get a better idea about what lies beyond our current knowledge and understanding.

When we consider mental issues that do not have tangible features like the table example, we have to interrogate them very carefully. We must bear in mind that there are aspects of mental and social things that are generally consistent and other aspects that are dependent upon the situation. By using imaginative variation, we can do mental comparisons regarding the mental issue at hand to determine which qualities or characteristics of the issue are essential and which are merely circumstantial. Imaginative variation is not a special skill. People use it all of the time when thinking about something hypothetical and imagining, "What if it was different?" (Husserl, 1983). When we have experienced something like an interpersonal conflict, we often reflect on the argument and think about things we might have said, things we should have said, and that which we heard. We modify the argument in our heads to see if there are aspects of the conversation that are unclear or might have gone better, or even start thinking about the next conflict with that person if the problem wasn't satisfactorily resolved. In descriptive phenomenological research, we do the same with the transcripts of the research participants who gave us their account of a particular real-world experience. We go through the story and consider each issue of the narrative using imaginative variation to help us to formulate expressions about the essential meanings of the experience. With those essential meanings, we create a unified descriptive account of those essential meanings to elucidate the general aspects of the experience that make it what it is (Giorgi, 1985, 2009). The purpose for using a human science approach to examining human experience is so that we can exercise caution during our analysis and avoid rushing to judgment. Science in this context provides us with a way to discover knowledge in a methodical and systematic way to render general understanding that can be critically reviewed by others (Giorgi & Giorgi, 2003). No scientific method should become dogma, but when we use a system of focused inquiry to explore our psychological worlds, we avoid jumping to conclusions and imposing our thoughts onto the experience of the others whose stories we intend to faithfully represent theoretically.

Being unsuccessful with his questions, Knowledge swung south to the White Water, climbed Solitary Confine and found Mad Stammerer, who claimed to have all of the answers (Zhuangzi, 1998, Chapter 22). Mad Stammerer is imposing one's will on something without considering its nature. In other words, it is operating on our presuppositions about the thing or state of affairs. We take what we already think we know, and impose it upon the thing or situation to define it without considering the best approach to it. Moreover, we often use tools within our approach that fashions the thing according to our will and skill with tools, rather than illuminating its natural essences. While "the Tao is eternal, nameless the Uncarved Block . . . Once the block is carved, there are names" (Yu-Lan, 1997, p. 95). Like much of Western psychology, imposing theoretical interpretations and models can have great utility, but it is carving the block. It is arbitrary, artificial, and has purpose toward achieving a goal. That goal is to produces answers to problems very much like Act-on-Impulse the Inspired Prophet proposed to do. But by getting dogmatically wrapped up in its theories, concepts, and medicalized terminology, mainstream Western psychology has forgotten what it is about—the study of the human psyche or soul as an embodied consciousness (Husserl, 1977; Giorgi, 2001). What it is like for the whole being to navigate his or her world is really what concerns us.

In the West, there are two distinct categories of psychology: scientific/academic and clinical/professional. These two streams of psychology were driven by different motivations. The first was driven by a political movement to achieve scientific status alongside of physics, biology, and other natural sciences (Giorgi, 1970). The medical model and a desire to be included among medical practitioners and the healthcare industry drove the second (Szasz, 2007). Behaviorism led by Watson (1913) proclaimed that psychology was a physical science of the study of behavior. Its scope and purpose was to study behavior so that human beings' actions could be predicted and controlled. Behaviorism made important contributions and politically took primacy in academia because it could "do something" (Giorgi, 1970). To some degree, we have learned to somewhat predict and steer people through psychological strategies. Clinical psychology fashioned theories and practice by adopting the metaphor of "mental illness" and its associated medical nomenclature (e.g., diagnosis, treatment, patient, etc.) (Szasz, 2007). By adopting the natural sciences paradigm and language, or by adopting the medical model and vernacular, psychology is a carved block of wood in the shape of things very contrary to the nature of the psyche. When people are having a crisis of their existence, these carved blocks readily provide superficial answers, but they are based on the forgotten subject matter of psychology, the human person.

Knowledge went last to the Palace of the Emperor Ti, and asked his questions of Ti. Ti replied: "To exercise no-thought and follow no-way of meditation is the first step toward understanding Tao" (Merton, 1965/2004, p. 137). That is to say that nobody can figure out truly the way he or she ought to go about living by following prescribed theories and practices fashioned by the human will and desires. The Third-Force psychology emerged out of the discontentment of psychologists who did not see their clients or subject matter as mechanistic things to be manipulated or fixed. Rather, the Third-Force (Existential-Humanistic Psychology) sought to honor the whole person as its subject matter with his or her human social and cosmological context (Bugental, 1964). What this means is to re-look at psychology through a new viewpoint and to honor human persons in their natural habitat. "To dwell nowhere and rest in nothing is the first step toward resting in Tao. To start from nowhere and follow no road is the first step toward attaining Tao" (Merton, 1965/2004, pp. 137–138). That is to say that one must observe the nature of his or her life and seek to follow the natural path rather than forcibly carve an inauthentic path for him or herself. Having no dwelling is to begin without an already-made ideology that defines things and determines its use. This concept returns us to an existential-phenomenological approach to *going back to the things themselves* (Giorgi, 1985; Husserl, 2001). A pure science of humanity or human science goes to the human person in his or her life-world to observe and figure out how it lives and experiences his or her life-world. By examining the lived experience of the human person, we can discover the natural patterns and flow of his or her world navigation against that which is not working. Very often, the aspects of living that are artificial and imposed on a person from other people are the dysfunctional parts of life when they are in their extreme forms.

Client Searching for Answers

I did some counseling work with a police detective who was troubled by some of the horrible things he had to face while investigating child sex-abuse crimes. One particular case troubled him, because it involved an adolescent girl who had been molested by her father for many years. At an overnight girl party, she shared a story about the molestation while innocently believing that all the other girls also had sexual relationships with their fathers. Needless to say, the girls disclosed this disturbing information to their parents, who called the police and initiated the investigation.

My client revealed some horrifying details about the case and what this abuse victim had suffered. He talked about how it had been years since the investigation, the man was in prison, and the house had been demolished incidentally due to some urban development. Nevertheless, the detective described how he avoided the intersection where the house once stood because it would conjure mental images of the horrific abuse that had taken place there. The detective spoke about how he would go into the restaurant where the girl was employed and she would always greet him excitedly with an embrace and a smile. It would break his heart to *know* what had happened to her and yet she still would happily greet him with such enthusiasm. How could he make the terrible feelings stop and the mental images of what had happened go away? That was what he came to me seeking help for.

Through our discussion, I asked what it would *mean* if he was able to forget completely what had happened. What would it mean if you could see that girl and feel nothing? He thought a long time silently. He replied to me, "Man, you're good." I realized that he thought I was posing a hypothetical question and would soon provide the answer for clarification of what was implied. I waited patiently, silently, and was present for his answer in the spirit of non-doing, the Speechless One (Zhuangzi, 1998, Chapter 22). I had asked the question for us to explore, but he was much like one who was seeking answers from Act-On-Impulse/Mad Stammerer whose many words would be forgotten as soon as they were said (Zhuangzi, 1998, Chapter 22). The answer really had to come from him. Finally, he told me that it would mean he was coldhearted. But I recognized the indictment that he had leveled on himself in relation to his feelings. Being coldhearted would mean that he didn't care, but it also carried with it that he was violating a duty to care as a police officer and more so as a human being. After asking him what coldhearted meant to him, he affirmed that being uncaring was not a normal human emotion to such sadness and he was afraid of becoming unsympathetic about others' pain.

The paradox is here, to continue to experience pain and horrifying images was disrupting his life and personal relationships. On the other hand, to become uncaring and coldhearted meant that he would lose the capacity to love, even in his personal relationships. So I asked, "Would you prefer to be indifferent to all of the victims and have your memory erased, or would you prefer to embrace the pain and keep them in your heart as people for whom you were their hero? Is forgetting the goal, and then what would that mean? *Is there a way of taking the painful memory and realizing that it only hurts because that person matters to you?*" It was in the final question that I saw my client's posture and facial expression relax. In facing directly the painful memories of the abuse victims' stories, he could see that they all had mattered to him. The detective's experience in the work had inherent meaning to it and his pain was the residue of having ushered these children out of their victimhood and into a new horizon of survival.

In no way was the pain or the search for meaning over. But in life, this is also true. It really is not about putting one's problems to rest, but learning how to dwell with them and understand them. Each problem that we face directly and successfully navigate prepares us to face future problems. The answers paradoxically come from observing the world and the natural order of things while also creating meaning by adding our own inner wisdom wrought by knowledge, experience, and understanding.

Conclusion

Our knowledge and understanding often come from sources that were there before us. We look for answers from authorities beginning with our parents. As children, we seek answers from our parents and exploring our worlds within the limitations they allow. We find that our parents' guidance gives us a sense of certainty and security. Like Western science, we feel comfortable with *knowing* facts, but there are always unanswered questions that leave our *understanding* incomplete. Science and philosophy provide some ready-made answers. Science and philosophy are knowledge resources and often provide very practical ways of dealing with problems. Both are knowledge-producing projects for people to come to a better understanding of our existence. Each person however, has to use the learning resources available to him or her, and having a mentor and guide is certainly helpful. But ultimately, living the Tao is living toward wisdom and truth. This is because "[t]he Tao that can be spoken is not the eternal Tao" (Lao Tzi, 2003, p. 5).

References

Becker, E. (1975). *Escape from evil*. New York, NY: The Free Press.

Bugental, J. F. T. (1964). The third force in psychology. In *The Journal of Humanistic Psychology, 4*(1), 19–25.

Dillon, M. C. (1998). *Merleau-Ponty's ontology* (2nd ed.). Evanston, IL: Northwestern University.

Giorgi, A. P. (1970). *Psychology as a human science: A Phenomenologically based approach*. New York, NY: Harper & Row.

Giorgi, A. P. (2001). The search for the psyche: A human science perspective. In K. J. Schneider, J. F. T. Bugental, & J. F. Pierson (Eds.), *The handbook of humanistic psychology: Leading edges in theory, research and practice* (pp. 53–64). Thousand Oaks, CA: Sage.

Giorgi, A. P. (2009). *The descriptive phenomenological method in psychology: A modified Husserlian approach*. Pittsburgh, PA: Duquesne University.

Giorgi, A. P. (Ed.). (1985). *Phenomenology and psychological research*. Pittsburgh, PA: Duquesne University.

Giorgi, A. P., & Giorgi, B. M. (2003). The descriptive phenomenological psychological method. In P. M. Camic, J. E. Rhodes, & L. Yardley (Eds.), *Qualitative research in psychology: Expanding perspectives in methodology and design* (pp. 243–259). Washington, DC: American Psychological Association.

Heidegger, M. (2008). *Being and time*. New York, NY: Harper Perennial.

Husserl, E. (1970). *Crisis of European sciences and transcendental phenomenology: An introduction to phenomenological philosophy*. (D. Carr, Trans.). Evanston, IL: Northwestern University.

Husserl, E. (1977). *Phenomenological psychology: Lectures, summer semester, 1925*. New York, NY: Springer.

Husserl, E. (1983). *Ideas pertaining to a pure phenomenology and to a phenomenological philosophy: First book: General introduction to a pure phenomenology*. (F. Kersten, Trans.). New York, NY: Springer.

Husserl, E. (2001). *Logical investigations, vol. 1.* (D. Moran & M. Dummett, Trans.). New York, NY: Routledge.

Landes, D. (2013). *Merleau-Ponty and the paradoxes of expression.* New York, NY: Bloomsbury.

Lao Tzi. (2003). *Tao Te Ching: The definitive edition.* (J. Star, Trans.). New York, NY: Penguin Group.

May, R. (1996). *The meaning of anxiety.* New York, NY: Norton & Norton.

May, R. (2012). *Freedom and destiny.* New York, NY: Norton & Norton.

Merton, R. (1965/2004). *The way of Chuang Tzu.* Boston, MA: Shambhala.

Szasz, T. (2007). *The medicalization of everyday life: Selected essays.* Syracuse, NY: Syracuse University.

Watson, J. (1913). Psychology as the behaviorist views it. *Psychological Review, 20,* 158–177.

Yells, D., Clark, S., & Johns, C. (2003). Psychology 1010 [video file]. *Utah Valley University* [Online]. Retrieved from http://desource.uvu.edu/videos/psy1010.php

Yu-Lan, F. (1997). *A short history of Chinese philosophy: A systematic account of Chinese thought from its origins to the present day.* (D. Bodde, Ed.). New York, NY: Free Press.

Zhuangzi. (1998). *Wandering on the way: Early Taoist tales and parables of Chuang Tzu.* (V. Mair, Trans.). Honolulu, HI: University of Hawaii Press.

5

KNOWLEDGE AND PSYCHOTHERAPY

Lessons from Zhuangzi's Parable "When Knowledge Went North"

Trent Claypool

FIGURE 5.1 Created by Natalia Mello

Psychotherapy is a difficult process to facilitate. Years of schooling and hundreds to thousands of hours of supervised training are typically required to begin practicing independently. Even at this point, there are typically requirements for continued education to remain licensed. However, education cannot be equated to competence. While education is critically important, there is also much power in the context of how this knowledge is brought into the therapeutic environment (Wampold & Imel, 2015). The following parable "When Knowledge Went North," found in Chapter 22 of the book *Zhuangzi*, offers some insight into the usefulness, or lack thereof, of knowledge.

Knowledge wandered north to the banks of the Dark Water, where he climbed the hill of Obscure Prominence and happened to meet Dumb Non-action. Knowledge said to Dumb Non-action, "I have some questions I wish to ask you. By what thought and what reflection may we know the Way? Where shall we dwell and how shall we serve so that we may be secure in the Way?" He asked three questions and still Dumb Non-action did not answer. Not only did he not answer, he did not know how to answer.

Being unsuccessful with his questions, Knowledge went back south to White Water, where he climbed upon Solitary Confine and caught sight of Mad Stammerer. Knowledge asked the same questions of Mad Stammerer. "Ah!" said Mad Stammerer, "I know the answer and will tell you." But right when he started to speak, he forgot what he wanted to say.

Being unsuccessful with his questions, Knowledge went back to the imperial palace where he saw the Yellow Emperor and asked him the questions.

The Yellow Emperor said, "Don't' think and don't reflect—only then may you begin to know the Way. Don't dwell and don't serve—only then may you begin to be secure in the Way. Have no departure and no way—only then may you begin to attain the Way."

Knowledge asked the Yellow Emperor, saying "You and I know the answers, but those two do not. Who's right?"

The Yellow Emperor said, "It's Dumb Non-action who's truly right. Mad Stammerer seems like he is, but you and I come last and not even close. Now,

One who knows does not speak;
One who speaks does not know.

Therefore, the sage practices a doctrine without words. The Way cannot be compelled and integrity cannot be forced. Humanness may be practiced;

righteousness may be slighted but ceremony is for being false to one another. Therefore, it is said,

> When the Way is lost,
>   afterward comes integrity,
> When integrity is lost,
>   afterward comes humanness.
> When humanness is lost,
>   afterward comes righteousness.
> When righteousness is lost,
>   afterward comes ceremony
> Ceremony is but the blossomy ornaments of the Way,
>   and the source is disorder.

Therefore, it is said,

> The practice of the Way results in daily decrease.
> Decrease and again decrease,
>   Until you reach non-action.
> Through non-action,
>   No action is left undone.

Now, is it not difficult for what has already become a thing to return to it's roots? Could anyone but the great man find it easy? "For life is the disciple of death and death is the beginning of life. Who knows their regulator? Human life is the coalescence of vita breath. When it coalesces there is life; when it dissipates there is death. Since life and death are disciples of each other, how should I be troubled by them? Thus the myriad things are a unity. What makes the one beautiful is its spirit and wonder; what makes the other loathsome is its stench and putrefaction. But stench and putrefaction evolve into spirit and wonder, and spirit and wonder evolve once again into stench and putrefaction. Therefore it is said, 'A unitary vital breath pervades all under heaven.' Hence the sage values unity."

Knowledge said to the Yellow Emperor, "When I asked Dumb Non-action and he didn't respond, not only didn't he respond, he didn't know how to respond. When I asked Mad Stammerer and he didn't tell me just when he was starting to do so, not only didn't he tell me, he forgot the questions just when he was starting to do so. Now, when I asked you, you knew the answers. Why did you say you weren't even close?"

"The reason Dumb Non-action was truly right," said the Yellow Emperor, "is because he didn't know. The reason Mad Stammerer seemed to be right is because he forgot. The reason you and I came last and were not even close is because we knew."

Mad Stammerer heard of this and considered the Yellow Emperor someone who knew how to speak.[1]

(Zhuangzi, 1998, pp. 210–212)

As this parable warns, the most dangerous practitioner is the one who "knows" and makes purposeful action based upon this "knowledge." We might call this blind knowing. This practitioner makes assumptions and disregards the client's truth. Take for example a therapy such as Eye-Movement Desensitization and Reprocessing (EMDR), which is a manualized therapy with eight phases, three of which are to be done verbatim in its orthodox protocol (Shapiro, 2001). In EMDR there are suggested scripts about several key elements of the therapy, including how to educate about the therapy process and how change occurs. With all of this in place to help the EMDR practitioner "know" how and what to do, there is still an element of wisdom, or wise knowing, required by the practitioner to appropriately apply the protocol. Guided by the moral of Zhuangzi's parable, a deeper look into the practice of EMDR appears to reveal three starkly different kinds of EMDR practitioners (and therapy practice in general): 1) the practitioner who knows; 2) the practitioner who does not know, but pretends to know; and 3) the practitioner who does not know and does not pretend to know. According to the ways of the Tao, it is only this third type of practitioner that may be able to wisely know.

Let's assess the danger of the first practitioner, the one who knows. Imagine the setting, if you will. A client walks into the practitioner's office adorned with degrees from prestigious institutions, certificates of achievement and competency from the appropriate accrediting bodies, and a license to practice psychotherapy. All of this is in service of one thing and one thing only: to bolster the practitioner into the role of expert, the one who possesses something worth paying for. The client agrees to consent forms that give permission for the treatment to begin. After a careful one-hour assessment, it is found that this particular client is afflicted with Posttraumatic Stress Disorder, a disorder of avoidance, disruptive intrusive experiences, and isolation. After careful consideration of the cluster of symptoms, the following treatment plan is made: one to three sessions of psycho-education on trauma-based disorders and learning skills to regulate emotions and soothe the central nervous system; one to three sessions learning mindfulness to develop the ability to observe internal experiences; and four to ten sessions reprocessing memories with EMDR. Being a well-trained practitioner and current with best practices, the sessions begin as indicated, the skills are taught with expert precision, and the reprocessing is done in a manner that would make Francine Shapiro, the founder of EMDR, proud. And so the therapy goes.

Now, there is nothing inherently wrong with this treatment plan, as long as it is used as a guidepost as opposed to a recipe to the treatment process. It is knowledge that is important to understand, and yet, it is advisable for the practitioner to leave this knowledge at the door, trusting that the spontaneity of connection and interaction will allow for the way to healing to reveal itself. This is the essential problem with blind knowledge; it does not allow for the lived experience and uniqueness of the client to shape the treatment process. Blind knowledge can readily produce brilliant interventions, but their application must go beyond this simple type of knowing. Embracing what is unknown (the idiosyncrasies of how the client is responding to the intervention, the client's strengths and limitations, their ability to relate to their internal world, and so on) will produce higher levels of client satisfaction and felt progress. It is based on a deep valuing and respect for the client. Intervening too quickly may have more to do with the practitioner's needs than the needs of the client. More specifically, when guided by blind knowledge, the practitioner is more in service of oneself than that of the client.

Indeed the parable of Action and Non-action found in Chapter 13 of the book *Zhuangzi* (Merton, 2010, pp. 80–81) tells us that the nature of those who comprehend is in not knowing and being centered in stillness. Zhuangzi explains further: as still water reflects back small details and becomes perfectly level, so too does pure spirit and a stilled heart become the mirror of all life. Pure spirit may be found in cultivating emptiness, stillness, calm, silence, and non-action, for resting in this spirit also allows for their opposite to emerge. The practitioner who is operating through non-action has no behaviors or sayings that are in anyway premeditated. Even with a scripted therapy with hundreds to thousands of hours of research substantiating its usefulness, none of it must be said or performed at any given moment. The practitioner is so in the moment and in tune with the client that her/his actions are completely spontaneous. The foundation for good therapy can be found through cultivating stillness, calm, and becoming actionless.

However, considering that this is the practitioner who knows, a few predictions can be made. This practitioner is going to be less likely to gather client feedback, more likely to continue the treatment when it's contraindicated, and thus more likely to experience client dropout. Keep in mind, it has been shown time and again that gathering client feedback about the progress of therapy and the nature of the therapeutic relationship has substantial positive influences on therapy outcomes (Lambert, 2010). This practitioner will likely be quite prescriptive, rarely lose command of the sessions, hold the belief that he/she can successfully read his/her clients, and be much less likely to consult with other professionals. This practitioner is likely to operate off of assumptions. For the practitioner who knows has no need to inquire about others' lived experience. Through these assumptions, one is all but guaranteed to miss the essence of the other's being. It is a dangerous lens, one of knowing, in therapy—perhaps one of the most dangerous mistakes a practitioner can make. Much like the Yellow Emperor was "last and not even close" to living in accordance with the Way, so too is the practitioner who knows. She/he is but the ceremonial ritual sourced from disorder. Recall, the Way cannot be compelled and integrity cannot be forced. The Way must be practiced through daily decrease until non-action is reached. From this place the practitioner can act without a sense of self, or according to Richard Schwartz (1995), from one's true self. This practitioner, however, is not operating in a place where this is possible.

Now, back to the case. This particular practitioner may be best described as an expert technician. The treatment will be wrapped in proficient technique. Every question the client may ask will be promptly answered, one wrapped in the shroud of mystery that only the practitioner may unravel. The client may or may not get better. If the client does not get better, the practitioner will almost certainly state that the reasons for a bad outcome are the client's problem, as the ingredients for healing, according to this practitioner, are held within the practitioner's knowledge.

Now consider the second practitioner, the one who does not know, but pretends to know. Even more so than the first practitioner, this practitioner's office will strive to convince the client, and themselves, that they know. Their accolades adorn their walls in service of mostly themselves, as the knowledge of not knowing combined with the posturing of knowing is too painful to experience. This practitioner, too, will forgo soliciting client feedback, as this may expose what they are attempting to hide. If they do solicit feedback, it will likely be taken quite personally and could be wounding. They too, will spend time creating an aura of mystery and omnipotence, but internally will be unsettled with the dissonance caused by their awareness that they don't really know. Their quest for knowledge, likely motivated by unconscious forces, is more about them than their client. They will gather information subtly through others and through this information may find a deeply unsettling feeling of being an imposter. Such practitioners will take pride in their relational abilities and will boast about the compliments from their clients.

Recall in the parable, when the Way was lost, along came integrity, a strong moral principle or virtue. The practitioner who pretends to know has not only lost integrity, but humanness as well. It is the loss of kindness. After all, what kindness can there be in selfishness, even if coming from a place of fear and lack of awareness? This practitioner clings to ceremony, as it provides the anxiety-reducing prescription necessary for the salvation of the ego while continuing to operate a practice. This person, though, at least has some awareness that they don't know and this could just be their path to salvation. In this way, what they see as their weakness is actually their strength and embracing this may lead to significant growth.

Now the third practitioner, the one who does not know and does not pretend to know, is truly in a place to be of best service to their client. This practitioner has what one might call a humble naïveté about the matters of their clients. Since they don't know, there are no assumptions and nothing is taken for granted. In this way, the practitioner is at once nothing and everything their clients may need. Through not knowing, an effortless attunement can be developed that allows for the natural ebb and flow of therapy to progress. In the Parable of the Woodworker found in Chapter 19 of the book *Zhuangzi* (Zhuangzi, 1998, pp. 182–183), this type of attunement is found through emptying oneself. The parable goes that an older man is swimming in water where no tortoise, alligator, fish, or turtle could swim. Confucius, having seen the swimmer, aligned his disciples along the current to rescue the man. However, after the man had gone several hundred yards, he emerged from the water by himself, singing and joyful. Confucius approached the man and inquired if he had a special way for treading water and the man responded that he had no special way. He began with what was innate, that he was born among the hills and feels secure in them; grew up with his nature, in the water, and feels secure in it; and completed his destiny, that he does not know why he is this way, yet that is how he is. He continued to explain how he entered the very center of the whirlpools and emerged as a companion of the torrents through following along with the way of the water, not imposing himself on it, and in doing so was able to fulfill his destiny. In therapy, every step of the clinician, including the impact of the therapy and the therapy relationship, is to be assessed and reassessed with humble openness. There is no moment when this stops. The clinician enters the whirlpools of their clients' lives and emerges a companion of the torrents of the heart, making no imposition. There is no moment when this practitioner will say that they understand the client. Understanding in this way is not necessary and certainly not possible. The moment that this is imposed, what is essential to good therapy is lost.

Now, a pivotal choice is to be made about how to practice in therapy. Is the practitioner to abandon the culture of psychotherapy today that requires elements of diagnosis and prescription—elements that are the ceremony of our time? Or, is the practitioner to practice within the givens of her/his existence in this time and place? It is essential to be aware of the forces that create opportunities of being "false to one another." This level of awake-ness, though, creates challenges, for as soon as this level is reached, a whole new level of responsibility is revealed. Being a part of and apart from the traditional ceremonies of practice is required. Actions come from non-action and true knowing comes from not knowing.

The following case example will serve as an illustration of the third type of practitioner. The client, who we will call Melissa, is a 37-year-old Caucasian female with a significant history of abuse. She has been married three times, always having found reason to leave her husband within the first few years. Her past partners were either too caring, physically abusive, or emotionally distant, leaving her with a deep feeling of isolation and victimization. She is currently on her fourth marriage. She works as a mental health technician at a local psychiatric hospital and found some of the stories of the patients triggering her past experiences with her parents. Her mother was an alcoholic and her biological father was never in her life. Around age 13, her mother remarried and this would start the most significant period of abuse in her life. Unbeknownst to her mother, her new husband was a sexual predator and would spend the next several years grooming her and her daughter to see and experience his sexual advances as not only acceptable, but an expression of love. With what appeared to be incredible precision and skill, he advanced from grooming behavior to peeping as Melissa bathed and changed clothes to groping and rape. There is no telling how far this may have progressed had Melissa not possessed the strength and courage to leave home at age 17. He would frequently tell her that she was the most precious thing in his life and that he deeply loved her. Melissa would later discuss how her sense of love had forever been distorted from these exchanges, especially as he was the most significant father figure she had known and she deeply wanted an adult figure to care about her.

She presents into therapy wanting first to decrease the number of intrusive experiences she has been having while at work and then secondly begin to understand what has been causing this distress. She initially had little insight into the connection of her past experiences with her stepfather and her triggers at work. The initial interview revealed this was because she had gone to extraordinary lengths to block out most explicit memories of the abuse she suffered at the hands of her stepfather, most notably through dissociation. Her disintegrated ego structure was observed to be similar to what might be expected given her history of many significant aversive childhood experiences. The ego structure was organized into parts that helped her to function and appear normal, parts that acted as defenses, and parts that held the trauma. Her apparently normal self was capable of going to work, exchanging pleasantries, and generally giving the appearance that there is no reason to be worried about her. Her defensive ego states protected her from reliving the trauma or potentially harmful events through producing deep shame and binge eating several times a week, followed by extreme guilt and obsessiveness about her body weight. In its extreme form, it resulted in derealization. After careful assessment, we came up with the following plan: 1) work on building her ability to experience emotions; 2) increase mindful awareness of her internal world; 3) develop skills to manage intrusive experiences through building alternative resources; and 4) begin to reprocess traumatic memories once she demonstrates the ability to experience distress and remain in control of her ability to dissociate. The goal was not for her to never dissociate, but rather to understand its functioning and begin to allow her to be in control of its role in her life.

Therapy progressed slowly at first, as there were many fires to be extinguished. At first, each week brought a new trigger along with anger and confusion. In a more memorable moment, she described her agony and fear while listening to an adolescent girl in a therapy group begin to talk about the sexual abuse she had experienced at the hands of an uncle. At this moment, her intrusive experiences shifted from being mostly somatic (gastrointestinal distress, weepiness, and a feeling of choking) to vivid flashbacks. She recalled the crippling effect of the flashback and her embarrassment that her peers were witnessing one of the tougher moments in her life. To a blindly knowing clinician, it might have been tempting to interpret this choking feeling as having been choked in one of the abusive experiences; however, the wise knowing clinician is able to suspend his "knowledge" and understand that this suggestion in and of itself could misdirect the trajectory of therapy into a witch hunt for that choking memory instead of allowing for the spontaneity of Melissa's own adaptive processing to properly place and heal that sensation. In this early stage of therapy, these moments were used to teach her how to contain her experience. Eventually, she was able to be aware of her triggers and had access to a plethora of tools and a more compassionate view of herself. That is, she had begun to have contact again with what Richard Schwartz (1995) would call her true self—that part of her that is acting from compassion and can openly relate and understand the parts of her that are angry, afraid, spiteful, demonizing, critical, sabotaging, and wounded. Over time (about a year) she began reporting a readiness to begin reprocessing her memories more directly and her therapeutic progress indicated that she became a reasonably good candidate for EMDR. Most notably, there was evidence of strong rapport from both the clinician's perspective as well as ratings from Melissa. She resoundingly showed the ability to tolerate emotional disturbance. Her life and relationship was more stable now. There were no medical or neurological conditions present that may interfere or make EMDR contraindicated. No alcohol or drug abuse, and the timing was appropriate, with no disruptions in her imminent treatment or any outside events in her life that would require her EMDR sessions to be delayed.

However, as Shapiro (2001) mentions, using EMDR with dissociative disorders is strongly discouraged without supervised training in advanced practices with EMDR—most notably, the cognitive interweave. We had also assessed the cost of healing, with Melissa coming to an acute awareness that processing her memories with her stepfather could potentially lead to an acknowledgement that she would have to part with the idea that her stepfather truly loved her. This clinician immediately sought supervision and consultation from his work colleagues, one of which happened to be an approved consultant for the EMDR International Association (EMDRIA). Through use of the cognitive interweave and integration of ego state treatments and dissociative symptoms, the clinician was able to successfully begin EMDR and she made substantial gains in reprocessing her traumatic memories. She was also able to reevaluate her life's purpose. Prior to therapy she had been secretly holding the idea of going back to school to become a clinical social worker, but her self-concept would not allow for her to really believe she was capable of such lofty accomplishments. As therapy concluded she had been accepted into a graduate program and adamantly believed that she deserved to have life-fulfilling experiences.

Key points that are relevant to our discussion involve the nuanced level of knowledge that is a prerequisite to having helped this client with this particular plan: 1) basic training in EMDR, 2) advanced training in EMDR and supervision, 3) continually checking in with the client about the impact of treatment and her readiness to proceed, and 4) deep respect for her healing process to be of paramount importance over theory and protocol. All of this training was quite necessary for this treatment plan. However, with only blind knowledge one is, at best, a tactician dispensing treatment. A true clinician, one that wisely knows, takes this knowing and allows it to inform with respect to also not knowing what may unfold. That is, the clinician must embrace the unknown to allow for the most authentic path towards healing to be revealed. At times, EMDR was started only to have Melissa soon report that she was nearing the limit of her ability to tolerate the impact of the session. During such times, we would work on containing Melissa's emotions and then allowing her to choose where therapy should go next. At no point did the clinician attempt to interpret the meaning of her feelings or sensations. For example, her choking sensation might readily be a somatic abreaction to having been choked in one of her previous experiences; however, harm can be done in suggesting this, and so the clinician opted to instead acknowledge his keen analysis and then promptly let it go so as to not predetermine the direction of treatment. This clinician also embraces the idea that he made many mistakes and has much room to grow. Such growth involves participating in activities that both embrace the acquisition of knowledge and ones that help to embrace the ambiguity of not knowing to fully honor the client and their path to healing.

Zhuangzi's parable of When Knowledge Went North is of tremendous importance for mental health clinicians. While good clinicians may practice in many ways, there are qualities that each possess in how they encounter their clients. In applying lessons from Zhuangzi's parable, we see these qualities. Most notable, these clinicians have developed an attunement that can only be found through emptying oneself of simple knowing. They become vessels of emptiness, stillness, and non-action. Full therapeutic utility is found in an attunement with the client that is based in humble openness and in full service to the client. From this foundation action and wise action can emerge.

Note

1 Permission to republish granted by University of Hawaii Press. Zhuangzi. (1998). *Wandering on the way: Early Taoist tales and parables of Chuang Tzu.* (V. Mair, Trans.). pp. 210–212. Honolulu, HI: University of Hawaii Press.

References

Lambert, M. J. (2010). Yes, it is time for clinicians to routinely monitor treatment outcome. In B. L. Duncan, S. D. Miller, B. E. Wampold, & M. A. Hubble (Eds.), *The heart and soul of change, delivering what works in therapy* (2nd ed., pp. 239–266). Washington, DC: American Psychological Association.

Merton, T. (2010). *The way of Chuang Tzu.* New York, NY: New Directions Publishing Corp.

Schwartz, R. C. (1995). *Internal family systems therapy.* New York, NY: The Guilford Press.

Shapiro, F. (2001). *Eye movement desensitization and reprocessing: Basic principles, protocols, and procedures* (2nd ed.). New York, NY: The Guilford Press.

Wampold, B. E., & Imel, Z. E. (2015). *The great psychotherapy debate: The evidence for what makes psychotherapy work* (2nd ed.). New York, NY: Routledge.

Zhuangzi. (1998). *Wandering on the way: Early Taoist tales and parables of Chuang Tzu.* (V. Mair, Trans.). Honolulu, HI: University of Hawaii Press.

PART III
Miscellaneous Chapters

6

ON THE POWER OF BUTTERFLIES

Dreaming, Waking, and the Therapeutic Potential of Nocturnal Beings

Erik Craig

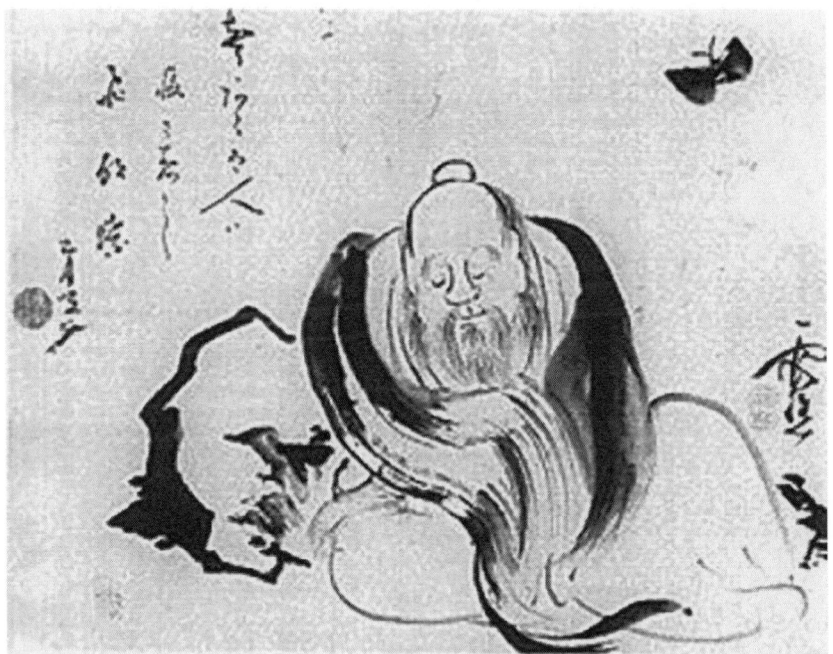

FIGURE 6.1 Zhuangzi dreaming of a butterfly (or a butterfly dreaming of Zhuangzi) by Ike no Taiga, retrieved from https://commons.wikimedia.org/wiki/File:Zhuangzi-Butterfly-Dream.jpg

> Once upon a time, I, Chuang-Tzŭ, dreamt that I was a butterfly fluttering hither and thither, to all intents and purposes a butterfly. I was aware only of following my fancies as a butterfly, and I was unconscious of my individuality as a man. Suddenly I awaked, and there I lay, myself again. Now I do not know whether I was then a man dreaming I was a butterfly, or whether I am now a butterfly dreaming I am a man.
>
> (Chuang-Tzŭ, 1926, p. 32)

Zhuangzi: Gadfly, Fox, and Trickster

The above allegory from the mischievous, enigmatic Taoist sage and story teller, Zhuangzi,[1] is often used in epistemological arguments to suggest that we cannot trust the evidence of sense experience to evaluate what is real. However, this was probably not Zhuangzi's actual concern, either in the allegory or in the chapter that it concludes, the second of his so-called "Inner Chapters." Rather, he seems to be ridiculing philosophical arguments that remove us from the joys and challenges of our everyday lives. Again and again he shows that the philosopher's efforts to infallibly distinguish between even the simplest of realities—for instance, this from that, here from there, right from wrong, being from non-being, dreaming from waking—invariably lead to more doubt than certainty. In Zhuangzi's allegory, for instance, we might conclude that reality is any one of the following: that he is actually himself the awakened human being, Zhuangzi, who had just dreamt he was a butterfly; that he is now actually a butterfly dreaming of being the human being, Zhuangzi; that he is neither a butterfly nor himself; or, perhaps, that he is both. Throughout the entire second chapter (Zhuangzhi, 1996) and its famous culminating allegory, the philosopher devilishly wrecks our facile, taken-for-granted convictions about reality, whether based in logic or sense experience, raising doubts about what we consider most obvious and certain. His chapter and the allegory itself thus stand as an indictment of epistemo-logical arrogance and useless philosophical debate aimed at proving the validity of our distinctions between one apparently obvious reality and another. In mocking our human hubris at thinking we can even know what is and is not, Zhuangzi dares us to recognize and accept our fundamental finitude and, instead of engaging in futile philosophical quibbles, get on with our lives. Essentially his butterfly allegory invites us to forget about our useless arguments over which is more real, dreaming or waking. What if, rather than arguing about which is more real than the other, we looked at the phenom-enon of human dreaming as such, granting it the same respect we do our waking existence without holding it accountable to the standards of the latter. Could it be that our dreaming and waking modes of existing are equally but differently real and meaningful modes of being in the world? If that is the case, what light might that shed on the therapeutic value and potential of the analysis of dreams?

Dreaming as Inconvenient Reality: Gadfly of the Soul[2]

Zhuangzi's impatience with our endless arguing in search of infallible episte-mological distinctions does not mean that practical, everyday distinctions are useless in our quotidian lives. Obviously, quite the opposite. Mothers and babies are dependent on knowing the difference between crying and laughter, drivers the difference between red and green, workers and employers the difference between 7 and 8 AM, and so forth, ad infinitum. We must always live our lives in the realm of everyday experience and in accord with the unavoidable prag-matic distinctions given to us in that experience.

We also live in an everyday world as therapists, a very specialized world of pragmatic being, a world constantly requiring discerning perception, understand-ing, and response. We must, for instance, discern what is well-being or not, healthy or not, helpful or not, fitting or not, authentic or not, ethical or not, etc. Sometimes we are called upon to distinguish what is truth or a lie, abuse or discipline, side effect of drugs or medication or a thought disorder, a genuine religious value or a compulsion for control, self-deception or an effort to deceive others, and so forth. In many cases, even within the realm of our practical understanding of things, we often find ourselves uncertain and compelled to hold opposing possibilities openly with patience and equanimity. In the follow-ing, I will attempt to address three basic discernments with respect to the phe-nomenon of dreaming and its relation to waking existence: Are dreams real? What is the difference between our experiences of dreaming and waking and how are they each related to our lives as a whole? What is the existential and therapeutic potential of dreaming?

In raising these questions, I may appear to be stepping into territory occupied by long-standing and highly contentious philosophical and scientific debate about what dreams are, whether they actually exist, whether we are conscious while "having" them, whether they can be called experiences, and even whether there is anything like consciousness or experience at all. I have no wish to join these conversations but focus instead on the everyday significance and potential of dreaming for both personal and professional existence. I will do my best to remain as faithful to experience as possible.

Before going forward, here are some perspectives and assumptions that will guide me. Since I am grounding this inquiry on what is called lived experience, I should say that what I mean by the term *experience* and that is *all that I live through, endure, or undergo*, in other words, *everything that occurs within the realm of my existing, whether or not I am conscious or aware of it*. Within this context of lived experience, I find both my dreaming and waking existence to be meaningfully organized by familiar, inextricably relational patterns of thought, feeling, and behavior or responsiveness. I find these meaningfully structured patterns both constant and ever-evolving in accord with new experiences that come toward me from my own future, even now as I write. My anticipation of this "still-to-become," "not-as-yet" future that includes my own death, draws me on with both, on the one hand, love and longing and, on the other, to borrow from Kierkegaard, "fear and trembling." This constantly evolving forward movement of our human existence has been called, among other things, individuation, self-organization, self-actualization, self-realization, selfing (Craig, 2000),[3] being-towards-the-future, becoming, and, most broadly and simply, human development. Whatever we call it, clearly both dreaming and waking exist in the service of our unfolding existence as a whole, an existence that is thoroughly constituted and structured by and as our relatedness with the world, especially the world of others, but belongs entirely to ourselves alone.

Having laid out these foundational assumptions, let's return to the three basic questions about dreams and dreaming mentioned above. The first of these concerns the realness of dreams.

The Realness of Dreams

Dreaming's status as reality has suffered considerable insult in the hands of the academy, including the field of psychology and even psychotherapy; this, in spite of the fact that the study of dreams was an indispensable aspect of the founding of modern scientific psychotherapy and the field of depth psychology as a whole. With the exception of those who thought of dreams as Divine direction or demonic misdirection and those who considered them in some way pre-cognitive or prophetic, the overriding historical attitude toward dreaming experience was, in one way or another, to dismiss dreams as unreal, unworthy of consideration and reflection. The majority of thinkers before Freud considered dreams either to be the result of somatic or environmental stimuli or to be some kind of pathogenic or hallucinatory process; that is, not at all a thematically or structurally meaningful dimension of human existence.

However, the status of the reality and significance of dreams changed dramatically with the very first sentence of Freud's Interpretation of Dreams (1900/1953), in which he boldly and historically declares that with thoughtful analysis "every dream reveals itself as a psychical structure which has a meaning and which can be inserted at an assignable point in the activities of waking life" (1900/1953, p. 1). In asserting the importance of dreams as an essential resource for understanding the mysteries of what he called "the life of the soul" (*Seelenleben*),[4] even describing them as "the royal road to the unconscious" (1900/1953), Freud opened the door to civilization's respect for the meaning of dreams and its relevance for our personal and professional understanding of individuals, including ourselves. As mighty a recognition as this was, Freud still failed to acknowledge the significance of the lived experience of dreaming as such, its so-called manifest content, by dismissing it as a mere, usually disguised, representation of the "real" underlying meanings, the so-called latent content. Understanding dreams this way, while opening the door to taking human dreaming more seriously, led to the widespread assumption that dreams merely represent reality and are not, in themselves, reality. Consequently, analysts and lay people alike rushed toward the dream, determined to dismantle its so-called facade of symbolic content, whether that symbolic content was intended to deceive, as Freud largely held, or to reveal, as C. G. Jung believed.

It was not until the Swiss psychiatrist Medard Boss (1953) took up a systematically phenomenological approach to understanding dreams that dreaming existence was restored to its full and legitimate status as human reality, a way of being that was, in and for itself, as real and meaningful as waking. Boss's foundational proposition for this oneiric rehabilitation is that dreaming and waking are simply two different modes of carrying out each individual's one-and-the-same historical human existence. The simple premise that the I who dreams and the I who awakens and carries on through the day are one and the same was hardly new in philosophy but radical in psychoanalysis, psychology, and psychotherapy. And it was just this premise that enabled Boss to build an argument for dreaming as being equally albeit differently, first, as real as waking and, second, as potentially as disclosive of the meaning of our existence as being awake.[5] But what do I mean when I speak of the reality of dreams?

Realness as Actuality

The most basic meaning of the realness of dreams is simply that our dream worlds actually exist, that we actually carry on worlded lives while dreaming just as we do while awake. Thanks to thousands of sleep studies, we now know that human beings never really stop experiencing, thinking, feeling, and responding to their worlds even in what sleep scientists refer to as non-REM sleep or what the East calls deep memoryless sleep. Although the kind or quality of experience, thought, and feeling may change, our experience of mental activity and worlded engagement never ceases but continues through every minute of our lives in both wakefulness and sleep. Whether or not we are able to recall our experiences while sleeping, our thoughts, feelings, and responses to them still occur, whether or not there is anyone able to bear witness to their having occurred. As in waking, the failure of memory is not an argument for the non-existence of any event. Dreaming and many other sorts of mental activity actually do occur throughout the night whether or not we are capable of recalling or describing them.

Realness as Lived Experience

As Western philosophers and Zhuangzi himself have always seen, dreaming and waking experience are so similar in their basic existential structure, so inescapably worldly and alive, that it is difficult, though not at all impossible, to realize while dreaming that we are not actually awake. If while dreaming we did not actually experience ourselves and our world as so real and alive, it would likely be far easier to know we are dreaming when we are dreaming. The very fact that, for the most part, we take our dreaming experience for our waking one is evidence of dreaming's worldly, experiential realness. Unfortunately, when awake, back in the same bed in which we fell off to sleep, we so often dismiss our dreaming existence by saying, "It was only a dream," and, with this, banish dreaming's realness as an experientially vital dimension of our lives. This common tendency to prioritize our waking mode of being over our dreaming one goes back as far as the early Greeks and continues today, even among some of our most scientific dream investigators. Simply because our being in the world while dreaming dissolves, lacks the continuity of waking, and allows us the freedom to be in ways that are impossible while awake—for example, by flying or talking with a deceased friend—does not mean these experiences are not real in and for themselves. Indeed our central nervous system, affects, and bodies (with the exception of the employment of large striated muscles) are mostly as active as when we are fully awake. So real to us are our experiences while dreaming that Nietzsche even considered the experience of flying in dreams as such a "privilege" and "peculiarly enviable happiness" as to alter the color and our very definition of happiness in our lives.

Realness as Meaningfully Disclosive

Since dreaming and waking modes of being are equiprimordial and arise coequally from our one and only existence, how can dreaming not be structured and disclosive of that one existence as a whole? How can dreaming ever be anything but meaningfully homologous (having the same relations, structures, and meaning content) with our lives as a whole? Don't we recognize both while dreaming and waking that it is our very own existence we are living? Even if we dream we are someone or something else, don't we still experience that existence as belonging to ourselves? Finally, does not our experience, our very being in the world while dreaming, run seamlessly into our being in the world while awake, even if we don't understand, upon waking, how the two are related? Anyone familiar enough with their dream life has certainly had the experience of altering or revising their memory or account of a dream as they begin to wake up, a phenomenon first identified by Freud (1900/1953) and called secondary revision or secondary elaboration. This sort of waking participation in the memory and understanding of our dreaming experience is only one way in which both waking and dreaming existence are actively engaged in the experience, perception, organization, and understanding of our spatially and temporally situated and destined existence, whether awake or dreaming. Dreaming and waking both contribute to and exist in the service of the ever-changing meaningful patterning of our existence, our selfing. Even Aristotle (2015) somehow recognized this when he declared that "the most skilled interpreter of dreams is one who can observe resemblances" (p. 115). How could any such statement make sense if there was not, whether recognized or not, an implicit understanding that our waking and dreaming modes of existence belong to and serve the ongoing meaningfully structured development of the one and the same individual? How can dreaming not be a meaningful living out of the one existence of which waking is an equiprimordial mode of being?

Though dreaming and waking are equally real in that they both actually occur, have a palpable quality of experiential reality, and are meaningfully disclosive of the single human existence to which they alone belong, in what ways might they actually be different?

The Difference between Dreaming and Waking Worlds

Although, for the most part, we presume our immediate worlds to be real whether we are dreaming or awake, this does not say how they are distinct from one another and what their differing kinds of realness might imply for a richer understanding of our existence as a whole.

As we know from Zhuangzi, we are not the first to ponder the question of how to distinguish between dreaming and waking based on experience itself. Even before Zhuangzi was born, the Greeks, beginning at least with Socrates, wondered, "what evidence we could offer if we were asked whether in the present instance, at this moment, we are asleep and dreaming all our thoughts, or awake and talking to each other in real life" (Plato, 1992, p. 22). Descartes, too, puzzled over this question, writing that he could "see so plainly that there are no definitive signs by which to distinguish being awake from being asleep [and dreaming]" (Descartes, 1641/1998, p. 60, brackets mine). In fact, thinking over the difference between dreaming and waking was what eventually led him to come to his famous conclusion, "*Cogito ergo sum.*"

Such questions about the ontological status of dreaming relative to waking have obviously perplexed geniuses for ages. However, with the exception of the kinds of individual observation and reflection described above, we have not had any scientific or philosophical means or methodologies to provide the breadth and depth of information required for adequately distinguishing these two ways of existing. It was not until the last century that we finally developed methodologies and sample sizes sufficient to draw significant and reliable conclusions as to the similarities and differences between dreaming and waking. With the advent of psychoanalysis and psychotherapy in the early 1900s, we finally had human scientific methodologies and sufficient numbers of dreamers willing to share their experiences of dreaming and waking from which we could begin to draw some conclusions as to the relative natures of these two modes of existing. Then, toward the middle of the century, technical laboratory studies of sleeping and dreaming were made possible with the invention of the scientific equipment capable of identifying and measuring physiological and neurological correlates of dreaming and waking.

Physiological Similarities and Differences

These later natural scientific laboratory studies led to the discovery of what is called "rapid-eye-movement sleep" (REM) which occurs regularly through-out the night as the last of the five stages of every standard 90-minute sleep cycle. Whereas in "non-rapid eye movement sleep" (non-REM or NREM) when our eyes move slowly and randomly, sometimes even independently, during REM ocular activity is highly coordinated and as rapid as waking. Furthermore, it was found that awakening individuals from REM sleep yielded significantly higher rates of dream recall, even as much as six times higher than awakenings during non-REM. These scientific laboratory studies also soon revealed that REM sleep (or "Dream-sleep") and waking modes of being have a surprising number of similar characteristics by a number of physiologi-cal and neurological criteria. For example, as opposed to non-REM sleep when our pulse, blood pressure, respirations, and electronic rhythm rates slow to a virtual crawl, during REM, these rates very closely approximate the respective rates while awake. Finally, though we are in many ways physiologi-cally active during REM, when awakened during REM, sleepers typically report that they are sleeping "soundly" or "deeply" as compared to NREM, when physiological indications are exceptionally quiescent, sleepers report they are "just falling asleep" or, at most, "sleeping lightly." So striking were these and other apparent oppositions in REM sleep it came to be called "paradoxical sleep."

Psychological Similarities and Differences

Just as natural scientific technological invention allowed for the study of biological and physiological difference between dreaming and waking, the human scientific invention of clinical methods for the study of dreams allowed for the study of psychological similarities and differences, especially as a result of suddenly having access to hundreds of thousands of first-hand reports. At least to begin with, the conclusions drawn from these methodologies were largely concerned with theoretical explanations and, unfortunately, based on the assumption that dreams were symbolic of reality, not reality as such. This only began to change when two phenomenologically oriented Swiss psychia-trists, Ludwig Binswanger and Medard Boss, independently began analyzing dreaming worlds based entirely on the meaningfulness of what appeared in the dream world as such. In addition to the analysis of patients' dreams as such, Boss also attempted to study systematically the phenomenologically given similarities and differences between the dreaming and waking modes of exis-tence. As with the laboratory studies, Boss's clinical analyses revealed the dreaming mode of existing to be profoundly paradoxical from a psychological perspective as well.

Medard Boss's Discovery of the Paradoxical Nature of Dream Worlds

The original intent of Boss's (1977) systematic, phenomenological analysis of "The Nature of Dreaming and Waking" (pp. 175–215) was to convince us to take "the dreaming world seriously, as one of the most integral facets of human 'reality'" (p. 215), equally, albeit differently as real and significant as waking. Claiming to draw his conclusions "on the basis of over 50,000 dream accounts," Boss distinguishes the dreaming and waking modes of existence based on phenomenologically observable characteristics that tend to typify each in contrast with the other. Since we exist as fully human and as precisely and uniquely ourselves in both modes of being, the differences between them can't possibly be sharp categorical ones but, rather, somewhat subtle relatively consistent tendencies. Nevertheless, Boss eventually identified three relatively stable characteristic distinctions from which we might conclude that, in comparison to waking, while dreaming, we are paradoxically both more and less open, more and less free, and more and less capable than we find ourselves while awake. Here are Boss's own paradoxical distinctions.

Waking versus Dreaming Worlds

First, compared to the world in which we find ourselves while dreaming, our waking worlds are relatively limitless with respect to the time-space continuum of our existence and, within that world, we are relatively free to choose the distance and quality of our relations to our spatially and temporally contextualized worlds and the phenomena appearing therein. For instance, as you sit there now awake and reading, you can think and act freely and widely with respect to your world. You can get up and go to the kitchen, walk outside, go to a nearby restaurant, drive to your workplace, or make arrangements to fly somewhere for a vacation then actually fly there at some point in your future, a future that comes steadily, reliably, continuously, and even roughly predictably toward you in time. This world is intact, the phenomena and possibilities within it stretching seamlessly in all directions with respect to the time-space continuum within and as which you exist.

In contrast, while dreaming, you generally find yourself engaged in a strikingly more *pre-delimited world*. The room in which you find yourself while dreaming comes with certain aspects pre-selected, not in the richly textured, continuous way that appears to you when awake. Furthermore, if, while dreaming, you leave the room where you are reading to go to the kitchen just a few steps away, you might just find yourself, without warning or forethought, suddenly in the kitchen of your childhood, or in an open market, classroom, or dungeon, or even in some unknown foreign country. Whatever the case, the next spatio-temporal context is much more often than in waking "pre-selected" for you and pre-delimited as to your options within it. In other words, our dream worlds are more often than in waking given to us *post facto*.

Paradoxically, although your dream world is relatively pre-delimited, it is also often far less limited than your waking world by various social, historical, or physical constraints. When dreaming you might find yourself strikingly uninhibited, and able to walk through a wall or fly through space, or thrown into an intimate conversation with a movie star or president, or talking to long dead relatives, or even standing on a distant planet looking back awestruck at Earth. Although none of these events could ever occur in waking life, they still all can occur within an already predetermined pre-selectively featured world. And, to add to the complexity, sometimes while dreaming, you find yourself completely unable to do what is so easy while awake, such as scream out in terror for help or run quickly away from danger. Thus, while dreaming, our worlds are both more and less open than while awake and we ourselves both more and less free than while awake. Likewise, with respect to memory and our freedom to choose among a variety of behavioral options, while dreaming, we are both more and less able than when awake. For instance, though we are occasionally uncannily hypermnesic in dreams, for the most part while dreaming we are generally much less capable of the kind of free-ranging memory we experience when awake. Rene Descartes actually described this difference over three and a half centuries ago, finding his own mnemonic capacity to be a crucial distinction between his dreaming and waking life. He even closed his famous *Meditations* with a paragraph containing these words: "Dreams are never joined by the memory with all the other actions of life, as is the case with those actions that occur when one is awake" Descartes, 1641/1998, (p. 103).

Waking versus Dreaming Distance and Proximity

Boss also noticed that, while dreaming, we more often than not encounter rather familiar persons or everyday situations even though they often do not appear in precisely the same way as they appear in waking. Furthermore, quite often the beings who "visit" our dream worlds appear as almost completely incompatible or foreign to our everyday waking experience. Though we most often dream of the familiar as largely familiar, we also dream of the familiar as foreign; that is, as thematically embodied in the strange or distant. For example, we may unwittingly dream of familiar and nearby meanings or themes but not as associated with those, including ourselves, who are actually familiar to our waking worlds, but as embodied in the presence of such phenomena; for example, as saints or soldiers; exotic lovers; cruel tyrants or dull-headed officials; strange or exaggerated body parts; birds or beasts; other-worldly spaces, times, or structures; or extreme circumstances such as fires, floods, tidal waves, and all manner of apocalypses. In other words, while dreaming, the meanings which are closest to us while awake appear as embodied in the foreign and unfamiliar presences; that is, as distant. And yet, paradoxically, it is those very same foreign characters to waking that impose themselves most closely upon us while dreaming. As Boss (1977) observed, "the beings of our dream world . . . come impressively, and at times uncomfortably close to us" (p. 199). In fact, such dreamt beings come so close to us we often wake with a silent exclamation of relief or disappointment, declaring that "it was only a dream." It is this richly paradoxical quality of simultaneous distance and closeness that, I have observed, gives our dreaming worlds their consistently life-illuminating power. It is *as if* while dreaming we place what is closest to us in our existence at a distance just in order to bring it near. In this way, as my friend and colleague Perikles Kastrinidis once observed, dreams are very much like the warnings we read on our passenger side rear view mirrors: "Objects in mirror are closer than they appear!" In other words, what appears as sensuously, *manifestly foreign*, and *unlikely* while dreaming is actually what is *meaningfully closest and real.* This will be seen quite clearly in the examples found later in this chapter.

Of course, while dreaming, we rarely perceive the existentially thematic meaningfulness of our dream worlds but, rather, when pressed upon by the sensually alive beings of our dreams, we respond pre-reflectively "in kind"; that is without pausing to consider what these beings might mean as they approach or fade away. It is only upon awaking that we find ourselves, hopefully, wondering what "all that was about." In this way, we are indeed much freer while awake than dreaming, which leads to Boss's last phenomenologically given difference between our dreaming and waking modes of existence.

Waking Versus Dreaming Self Reflection

This third phenomenologically observable difference Boss (1977) noted was that, while dreaming, we not only tend to ignore the "meaning content" of the beings that appear to us as so sensually alive but also that we "rarely reflect on ourselves in an attempt to gain insight into our existential state" (p. 199). In waking life, we are able not only to experience sensually present phenomena but also are considerably more able to recognize their meaningfulness with respect to our lives as a whole than we are while dreaming. For the most part, such existential reflection occurs only once we have woken from a dream. Even though, while dreaming, we may make profound statements about ourselves and human existence, it is usually only once we are awake that we realize their full profundity. Recently, for instance, I dreamt of walking with a much older analytic colleague and, just as we were parting, saying "I'm 70 years old, is there anything I need to be milking?" by which I meant the "senior benefits" I may now be eligible to use for my own benefit and well-being. My colleague, who had lived several more years as a senior than I, said nothing, apparently intentionally. As I casually walked away, I said, "Oh yes, of course, only my days." I immediately awoke and, recalling the dream, suddenly realized the existential profundity of my remark: what I most need to drink in (milk) was time, not just the hours of my days but the days of my week, and the rapidly diminishing number of months and years remaining to me. Although my statement while dreaming was true, it was only upon waking that I could realize its full existential profundity, and I could immediately exclaim aloud to myself, "Oh my god, don't ever forget this!"

Transdisciplinary Reflections

We should notice that our attention to the differences between dreaming and waking modes of being has primarily focused on the lived experience of our dreaming mode of existence. Obviously neuro-biology and psychodynamics also bear heavily on this question, albeit from different epistemological directions. Although a discussion of the psychoanalytic or psychodynamic perspectives on the problem is beyond the reach of this present paper, I would like to return briefly to the impressive advances in the neuro-biological study of sleeping and dreaming and note that these advanced natural-scientific studies have not contradicted a single one of Boss's phenomenological observations but, actually, have positively confirmed them. As one specific example, many dream scientists including, for instance, Hartmann (2011, p. 64f) and Thompson (2015, p. 158f) have underscored the importance of the circumstance that a portion of the frontal cortex called the dorsolateral prefrontal cortex (which is crucial for, among other things, focused waking thought, memory, problem solving and self-reflection) is deactivated during REM sleep. Not only does this corroborate Boss's findings regarding memory, choice, and reflective self-awareness described above, but also Descartes's self-observations of reduced mnemonic capacity while dreaming. A more general but exceedingly important finding from this research is that dreaming sleep is fundamentally constituted by a much freer, wider ranging capacity for imaginative emotional connections than almost any other ordinary state of consciousness (Hartmann, 2011). Anyone interested in the study and meaning of human dreaming would be greatly enriched by the now enormous body of experimental and neuro-scientific investigation of sleeping and dreaming. The impressive knowledge we have acquired over the last sixty years is potentially helpful not only for dreamers who would like to further develop their capacity for dream recall but also for persons suffering from insomnia, trauma, nightmares, or any of the variety of parasomnias. As students of the night, both waking and dreaming, we owe it to ourselves and those we serve to be as cognizant as possible of what it is to be human twenty-four hours a day!

In preparation for our final concern regarding the distinctive existential and therapeutic potential of dreaming, I will summarize the above points regarding the distinctive characteristics of dreaming experience as compared to that of waking:

1. In comparison to waking, our average dreaming presents us with a *preselected world* that, taken as a whole, is far more delimited with respect to the spatio-temporal context into which we are typically "thrown" while awake. Likewise, while dreaming, we ourselves most typically find ourselves correspondingly delimited in terms of our existential possibilities for responding.

2. Within this existentially delimited world, we also find that which appears to come toward us, come closer to us, often stretching our comfort zone with either discomfort or desire. One could say our dreaming world gets our attention by emphasizing, sometimes to the point of extreme exaggeration, certain meaning-bearing phenomena, while at the same time excluding other potentially distracting or contradictory phenomena, thus seizing our existence with what is *affectively most salient or alive*.

3. While dreaming, we are generally far less capable of grasping the psychological meaningfulness of the beings and circumstances that approach us, especially with respect to our existence as a whole. Once awake, we are generally more capable of grasping the meaning of dreams through self-reflection and analysis.

The Personal and Therapeutic Value of Dreaming

Having considered the questions regarding the realness of dreams and the differences between our lived experience while dreaming and waking, we can now ask how dreams may contribute to our personal and professional lives while awake.

The first and most obvious value of dreaming is as pure experience. Dreaming is a fascinating, surprising, and sometimes even magical mode of being in the world. Whether our dreaming is pleasant or miserable, satisfying, or frustrating, our dreaming existence transports us to vital, often dramatic worlds of living experience without the slightest effort required on our part. No plane tickets necessary, no plans or arrangements, no need to arrange schedules or get packed. We are just delivered immediately and straight away, kerplunk, into worlds often inconceivable in waking but nevertheless real and full of both natural and unnatural possibilities. Whether we encounter danger or delight, wisdom or silliness, friends or foes, familiar dear ones or puzzling ridiculous strangers, earthly or other-worldly settings, each dream presents us with its own unpredictable contingencies and challenges. I remember as a young child of 7 or 8 sometimes wondering what might come in the night and went to bed wondering where and how I might find myself while dreaming. Even today, I think that above all dreaming is to be enjoyed for this richness of experience in and for itself. There, we can fly. There, we can meet living embodiments of dear ones long gone. There, time and space are magically, instantaneously transcended. If nothing else, enjoy, savor, wonder! Enlarge your life. Sleep on, dream on.

Years later as an adult, as a psychotherapist, and as a student and teacher of dreams, I added to my purely experiential wonderment an intellectual and emotional fascination with what these brief nocturnes might signify in our lives as a whole. As a "bio-existential state" inseparable from waking, dreaming participates uniquely in the ever-unfolding process of our organizing and becoming who we are as individual human beings. Self-organizing process "is a regnant feature of being itself, particularly living beings" (Craig, 2008, p. 253) and is that by which we as human beings create meaning from our lived experience in a way that "rounds it into the unity of a significant whole" (Gadamer, 1960/1988, p. 60). Although during the day we participate in this meaning making process more consciously and deliberately than while asleep, our meaning making, self-organizing process goes on all night long, particularly while dreaming. One could even say that the dreams we remember each morning give us the freshest update on our existential standing in the world. They deliver the latest newsflash on just where we are and are going, who we are and are becoming. Remarkably, while dreaming we don't have to do a thing to make the meaningful emotional connections our dreaming existence make for us (Hartmann, 2011). It seems that while dreaming we gather thoughts, experiences, and feelings from the day before while anticipating the one just ahead. Generally these "gatherings" concern matters that we have not had the time or even inclination to consider thoughtfully or even at all while awake. But the gatherings return at night, seemingly begging our attention.

Whereas Freud considered dreams to be an expression of our passions, fears, and desires, Jung thought them expressions of the human personality striving for its own fulfillment or individuation, and Adler believed they were attempts to develop power or mastery in our lives, existentialists are unwilling to attribute dreams to any single theme or Ur-motive. Instead, for the existential therapist, dreams show us our possibilities for being in the world, albeit possibilities we may still not feel comfortable or at home with. But what is a possibility? In German the word for possibility is *möglichkeit*, from the German *mögen*, which means to like or want. One could say, then, that upon waking from a dream with its fresh images and affects, we are presented with that which wants us, wants our attention, whether or not we want or desire it.

This is precisely where the personal and therapeutic advantage of our dreaming mode of existence lies. While lying peacefully and physically at rest in our beds at night, we are organismically more relaxed, private, safe and free than we are at any other point in our twenty-four-hour day. It is just in this fundamental biological state that we can be open to that which is unrecognized, unfinished, undesired, still unorganized for us as we turn in for the night. It is in just such a relaxed, private, safe, and free state that a wider range of possibilities and emotionally guided connections can occur in ways our demanding pre-occupied waking existence does not permit. Here is an example.

An intelligent middle aged woman, let's call her Julie, dreams of standing in a stark, plain room with a single bed against the wall while vomiting violently all over herself and the room. When she first shared the dream, it seems completely bizarre and unintelligible, having nothing to do with her waking life. Plain nonsense. However, upon recalling and discussing more of the details of her dreamt world along with some surprising connections to her waking world, some striking similarities between her dream world and a particularly poignant dilemma in her waking world began to dawn on her.

Due to some extreme financial circumstances in her family, she had been forced to return to her old work as a hotel room service manager and give up on her lifelong wish to obtain a doctoral degree in psychology. A few months before her dream, she had been making considerable progress with her professional goals and was even in the practicum stage of her education and training when the financial crisis arose. Although this situation made her "sick to her stomach," she did not realize until reflecting on her dream just how violently disgusted and angry she felt about it and was then determined not to let her circumstances interfere any further with the fulfillment of her life's ambition.

Here we see an example of how what appears to us while dreaming may initially seem so foreign and far from reality but upon thoughtful, gentle analysis, turns out to be very real indeed. Again, as we read in our automobile passenger side rear view mirrors, we can also say of our dreaming worlds, "The beings of our dreams are closer than they appear!"

The gift and power of our dreaming mode of existence lies in the circumstance that, as two modes of our one and the same human existence, they are homologous with one another, sharing the same structure, form, concerns, and patterns of a single, meaningfully organized self (Craig, 1987, pp. 128–134). This is why Aristotle's statement of millennia ago that "the most skilled interpreter of dreams is the one who can observe resemblances" (1996, p. 15) remains so pertinent to everyone who studies dreams even today. It is the way of dreams to shepherd our very own forgotten, denied, overlooked, or neglected possibilities back into our awareness as awakened ones. It then remains for us to shepherd those same lost or forsaken existential possibilities shown to us while dreaming fully into the full history-making power of being awake. Those evanescent butterflies of our dreaming, once seen and understood in their fullness as meaning-bearing beings, have the power, once we are awake, to change the world, not only our world but the world of many others as well. This reminds me of a portion of W. H. Auden's (1945) poignant 1939 *Tribute to Sigmund Freud*,[6] with which I will close:

> But he would have us remember most of all
> To be enthusiastic over the night
>   Not only for the sense of wonder
>   It alone has to offer, but also
>
> Because it needs our love: for with sad eyes
> Its delectable creatures look up and beg
>   Us dumbly to follow;
> They are exiles who long for the future
>
> That lies in our power. They too would rejoice
>   If allowed to serve enlightenment like him . . .
>   (p. 167)

Notes

1 Of the three great Chinese Taoist Sages—Lao Tzi, Lieh Tzu, and Zhuangzi—only Zhuangzi (approximately 370–287 B.C.E.) appears to have actually existed and is believed to have been born in the town of Meng in the Anhui province lying just to the West of the former capital city of Nanjing. The reason all three Taoist masters share the same name, Tzu, is that Tzu is a title of reverence given to venerable ancestors. Zhuangzi's original name was Chang Chou.

2 I trust the reader will accept my use of the term "soul" here, a word with which I intend no metaphysical or transcendental reality, but rather a purely experiential meaning, namely, our "very own situated gathering of lived experience" (Craig, 2008, p. 257).

3 I quite like the fact that the term "selfing" in biology refers to the "self-fertilizing." However, today I use this term reluctantly because of the possible interpretation being that one does not need the world or even others in the process of "becoming oneself" when precisely the opposite is the case. We now know that our entire central nervous system is inescapably relational in all of its self-organizing activity. Unfortunately in contemporary popular culture, the term "selfing" also refers to such activities as taking "selfie" photos, autoerotic stimulation, or inappropriately changing the focus of conversations to oneself.

4 In the original German, Freud consistently described psychoanalysis as his "science of the life of the soul" (*Wissenschaft vom Seelenleben*). Unfortunately, Strachey's scientifically conservative translation translates Freud's *Seelenleben* as merely psychic life, thus watering down Freud's own more poignant, passionate intention.

5 Rollo May also attempted to take up a phenomenological approach to understanding dreams in a 1968 book, authored by himself and Leopold Caligor, entitled *Dreams and symbols: Man's unconscious language* (May & Caligor, 1968). Although he aspired "to take the dreams [of Caligor's patient, Susan] phenomenologically," "to stick as closely as possible to the dreams themselves," and to study "only the dreams themselves and let them, so far as [he] could, speak to [him]," his actual understanding of Susan's dreams repeatedly returned to stock theoretical interpretations straight out of classical Freudian theory. So in spite of his admirable intention to let the dreams themselves "speak to" him, what he ended up "hearing" was not the dreams themselves but his own unexamined Freudian theoretical assumptions.

6 "In Memory of W.B. Yeats," copyright © 1940 and renewed 1968 by W.H. Auden; from *W.H. Auden collected poems* by W.H. Auden. Used by permission of Random House, an imprint and division of Penguin Random House LLC. All rights reserved.

References

Aristotle. (2015). *Aristotle: On sleep and dreams*. (D. Gallup, Ed. and Trans.). Havertown, PA: Oxbow Books.

Auden, W. H. (1945). *The collected poetry of W.H. Auden*. New York: Random House.

Boss, M. (1953/1957). *The analysis of dreams.*. (A. J. Pomerans, Trans.). London: Rider and Company.

Boss, M. (1977). *I dreamt last night. . . .* (S. Conway, Trans.). New York, NY: Gardner Press, Inc.

Chuang-Tzū. (1926). *Chuang-tzū: Mystic, moralist, and social reformer*. (H. E. Giles, Trans.). Shanghai: Kelly & Walsh, Limited.

Craig, P. E. (1987). Dreaming, reality and allusion: An existential-phenomenological inquiry. In F. J. van Zuuren, F. W. Wertz, & B. Mook (Eds.), Advances in qualitative psychology: Themes and variations. Berwyn, PA: Swets North America.

Craig, E. (2000). *Self as such: Self, spirit, and the existing human*. Unpublished paper presented at the Old Saybrook 2 Conference, May 11–14. University of West Georgia, Carrollton, Georgia.

Craig, E. (2008). The human and the hidden: Existential wonderings about depth, soul, and the unconscious. In *The Humanistic Psychologist, 36*, 227–282.

Descartes, R. (1998). Meditations on first philosophy. In D. A. Cross (Trans.). Discourse on method and Meditations on first philosophy, pp. 59–103). Indianapolis, IN: Hackett Publishing Company. (Original work published 1641).

Freud, S. (1953). The interpretation of dreams. In J. Strachey (Ed. and Trans.), *The standard edition of the complete psychological works of Sigmund Freud* (Vol. 4 & 5, pp. 1–625). London: Hogarth Press. (Original work published 1900).

Gadamer, H-G. (1988). *Truth and method*. New York: The Crossroad Publishing Company.

Hartmann, E. (2011). *The nature and function of dreaming*. New York: Oxford University Press.

May, R., & Caligor, L. (1968). *Dreams and symbols: Man's unconscious language*. New York, NY: Basic Books.

Plato. (1992). *Theaetetus*. (B. Williams, Ed., M. J. Leavett, Trans.). Indianapolis, IN: Hackett Publishing Company, Inc.

Thompson, E. (2015). *Waking, dreaming, being: Self and consciousness in neuroscience, meditation, and philosophy*. New York, NY: Columbia University Press.

Zhuangzi. (1996). *The book of Zhuangzi*. (M. Palmer & E. Breuilly, Trans.). New York: Penguin Books.

7

MASTER HUI'S GRAVE

To Sharpen Your Character, Rub It up against Something Abrasive

Richard Bargdill

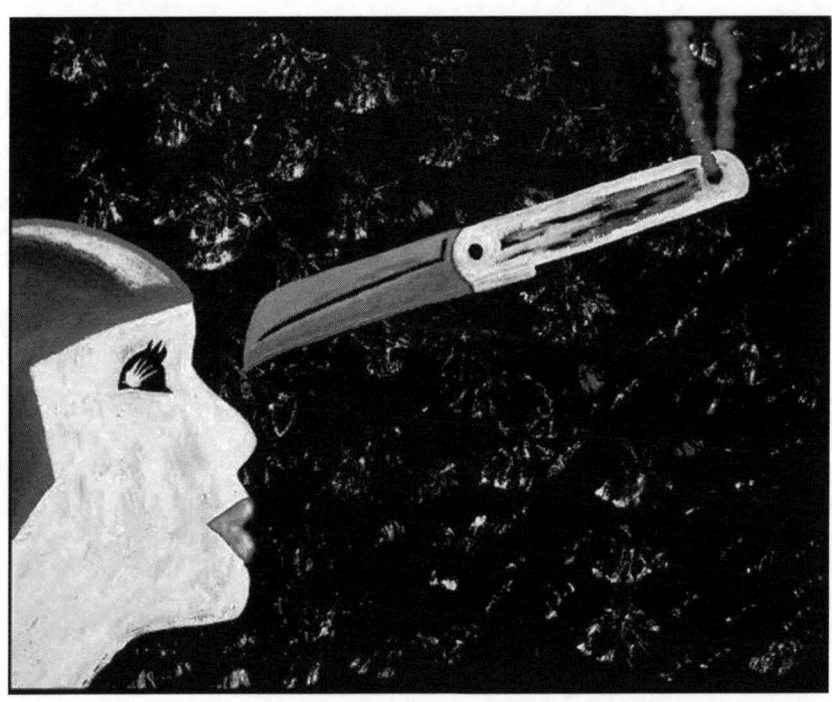

FIGURE 7.1 Created by Nesreen Frost

There are a number of elements in the short parable "Master Hui's Grave" that resonate with Existential Psychology. The parable will first be presented so the reader can gather some of the nuances that are available from this short anecdote. Then we will look at some of the elements that an Existential Psychologist might highlight. First, this parable draws our attention to how death can enlighten us about those significant things in our life. Second, strong interpersonal relationships are important to bring out the best in one's self and also help us to begin caring for others and our community. Third, our greatest achievements are likely to come from our most difficult journeys. Fourth, maturity includes coming to terms with no longer being the person we once were. Finally, the acquisition of our values will take daily practice and self-reflection, and often requires us to rub up against something abrasive.

Master Hui's Grave

> Master Zhuang was accompanying a funeral when he passed by the grave of Master Hui. Turning around, he said to his attendants, "There was a man from Ying who sent for carpenter Shih to slice off a speck of plaster like a fly's wing that had splattered the tip of his nose. Carpenter Shih whirled his ax so fast that it produced a wind. Letting the ax fall instinctively, he sliced off every last bit of the plaster but left the nose unharmed, while the man from Ying stood there without flinching. When Lord Yuan of Sung heard about this, he summoned carpenter Shih and said, 'Try to do the same thing for me.' 'Your servant used to be able to slice off plaster like that,' said carpenter Shih, 'but my "chopping block" died longed ago.' Since your death, Master Hui, I have had no one who can be my 'chopping block.' I have had no one with whom to talk."
>
> [1](Zhuangzi, 1998, p. 244)

Existential Parallels

A Friend Allows Me to Become More Myself

Master Zhuang recognizes that his friendship and intellectual rivalry with Master Hui has been one of the most important relationships in his life. We often hear that competition helps to raise the level of each of the participants on a given task. The conversations between Zhuangzi and Hui allowed each of them to strengthen their respective philosophies.[2] Master Hui allowed Zhuangzi to craft his arguments in the company of someone whose thinking Zhuangzi appreciated. The fact that they are often walking together suggests that they enjoyed each other's company. We walk with those that we like and walk away from those we don't. Siblings can often be great friends and our fellow competitors; however, we can often appreciate the point of view of a friend from outside of our family because we don't see the influences of their upbringing like we do with our own brothers and sisters. We frequently believe that siblings act in certain ways, or believe certain things, because they are trying to get in the good graces of a particular parent. Our friends' actions and intentions seem a little more mysterious to us and they seem to laugh more with us than at us—that is not always the case with siblings.

Another great aspect of friendship is that we choose to be friends, and of course, don't have any obligation to continue being their friend if they treat us badly. It's hard to get rid of a sibling. For many people, a great friend will eventually replace a brother or sister as the most important peer in their lives. We can trust friends more than siblings because friends have less to gain by sharing our secrets. Every brother or sister has "told on" each other. A friend will often go out of their way to protect the other from getting in trouble. Aristotle points out that friendship is an essential element of the good life. A friend expands our world as they show us that there are other ways to do things than the way our family taught us. A friend might expand our horizon by sharing their favorite music or favorite game. Sometimes what they show us becomes a new and integral part of our lives. Friends can often change us by showing us a side of ourselves that we can't see. A sibling might try to do this by teasing us, but the meanness of spirit makes us defensive. A friend can chide us a bit and in their humor we can glimpse something we might want to change. Friends don't always last forever but their impact can be enormous. Nietzsche (1974) in his aphorism "Star Friendship" speaks to the changing nature of friends as time goes by. He writes:

> We are two ships each of which has its goal and course; our paths may cross and we may celebrate a feast together, as we did—and then the good ships rested so quietly in one harbor and one sunshine that it may have looked as if they had reached their goal and as if they had one goal. But then the almighty force of our tasks drove us apart again into different seas and sunny zones, and perhaps we shall never see one another again— perhaps we shall meet again but fail to recognize each other: our exposure to different seas and suns has changed us!
>
> (Nietzsche, 1974, pp. 225–226)

Nietzsche suggests that friends can have great influence on each other because they help us shape our own philosophies of life. We are sometimes inspired to go in a different direction because of them. Our friends can encourage us to take chances that we do not think we are ready for. They can tell us: "You should apply . . . You should go . . . You're as good as they are." They give us the confidence to even leave them because we know that is what we need to do for our own betterment. This might remind us of Herman Hesse's (1981) Siddhartha and his friendship with Govinda. The two start out on the same spiritual journey beginning as ascetics then moving on to a monastery. Govinda finds the teachings of the spiritual leader powerful, but Siddhartha feels that he needs to keep looking for answers and he leaves. Their paths will cross two more times; both times the men have trouble recognizing each other. The final time Govinda seeks out the enlightened ferryman Siddhartha, and Govinda becomes enlightened through Siddhartha.

Friendship is important for our psychological growth because a friend allows us the confidence to show more and more of who we are to another person. Generally speaking, we all have public and private selves. Most of the time when we meet new people, we show them our public face that often includes socially approved ways of communicating. We are polite and might begin with some canned conversation about the weather or a sports team. If our conversation moves toward something more meaningful, we might find that we like the person. If we should meet again, we are likely to share more of our deeper views with this budding friend. We are getting to know each other now and we will continually let down our guard a little more as the person seems to appreciate our "private me." So one of the great compliments a person can say about a true friend is, "When I'm around you I feel that I can be myself." In other words, a friend is a person who you can show yourself to in all your glory. A friend is able to see the good and the bad. A friend is someone who hears your dirty language and your spin on politics and likes you anyway. When we have one person in our life that loves us regardless (unconditional positive regard), it allows us to feel comfortable in our own skin (Rogers, 1961). Freedom is when you stop caring what everyone else thinks and a great friend gives you that.

Too many of our relationships, including those with family, marriage, and colleagues, place limits on us as to how free we can act. Parents are often always parents and seem to want to shape our actions. Marriage partners often seem to want to take over the role of the super-ego and boss us around. Fellow work-ers sometimes leave us feeling like we have to be cautious about what we say or do around them because those things might come back to haunt us. A friend gives us a sense of freedom. There is someone I can tell a dark secret to because I have to get this off my chest. I trust this person, just as the workman trusts the ax wheeler in the story. In Existential Psychology, the client must develop a sense of trust with the therapist so that the client can also share the dark secret. Naturally, the client will need some time to develop a relationship. So, therapy will probably begin with some less significant problems and the main issue will be avoided until the client feels that therapist is trustworthy.

Little that is Worthwhile Comes Easy

Existential Psychology encourages people to search for meaning and purpose in the way they are living their lives. Clients often come to therapy because these are two things that they can't quite find yet. The Grave Parable suggests that struggling with difficult tasks, ideas, and matters is something that ultimately will bear fruit. When the carpenter "accepts the assignment" of slicing the mud off of the plasterer's nose, we see a project that is a true test of skill—an opportunity for authenticity. Authentic experiences are generally accompanied by anxiety for the person involved since at the same time there is the opportunity to do something death defying, there is also a chance at failure. Our authentic opportunities, in Heidegger's (1962) sense, are more likely to be moments that make us nauseous instead of being experiences we are looking forward to. Most of such opportunities require a great deal of courage so that we respectfully decline the invitation or even avoid taking up those possibilities. For example, each day we see an injustice and even recognize it as something that "someone" should stop. This is our opportunity for courage. But, *of course*, it is none of our business. Courage is often confused with fearlessness. Courage means to be afraid but to continue to act towards what is just in the face of one's own fear. Our authentic moments are defining experiences that occur in the face of un-pleasantries and if we are proud of our transformation from them it is usually only after the fact.

In the first part of the parable, the carpenter and the plasterer are both at ease with this daring act and we don't see any anxiety; probably because the event has taken place many times before. It is old hat. Of course, we can imagine that the first time this trick was performed there must have been doubt in one or both of the participants. We might imagine a similar situation at a carnival where the expert knife thrower slings his blades at the beautiful young lady. No matter how many times one practices on boards or mannequins, there must be some anxiety when a person who can be hurt by our slightest mistake is involved. Authenticity does not occur when someone is supremely confident. Anxiety shows us that we care for the project we are engaged in. Once we have mastered the task, the anxiety dims down and now we have to find another challenge or face boredom (Bargdill, 2014). Our lives ebb and flow; we have rare authentic moments but then our life settles down into a mundane routine.

It is interesting that the plasterer is the one who originated this spectacle and he is the one who is supremely confident in the carpenter's skills. Again, this speaks to how other people sometimes have more faith in us than we have in ourselves. In Existential Psychology, often the therapist takes a client-centered approach. This means that the therapist does not give advice or try to "fix" the client. Rather the therapist attempts to help the client find one's self. In a sense, client-centered therapy means that the therapist has confidence that the client knows how to live life and that she will be able to find meaning in a life project—either one she has already begun or one that will emerge for her. This is not an easy stance to take since therapists are sometimes conceived as authorities that "prescribe" acts. But all the other people, such as family, spouse, and co-workers, have led the client away from herself so the therapist must be different. When the client finds something she loves doing, other people—who she highly values—have talked her out of it. They say, "You'll never make any money doing that. You'll starve. Take the safe option. You'll have reliable income and benefits." The client has turned down this *easy and safe road* that has left her alienated from her own self and sense of vitality.

The therapist realizes that the person in therapy is already moving in the right direction. This person is unhappy with something in his or her life and they are willing to admit it and seek help. A client is already a courageous person because he has decided he needs help. The Existential therapist helps this process by being a sounding board for the client's own personal wandering. The therapist acts metaphorically as a guide who walks with the client as he verbally processes how he understands the events that are occurring in his life. The therapist's skill, almost like a traffic cop, is to get the client to pause at certain moments of insight, allowing it to sink in. Sometimes the therapist has the client do a U-turn and go back to something he was talking about but sped past too quickly. Other times, the therapist must get him to move along if he gets stuck ruminating on a particular problem. But the aim is to allow the client to discover what he already knows about himself but lost touch with and what really makes him happy. The goal of therapy is to help the client discover what makes his life meaningful and help him then pursue that.

Self-Knowledge is an Aspect of Maturity

Another part of the parable that relates to Existential Psychology is the maturity that the carpenter shows by declining to repeat his trick. Summoned to perform a task as a sort of novelty, the carpenter realizes that his skills are rusty and that he is out of practice. Rather than trying to please the Lord of Sung and the audience, the carpenter shows the self-awareness that his skills have deteriorated and he is out of practice. He realizes that the task that he performed years earlier was a feat of great skill and had a real risk to both he and the participant. Many people are talked into performing acts that they are not properly prepared for or are asked to mechanically repeat an action that was originally genuine. Think of how many times you have been asked to do it again for the camera—lost is the spontaneity of the moment, the improvisation of the unfolding, and now it is just spectacle.

Many people struggle with hanging on too long when it comes to things involving physical prowess, but not this carpenter. We might be reminded of the John Cheever (1978) story "O Youth and Beauty." In this story, a middle-aged man tried to show off his former athletic skills by arranging his living room furniture into series of hurdles. He then races against his house guests through this obstacle course. He won every race-until the day he broke his leg tripping over a couch. Afterwards, he fell into a deep depression as he learns that he is aging much to his chagrin. Instead of risking a horrific accident, our carpenter knows not to go forth. He understands his limitations and is not goaded into some act that might temporarily restore a feeling of past glory. He knows himself enough to realize that what he could do in the past he is no longer capable of doing now.

The Existential therapist will be interested in where in time the client is living. Some clients are living in the past. They can talk only about past glory but more often they talk about past trauma. The past can be a weight that seems to keep the person from fully living in the present. Other clients live too far in the unobtainable future. They fantasize about a future when ideal conditions will exist (Bargdill, 2000). They may win the lottery or be discovered for their talent but usually they will say, "I'll be happy when. . . ." This means that happiness is not there for them now but off in the unlikely future. People can also be negatively caught in the hedonistic now. We sometimes hear others claim that we need to "seize the day"—*carpe diem*. This can be problematic if we are not paying attention to the future and ignoring the lessons of the past by repeating the same mistakes. Existential therapists try to help clients integrate these three temporal regions with the goal that we learn from the past, we appreciate the "here and now," and we have an eye toward the future.

Values Also Require Practice

Another admirable lesson from this parable that Existential Psychology would promote is the idea that all virtue needs to be practiced on a daily basis. Master Zhuang recognizes that his intellect is not as sharp as it used to be because his friend and intellectual rival, Master Hui, is no longer there to play devil's advocate. Master Hui often took the opposing side in debates with Master Zhuang, enabling him to craft his arguments into fine theories. An opponent can think of counter points that might not cross the mind of the proponent and thus the thinker has to find a way to handle the opponent's question or objection. When someone is asked a good question, she has to stop and think about how to align the proposal within its own parameters to the new condition that the question imposes. Master Hui challenged Master Zhuang in this way but was also able to maintain a friendship with him. Mostly when someone opposes us, we end up seeing him as an enemy or nemesis and do our best to avoid him. We don't want to be around them because they are always challenging what we say and in a sense trying to make us look bad. Plato (1993) recounts that the Western father of philosophy, Socrates, was put to death because the people of Athens felt he was teaching young people to question the authority of the city officials.

We have to practice virtue almost in the same way we would exercise our body. Any physical act that requires an amount of skill we know requires maintenance. If we dance or play basketball, we know that to keep our abilities we must do that every day or our skill will get rusty. Anyone who has gotten injured or taken a long break from a sport realizes that only the repetition of daily practice will return one's skill. However, we tend not to see "mental" actions such as thinking and being virtuous as activities that also require daily dedication. It is interesting that some people start each year with a "New Year's Resolution" that almost inevitably is about a physical activity. So people try to lose weight, exercise more, or eat more vegetables. An equivalent task would be to pick a virtue that we want to exhibit more and then consciously attempt to make or simply take advantage of the opportunities that come our way. If we want to be more courageous, we will find there are many opportunities to stand against injustice every day. We see someone litter and shake our head because we want to say something to them but we don't. Any virtue can be exercised if we keep in mind to make this part of our lives.

Existential therapy is ultimately about helping people find meaning, purpose, and values in their lives (Frankl, 1959). The therapist doesn't need to impose values on the client but rather help the client find the values that she is half living out. Clients often discover that they have given up on their own passions and dreams to live in a way that pleases others. Often, neither end up pleased. Cultural, religious, and family expectations can have the client living a life completely drained of vitality. Therapy challenges clients to re-imagine what they want to do with their lives and to develop the courage to fight for that life as well as fight against those who are not going to want to see anything change; there will be many more against this growth than one might think. There are some well-known ways to find what we love to do by reflecting on: what makes time seem to fly, what would we do if we didn't need to make an income, what experiences consistently gives us chills or produces awe, and what situations in the world do we see as a unjust. These are the signs that something is alive in us. These are things we care for and there are virtues that we can cultivate if we bring it from the back burner to the front burner. Aristotle tells us we have to know what a virtue is, we have to know how to act in accordance with that virtue, and we have to have the courage to put that virtue into action (Bartlett & Collins, 2011).

Zhuangzi's parable about Master Hui's grave resonates with Existential Psychology in many ways, only some of which have been outlined here. Death shows us what is important in life because it reveals that we, and significant people in our lives, are here temporarily. Our friends allow us to be free because they both challenge who we are and accept us for who we are—we benefit from both. The obstacles in our life will provide the opportunities to stretch our skills and be more authentic rather than to do activities that come easy. Maturity means coming to terms with some of our limitations and this requires the ability to self-reflect. Virtues need to be practiced every day because our character can only be sharpened by rubbing it up against something abrasive.

Notes

1 Permission to republish granted by University of Hawaii Press. Zhuangzi. (1998). *Wandering on the way: Early Taoist tales and parables of Chuang Tzu.* (V. Mair, Trans.). p. 244. Honolulu, HI: University of Hawaii Press.
2 One of the most famous debates that occurred between Master Zhuang and Master Hui involved Zhuangzi's Parable of the Joy of the Fishes. An excellent exposition of the existential themes in this parable can be found in Chapter 4 of the book *Existential psychology: East West, Vol 1*, published by University of the Rockies Press.

References

Bargdill, R. W. (2000). The study of life boredom. In *Journal of Phenomenological Psychology, 31*(2), 72–103.
Bargdill, R. W. (2014). Toward a theory of habitual boredom. *Janus Head, 13*(12), 93–111.
Bartlett, R. C., & Collins, S. D. (2011). *Nicomachean ethics.* Chicago, IL: University of Chicago Press.
Cheever, J. (1978). *The stories of John Cheever.* New York, NY: Alfred A. Knopf.
Frankl, V. (1959). *Man's search for meaning.* Boston, MA: Beacon.
Heidegger, M. (1962). *Being and time.* (J. Macquarrie & E. Robinson, Trans.). San Francisco, CA: Harper.
Hesse, H. (1981). *Siddhartha.* (Hilda Rosner, Trans.). New York, NY: Bantam Classics.
Nietzsche, F. (1974). *Gay science: With a prelude and appendix of songs.* (W. Kaufmann, Trans.). New York, NY: Vintage.
Plato. (1993). *The republic.* (A. D. Lindsay, Trans.). New York: Everyman's Library.
Rogers, C. R. (1961). *On becoming a person: A distinguished therapist's guide to personal growth and creativity.* New York, NY: Houghton Mifflin Company.
Zhuangzi. (1998). *Wandering on the way: Early Taoist tales and parables of Chuang Tzu.* (V. Mair, Trans.). Honolulu, HI: University of Hawaii Press.

8

RELEASING THE JADE, GRASPING MEANING

Louis Hoffman

FIGURE 8.1 Created by Leah Pritchard

The Flight of Lin Hui (Chapter 20 in the book *Zhuangzi*)

Lin Hui of Kia took to flight.
Pursued by enemies,
He threw away the precious jade
Symbol of his rank
And took his infant child on his back.
Why did he take the child
And leave the jade,
Which was worth a small fortune,
Whereas the child, if sold,
Would only bring him a paltry sum?

Lin Hui said:
"My bond with the jade symbol
And with my office
Was the bond of self-interest.
My bond with the child
Was the bond of Tao.

Where self-interest is the bond,
The friendship is dissolved
When calamity comes.
Where Tao is the bond,
Friendship is made perfect
By calamity.

The friendship of wise men
Is tasteless as water.
The friendship of fools
Is sweet as wine.
But the tastelessness of the wise
Brings true affection
And the savor of fool's company
Ends in hatred.
                    (Zhuangzi, as cited in Merton,
                         2010, pp. 116–117)

Introduction

A myth is a way of making sense in a senseless world. Myths are narrative patterns that give significance to our existence. Whether the meaning of existence is only what we put into life by our own individual fortitude, as Sartre would hold, or whether there is a meaning we need to discover, as Kierkegaard would state, the result is the same: myths are our way of finding this meaning and significance.
                                                                  (May, 1991, p. 15)

Zhuangzi's "The Flight of Lin Hui," like any good myth, is packed with meaning. Rollo May (1991) stated, "The denial of myths . . . is itself part of *our refusal to confront our own reality and that of our society*" (p. 25, emphasis added). To state more positively, the embracement of myth is a way of facing our own reality and the reality of our society. "The Flight of Lin Hui" brings one face to face with a number of stark existential realities, and through this can promote or even incite reflection and self-awareness. This is the *power* of myth. Because myths speak to the existential givens, ultimate concerns that we all have to live with, we can relate to them directly; we can apply them to our lives.

In preparing for this chapter, the more I sat with this short myth, the more I recognized that one could spend many years, if not a lifetime, struggling with its deeper meanings and implications. Although it originated over 2,000 years ago, the struggle hidden within this myth is quite relevant today. This is the *beauty* of myth. All myths are written in a particular time and place, and thus influenced by the culture of the time. Yet, myths that wrestle with our existential condition can transcend time to remain relevant across many cultures and many generations (Hoffman, 2009a).

Symbolism of the Jade and Tao

> A symbol always transcends the one who makes use of it and makes him say in reality
> more than he is aware of expressing.
>
> (Camus, 1955, p. 124)

The jade and the Tao are two powerful symbols in "The Flight of Lin Hui." The power of symbolism is in its ability to remain simultaneously concrete and abstract, and through this hold together various meanings, or "truths," in a single symbolic expression. If the symbol is only able to represent a single meaning, it is severely limited in its instructive power, and the interpreter who reifies a singular meaning only impoverishes his or her own wisdom.

Artists, philosophers, and psychologists often endlessly play with symbols. This play is not for mere enjoyment, but rather it serves to promote insight. When we view symbols from different angles, including different cultural contexts, and when we push and stretch these symbols, we often find new meanings. Sometimes the new meaning only entails a small nuance of difference from previously held meanings; however, these nuances sometimes are quite profound, even life changing.

In "The Flight of Lin Hui," the jade and the Tao hold many potential meanings that can serve to illuminate and incite reflection. Some of this can be seen in the differing translations of this parable. What is translated as "the bond of self-interest" is alternatively translated as "profit" (Chuang Tzu, 1996; Zhuangzi, 2013). Merton's translation of "the bond of self-interest" reflects the broader symbolism of the jade representing self-interest, security, self-focused prosperity, or material gains.

Similarly, in the various translations of this parable, Tao (i.e., "My bond with the child was the bond of Tao") is alternatively translated as "heaven" (see Chuang Tzu, 1996; Zhuangzi, 2013), which may reflect a different reading through Western lenses. The Tao can be seen as reflecting a meaning beyond or greater than the self, potentially, though not necessarily, a spiritual or religious meaning.

The Jade

The jade is a rich symbol that brings together complex meanings. The jade is a strong stone that can be used in various ways, including as a tool, such as a knife or a weapon. However, it is more commonly used for jewelry. As a beautiful jewel, it has been particularly revered in China. The jade is a valuable material possession, representing financial gain or profit. However, in Zhuangzi's parable, it is also a symbol of power or prestige.

Throughout history and across many cultures, the temptation to seek power and material possessions for oneself and one's family has been pervasive. It is often believed that if one has power or material comforts, then one will be happy and satisfied. This belief in material possessions and power, however, is often denied, even to oneself. We voice one meaning and live another.

From an existential perspective, it's possible to differentiate sustaining meaning from meaning that is not sustaining (Hoffman, 2009b). Sustaining meaning is a deeper form of meaning that helps transform suffering and helps promote happiness or well-being. Meaning that is not sustaining may, instead of transforming suffering, contribute to it.

Meaning inevitably has individual and cultural influences. Thus, it is difficult to speak of a universal meaning. Even if agreeing to a particular source of meaning, such as relationships or love, it is unlikely that we could attain universal agreement as to how this is described, understood, and experienced. In other words, even if universal meanings exist, they always must be individually and culturally interpreted.

For Paul Tillich (1957), meaning was conceived in the context of one's ultimate concern. An ultimate concern is something that grips or holds the person, thus driving their life choices and behaviors. Again, people may not always be fully aware of their ultimate concern. Tillich uses nationalism as an example of an ultimate concern that often grips people or groups of people. In this instance, much of life is constructed around the protection of this nationalism.

Ultimate concerns have consequences beyond the individual. When we prioritize money and wealth over people, this has consequences. When nationalism is valued over compassion and concern for all people, it also has consequences. Thus, it is critical that we examine or are aware of our ultimate concerns. It could even be said that self-awareness is necessary for responsible and ethical living (Riker, 1997).

The Child

Does a true hero have to be heartless?
Surely a real man may love his young son.
Even the roaring, wind-raising tiger
Turns back to look at his own tiny cubs.

(Lu Xun, 2000)

What is the ideal for mental health, then? A lived, compelling illusion that does not lie about life, death, and reality; one honest enough to follow its own command-ments: I mean, not to kill, not to take the lives of others to justify itself.

(Becker, 1973, p. 204)

As a father, reading about a consideration of leaving behind or selling a child feels violent. Yet, it is important to avoid a literalized interpretation of this aspect of the parable in a contemporary context. While I would never literally sell any of my sons, when holding this part of the story at the symbolic level, I immediately feel convicted. I think of the times that I chose work or financial security over the relationship with my sons. These can be rationalized as the responsibility to provide economic security for my family, the need to role model to them the importance of work, or through stating these were small transgressions that do not impact the physical safety of my sons. Yet, these are still rationalizations. The reality is that I too often have valued the jade over my sons in my actions and this has consequences.

The Western world, particularly the United States, has decentered the impor-tance of the family and relationships, replacing it with the supreme valuation of the individual and personal happiness. This has increasingly become the center-piece of Western ethical, and even legal, systems. Western perspectives on hap-piness, at least at the implicit level, have further been connected to possessions, financial profit, and valuing working hard, even excessively. Compounding the problem, the West has aggressively exported this value system to other countries with attempts to impose it upon them as a universal truth.

As someone raised and influenced by the Western ideal of the individual, I am frequently aware of the deep ache or longing to reconnect with a more relationally centered world. May (1991) states:

Americans cling to the myth of individualism as though it were the only normal way to live, unaware that it was unknown in the Middle Ages (except for hermits) and would have been considered psychotic in classical Greece. We feel as Americans that every person must be ready to stand alone, each of us following the powerful myth of the lone cabin on the prairie. Each individual must learn to take care of himself or herself and thus be beholden to no one else.

(p. 108)

For May, this individualism breeds a type of narcissism that is destructive and, in the end, unsustainable.

The deep ache of loneliness is pervasive in the United States, and much of Western culture and even the world. While this cannot solely be attributed to the burden of individualism, it certainly has contributed to the problem. May (1991) believed this contributed to the common problems of gambling, addiction, and drug use. I would add that this has likely contributed to many forms of violence in contemporary society, including school and workplace shootings. Often, the individuals who carry out these terrible acts were people who were lonely, isolated, misunderstood, and rejected by society.

Friendship

> Sometimes I see myself fine
> Sometimes I need a witness
> And I like the whole truth
> But there are nights I only need forgiveness
>
> Sometimes they say, "I don't know who you are
> But let me walk with you some"
> And I say, "I am alone, that's all
> You can't save me from all the wrong I've done"
>
> But they're waiting just the same
> With their flashlights and their semaphores
> And I'll act like I have faith and like that faith never ends
> But I really just have friends
>
> (Williams, 1997)

*Permission to reprint lyrics granted by www.mctartists.com Lyrics from the song "My Friends," in the album *End of the Summer* by Dar Williams.

> The gospel of "being one's self alone" ends up in becoming nothing. . . .
> All such narcissistic egocentricity leads to self-destruction.
>
> *(May, 1991, p. 190)*

The transition in the last two stanzas of Zhuangzi's parable at first glance gives the appearance of not being connected. However, upon closer investigation, it is carrying forth and deepening the meaning of relationship. This appears to clarify that the symbol of the child in the story represents relationships more broadly. Zhuangzi seems to be emphasizing that the deeper, sustaining meaning in life is of friendship and relationship.

Zhuangzi distinguishes between friendships that are self-serving from those that entail deeper connections. This parallels Buber's (1923/1970) distinction between I-Thou and I-It relationships. In the I-It relationships, the other person is treated as an object, as something that can be used. The I-Thou relationship signifies a much deeper relationship in which the two are deeply connected and impacted by each other.

"The Flight of Lin Hui" does not present an idealized view of friendship, even presenting it as "tasteless." The tastelessness of true friendship is contrasted with the sweetness of being friends with fools. While this could be interpreted as saying that true friendship is boring or should not involve enjoyment, I do not believe this is what Zhuangzi is getting at.

Wine, soda, and other sweet beverages often are enjoyable to taste; however, they do not sustain us, and if over-indulged can even be destructive. Water, in contrast, does not have the same enticing taste, yet it is one of our most basic needs for survival. When we seek friendship for enjoyment, we often build relationships that cannot sustain us in difficult times. However, when we seek relationships based upon wisdom, we are drawn toward relationships capable of providing a sustaining meaning.

The Dar Williams (1997) lyrics cited at the beginning of this section provide a beautiful example of friendship. Like Zhuangzi, Williams does not present an idealized view of friendship. Relationships are hard, particularly when we seek out I-Thou relationships. Often, these relationships challenge us and confront us; they push us to examine parts of our life we would rather leave in the dark and out of our awareness. Yet, these friendships stay with us when we are in need of forgiveness, and when we are in need of someone to walk with us for a while.

However, this only speaks to one half of the friendship. Just as friendship asks for forgiveness, it also calls us to forgive. Just as friendship asks for someone to walk with us for a while, it also calls us to walk with our friends. Just as friendships treasures the faith our friends have in us, it also calls us to have faith in our friends, even when they have lost faith. It is in this type of relationship where "friendship is made perfect in calamity."

Loyalty

In contemporary Western culture, loyalties too often are shallow or self-serving. We can see this even in our allegiance to sports teams. Fans frequently follow the teams that win instead of sticking with their teams through the difficult times. Similarly, professional athletes quickly accept the most prestigious offer or highest pay instead of staying loyal to their teammates. In the workplace, people are often pressured, and sometimes even directly told or ordered, to put their work over their personal relationships. Transgressions made against our friends are often justified by our professional roles, work responsibilities, or financial necessity. "Business ethics," which often represent shallow ethical systems based upon easily manipulated rules, are seen as superior to relational ethics and values.

Contrary to how it is often portrayed, loyalty to relationships is not easy. Yet, I would maintain that the lack of loyalty to relationships, and the decreasing prioritization of relationships, is one of the great threats to psychological and social health in the world today. When self-interest is prioritized over relational loyalty, loneliness often results. When being "loyal" to our workplace or financial security is prioritized over relationships, relational transgressions are common.

Yet, loyalty is not easy. To write personally for a moment, I would say that loyalty has been one of the deepest sources of pain and greatest causes of stress in my adult life. Many times it would have been less stressful to end relationships than hold the tension between two friends in conflict. Similarly, on many occasions it would have been easier in my professional life to allow for relationships to fall astray and follow work expectations. Instead, I have several times taken great personal risk to remain loyal to people important to me.

Loyalty almost inevitably creates tension. Yet, loyalty is also connected to the deepest rewards of my life. I hope that most of my close friends, colleagues, and students recognize my loyalty to them and know that I will prioritize them over my own self-interests or the expectations that others place upon me. Even when not recognized, the loyalty and connected deep caring for these individuals remains deeply meaningful to me. These relationships, deepened by loyalty that is willing to endure suffering, are the greatest joys and deepest rewards of my life.

Loyalty is not a call to blind acceptance or agreement with our friends and loved ones. It is remaining committed and holding one's friends and loved ones just as close when there is dissent, anger, separation, and other challenges to the relationship. Loyalty, if based in blind acceptance or a lack of awareness, would not constitute the same depth of meaning. Rather, persevering through strife is a necessary component of loyalty.

To choose the jade is almost inevitably easier in terms of stress and strife. Yet, the jade also brings the deeper pain of loneliness and the recognition, even if sometimes largely on the unconscious level, of the betrayal and hurt one has caused to others. The joy that can emerge from the stress and strife of loyalty is worth the suffering for those willing to endure.

Contemporary Applications

This ancient tale of Zhuangzi is remarkably timeless in its lessons. When I look at the world and its problems today, I see the misguided placement of relationship as our biggest crisis. The "we" has been replaced with "I." The consequence of this can be seen in everything from social to environmental problems. The environment, other species, and other people are treated as something that serves the betterment of the individual, instead of valuing the collective. This section briefly examines a few issues that may threaten our future existence.

A vital problem in contemporary culture is the obsession with work. While work can be a source of deep meaning in life (Frankl, 1984), it can also be a source of destruction. Work is meaningful when it contributes to something beyond oneself, and when it is part of a balanced approach to living. Too often work is distorted to self-serving purposes, such as the attainment of wealth and power. Equally as dangerous as the misuse of work to attain power and excessive wealth is the overvaluing of one's work ethic or commitment to work. The lack of balance and misuse of work prevents work from achieving its potential of sustaining meaning. It is vital that we strive to preserve the sanctity of work, which is done by making sure work is centered in relational values, including a concern for others and loyalty to relationships.

Second, it seems that many in contemporary culture are replacing relational depth with quantity. The easy access to social media, which allows for people to interact with many individuals from around the world, contributes greatly to this problem. This is not to characterize social media negatively. Social media has the potential to help connect people in meaningful ways, but can also serve to promote a communication style that lacks relational depth. This may contribute to a culture of loneliness and isolation, which also connects to many other social problems.

Finally, it is sometimes not recognized that there is a relational component to contemporary environmental issues. As a father, I am deeply concerned about the environment because I want to preserve the environment for my sons, who will be impacted by environmental problems in ways I cannot yet imagine. Too often, the environment is understood as something that is there for people to use and consume. It is not recognized that the environment is something that we all share and that we relate to. When we treat the environment and nature with a lack of compassion and empathy, it has consequences.

"The Flight of Lin Hui" recognizes the central place that relationship should hold in our lives. For Zhuangzi, this has many meanings. First, relationship with others is central to his ethical understanding. In other words, Zhuangzi is suggesting that relationships should take priority in our ethical decision-making. This stands in stark contrast to an ethical system centered in individual rights, as is common in the West. Second, relationships are central to our well-being, and choosing the right type of relationship will have a powerful impact on our psychological health. Finally, relationships serve a purpose in our self-understanding and self-awareness. We cannot know ourselves apart from others.

Conclusion

In my life as a psychologist and professor, as well as in my personal life, I consider myself to be an existentialist. This label of "existentialist" has a deep symbolic meaning to me. While others share in many aspects of this meaning, I doubt that anyone else shares in the exact same understanding of the existential label. For me, part of the beauty of existential psychology is that there are no hard lines in defining what is existential psychology. Yet, it is an approach to psychology, and an approach to life, that is deeply meaningful to many.

In my own mixture of existential psychology and existential life, friendship and relationship are cornerstones. However, saying one is relational can mean many different things. When I speak of these in the context of an existential understanding, I mean relationship and friendship that is deeply rooted in compassion, love, authenticity, and openness. I do not always live up to these in my relationships, although I aspire to. Part of being authentic is acknowledging in humility our own lack of perfection.

Zhuangzi's parable "The Flight of Lin Hui" deeply resonates with my existential and relationship values. No doubt, some of this is what I read into Zhuangzi. Yet, I believe Zhuangzi's view of relationship is a powerful witness to the type of relationship we are in desperate need of in the world today.

References

Becker, E. (1973). *The denial of death*. New York, NY: Free Press.

Buber, M. (1970). *I and thou*. (W. Kaufmann, Trans.). New York, NY: Touchstone. (Original work published in 1923).

Camus, A. (1955). *The myth of Sisyphus: And other essays*. (J. O'Brien, Trans.). New York, NY: Vintage Books.

Chuang Tzu. (1996). *The book of Chuang Tzu*. (M. Palmer, Trans.). New York, NY: Penguin Books.

Frankl, V. E. (1984). *Man's search for meaning: An introduction to logotherapy* (3rd ed.). New York, NY: Touchstone.

Graber, K. (2010). *The eternal city: Poems*. Princeton, NJ: Princeton University Press.

Hoffman, L. (2009a). Gordo's ghost: An introduction to existential perspectives on myth. In L. Hoffman, M. Yang, F. J. Kaklauskas, & A. Chan (Eds.), *Existential psychology East-West* (pp. 259–274). Colorado Springs, CO: University of the Rockies Press.

Hoffman, L. (2009b). Introduction to existential psychotherapy in a cross-cultural context: An East-West dialogue. In L. Hoffman, M. Yang, F. J. Kaklauskas, & A. Chan (Eds.), *Existential psychology East-West* (pp. 1–67). Colorado Springs, CO: University of the Rockies Press.

Lu Xun. (2000). *Lu Xun selected poems*. (W. J. F. Jenner, Trans.). Beijing, China: Foreign Language Press.

May, R. (1991). *The cry for myth*. New York, NY: Delta.

Merton, T. (2010). *The way of Chuang Tzu*. New York, NY: New Directions Publishing Corp.

Riker, J. H. (1997). *Ethics and the discovery of the unconscious*. Albany, NY: State University of New York Press.

Tillich, P. (1957). *The dynamics of faith*. New York, NY: Harper & Row.

Williams, D. (1997). My friends. In *On end of the summer* (CD). New York, NY: Razor & Tie.

Zhuangzi. (2013). *The complete works of Zhuangzi*. (B. Watson, Trans.). New York, NY: Columbia University Press.

9

DRAGGING MY TAIL IN THE MUD

Personal Reflections on Authenticity

David N. Elkins

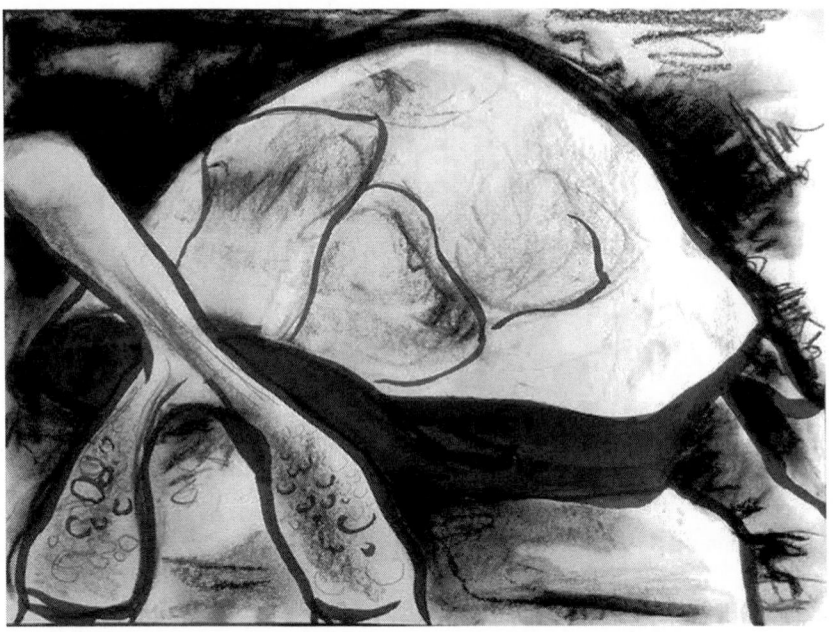

FIGURE 9.1 Created by Jyl Anais Ion

Zhuangzi with his bamboo pole
Was fishing in Pu river.

The Prince of Chu
Sent two vice-chancellors
With a formal document:
"We hereby appoint you
Prime Minister."

Zhuangzi held his bamboo pole.
Still watching Pu river,
He said:
"I am told there is a sacred tortoise,
Offered and canonized
Three thousand years ago,
Venerated by the prince,
Wrapped in silk,
In a precious shrine
On an altar
In the Temple.

"What do you think:
Is it better to give up one's life
And leave a sacred shell
As an object of cult
In a cloud of incense
Three thousand years,
Or better to live
As a plain turtle
Dragging its tail in the mud?"

"For the turtle," said the Vice-Chancellor,
"Better to live
And drag its tail in the mud!"

"Go home!" said Zhuangzi.
"Leave me here
To drag my tail in the mud!"
                         (Merton, 2010, pp. 93–94)

I was impressed by how simply, yet brilliantly, this story illumines one of the great themes of existential philosophy and psychology—the importance of living an authentic existence. Kierkegaard (1941), the founder of existential philosophy, said that the goal of life is "to be that self one truly is" (p. 29). Nietzsche, another great philosopher, gave a moving yet sobering description of authenticity:

> The soul in its essence will say to herself: no one can build the bridge on which you in particular will have to cross the river of life—no one but yourself. Of course there are countless paths and bridges and demigods ready to carry you over the river, but only at the price of your own self. In all the world, there is one specific way that no one but you can take. Whither does it lead? Do not ask, but walk it. As soon as one says, "I want to be myself," he discovers that it is a frightful resolve. Now he must descend to the depths of his existence.
>
> *(as cited by May, 1983, p. 80)*

A Personal Approach

As I write this chapter, I am 70 years of age. I have spent much of my life longing to be that self I truly am and wanting to build my own bridge across the river of life. However, unlike Zhuangzi, I have not always been successful. Far too often I have pretended to be a self that I am not. I have admired the bridges of others and have thought, at times, they could carry me across the river of life. Fortunately, I have also experienced moments of authenticity, times when I knew who I am and when I was building my own bridge. This chapter is personal. It's about my own search for authenticity, my failures, and occasional successes. Although each person's journey is unique, I believe that our personal journeys, if plumbed deeply enough, open up into the universal dimension of our common humanity. So I hope my journey, as described here, will touch the deeper dimensions of your journey as you, too, struggle to live an authentic life.

Authenticity: A Definition

The word *authenticity* has etymological roots in Latin, Greek, and French. The word can refer to a painting, a musical composition, a piece of writing, a bottle of wine, a signature, and many other things. Synonyms, or words that are close to being synonyms, include *genuine, real, true, bona fide, honest, pure, unfeigned, sincere, congruent, trustworthy, unhypocritical*. In psychology, the term is often associated with the existential-humanistic movement. For example, Bugental (1965), a major existential psychologist, published *The Search for Authenticity* and Carl Rogers (1957) considered congruence (i.e., genuineness) on the part of the therapist to be one of the conditions for client change.

Authenticity is also associated with existential philosophy. The quotes from Kierkegaard and Nietzsche above are about authenticity, even though they don't use the term. Also, Sartre (1988) said that if we define humans as having freedom within limits, then when we are confronted with certain situations, we can

exercise that freedom in either an authentic or inauthentic way. Defining authenticity, Sartre (1988) said, "Authenticity . . . consists in having a true and lucid
consciousness of the situation, in assuming the responsibilities and risks that it
involves, in accepting it in pride or humiliation, sometimes in horror and hate"
(p. 90). Sartre shows that authenticity is not simply about "saying what we really
think and feel" in social interactions. Instead, authenticity has to do with our
values, the decisions we make, and the actions we take, especially in situations
of gravity. For example, Sartre's definition comes from his analysis of anti-Semitism,
where he discusses bigotry and our existential responsibility to understand situations and to exercise our freedom to act authentically. Thus, authenticity not
only refers to being genuine in our interactions with others but it also has to
do with how we live our lives. It has to do with our way of being in the world.

Authentic Existence: All Hell Breaks Loose

In the above quote, Nietzsche said that "it is a frightful resolve" when one
decides "I want to be myself." However, what Nietzsche did not say is that all
hell is likely to break loose. The first time I learned this lesson was when I was
23 years of age. I had been trained in theology and was a minister of a conservative church in Michigan. Things were going great until I began to grow—which
is a dangerous thing for a conservative minister to do. I began to doubt some
of the rigid doctrines of my fundamentalist church. For example, although this
will seem ridiculous to most readers, my church believed that using instrumental
music, such as a piano or organ, in the worship services was a sin. In fact, this
was a major doctrine of my church that separated it from other churches. My
church was very proud of its non-instrumental beliefs and our ministers often
preached about how other churches were in "doctrinal error" because they used
a piano in their worship services. However, I had come to the "radical" conclusion that, while I had no desire to change my church's tradition, using instrumental music in the worship was probably not a sin. When my church leaders
got wind of my "liberal" leanings, they called me into a meeting and then fired
me. It was ironic that I was fired for being too liberal because at the time I was
one of the most conservative Christian ministers on the face of the planet!
During the meeting, my church leaders gave me an opportunity to recant but
I knew that if I did so, I would have to betray what I truly believed. I told them
that I respected our church's non-instrumental tradition and had no desire to
bring musical instruments into our worship services. This, however, was not
good enough. The leaders insisted that I also hold the "right belief" about
instrumental music. When they questioned me, I told them what I thought: I
believed using a piano or other musical instrument in worship was probably not
a sin and would likely be okay with God. This was very upsetting to my church
leaders and they concluded that they simply could not have a minister who was
in "doctrinal error" on such an important point. According to them, the Bible

was clear that using instrumental music in church was a sin and if I no longer believed that, then I had gone astray from the word of God. So even though they and the congregation liked me very much as a person, they could no longer allow me to be minister because I might taint others with my liberal ideas.

So they fired me. Then, for good measure, they defrocked me so that I could not spread my "false doctrines" to other congregations of my denomination. As I mentioned, I was only 23 years of age when this happened. I had a young wife, one child, and another child on the way. Now, because I had been true to myself, even if it was about a rather silly theological point, I was without a job and seemingly without a future. Many church friends, because they thought it was their religious duty to obey the church leaders, turned their backs on me and my young family. This was a difficult time. I had always wanted to be a minister, even as a child; so I had no idea what I was going to do. The world that I had known came crashing down. That was the first time that I learned that when you say, "I want to be myself," all hell is likely to break loose!

Eventually, things worked out. Through the help of a friend, I got a job at Fisher Body and built automobiles for a year. This put food on the table, a roof over our heads, and my health insurance paid the hospital bill associated with the birth of our second child. Then, a more liberal church in Connecticut heard what had happened to me and invited me to be their minister, even though I had been "defrocked" by the more conservative wing of my denomination. So my family and I moved to Connecticut and I returned to the ministry. However, by this time I was feeling pretty demoralized about religion and wasn't sure I wanted to continue being a minister. So after serving the church in Connecticut for two years, I went back to school in psychology. I got my master's degree in Connecticut and then we moved to California, where I got my doctorate in clinical psychology. And the rest, as they say, is history.

Today, I am no longer a minister. In fact, I'm not involved with organized religion at all. When I look back, I realize that being fired and defrocked as a young minister turned out to be a good thing. It helped me to leave my funda-mentalist religion and embrace a new profession. It released me to continue growing and to become more fully who I am. For me, fundamentalist Christianity was like a box. As long as I did not grow, I could fit into the box. However, once I began to grow, the box could not expand to accommodate me. Rigid systems have a difficult time tolerating diverse perspectives; they can't accom-modate those who want to be themselves; they have no place for authenticity of being. To use Nietzsche's language, rigid religious systems are among the "demi-gods ready to carry you over the river, but only at the price of your own self."

Sara's Illness: Mortality and Authenticity

Once I left the ministry and became a psychologist, my life settled down. I loved my new profession. I worked in a fairly large private practice in California and then in a community mental health center in rural Wyoming. Then, in 1982, I was offered a position as assistant professor of psychology at Pepperdine University in Los Angeles and we returned to California. During those years, I got along well with my colleagues. I was known as a "nice guy"—probably a product of my Southern upbringing and my former profession as a minister. I did my best to "fit in" and be a "team player." I was reasonably authentic during those years but maintaining my personal and professional persona as a "nice guy" and "team player" was more important to me than authenticity.

Then, in 2000, something happened that changed me forever. Sara, my wife, developed a life-threatening illness, a rare autoimmune disease in which her immune system attacked her own muscles. As the illness took its toll, her muscles became so weak that she could not get out of the bath tub by herself. She could walk but on several occasions, without warning, her weakened leg muscles gave way and she fell. Sara was only 55 years of age. Forty percent of those who develop her disease die within the first five years. Eternally optimistic and possessing a courage that I do not have, she told me numerous times, "Don't worry. This illness is not going to kill me." It has now been fifteen years and Sara is still here and doing well. She's on medication but her regular blood tests, which monitor the disease, have been normal for several years. What an experience in grace and gratitude to see one's life partner go to the brink of death and then return to life! Sara and I know that we are fortunate and we are grateful for every day we continue to share. We have now been married for more than fifty years. She is my best friend and the one who, better than anyone else, knows my heart and loves me for who I am.

Sara's illness had a major impact on my authenticity. When she almost died, I realized that life is indeed short and death is real. This was the first time that I knew—in the center of my being—that I, too, was mortal. If Sara, that strong woman who had never been seriously ill in her life, if she could develop a life-threatening illness, then I, too, was mortal and, at some point in time, would cease to exist. For me, Sara's illness was a "boundary event," an existential marker between how I had been and how I would be thereafter. As a result of Sara's illness, I became less concerned about what others thought and more concerned about being myself, and letting the pieces fall where they may. At first, I did not see the connection between my awareness of mortality and my increased authenticity. I was simply aware that I was being more real in my interactions with others. Being more authentic was not something that I had "decided" to do nor was it something that I understood at the time. However, I eventually made the connection and it was something like this: if we are all going to die and have only a short time on this earth, then why spend that time pretending to be someone we're not? Why *not* be oneself? Why *not* be authentic and let the pieces fall where they may? I also noticed that I had an edge of irritation and impatience with my own pretensions and the pretensions of others. I found myself wanting to say, "Let's stop this pretending. Let's talk honestly and sincerely with one another; let's say what we really think and feel. Life is too short to do otherwise." I also began to think to myself, "If people don't like me for who I really am, then I need to find new friends. Surely, there are people out there who also want to be real and who will not be 'put off' when I am being real. Besides, if friends don't like me for who I really am, then those friendships are vacuous anyway. Better to have one friend who loves the self I really am than a thousand friends who love a self I'm not! Even more important, if I pretend to be a self I'm not, then I have betrayed my own heart and will never know the peace of living from the center of my own being." Thus, Sara's life-threatening illness changed me in rather profound ways. I became more aware of mortality and more concerned about being myself. I came to agree with Kierkegaard (1941), who said, "The greatest despair is to be a self that one is not and the opposite of despair is to be that self one truly is" (p. 29). Zhuangzi, of course, understood all this . . . and more.

All Hell Breaks Loose Again

After Sara's illness, I stopped worrying about being a "nice guy" and a "team player" and began to say what I honestly thought and felt. The truth is, I sometimes overdid it. Out of my desire to be authentic, I was sometimes too blunt, forgetting that other people have feelings too. In recent years, I have tried to moderate my bluntness without sacrificing my authenticity. I've learned that in most situations one can be authentic and kind at the same time.

However, there's another side to this story. It wasn't all me and my bluntness. I found that many people, including even some psychologists, have difficulty dealing with honesty. For example, those of us who embrace existential psychology like to talk and write about authenticity but sometimes we're not very good at dealing with it in real life. I have found that some colleagues get very upset when I say what I really think. Some get mad; some get "hurt"; some end the relationship.

Thus, one of the lessons I've learned about authenticity is this: although authenticity is often romanticized in scholarly books and professional presentations, true authenticity is not romantic. It stirs up a lot of trouble. If you become more authentic, the most likely thing to happen is that all hell will break loose in your life. Nietzsche was right. As soon as you say, "I want to be myself" it is indeed "a frightful resolve"—in more ways than one. Nevertheless, it's worth it. Nothing feels better than knowing that, whatever others may think, you have been true to yourself. It's a lot better than knowing you're a hypocrite, pretending to be someone you're not. It's a lot better to build your own bridge than to use a bridge built by someone else. It's better to follow your own path than to follow the path of others. My only advice is this: be authentic but don't be a jerk at the same time. Other people have feelings too. Besides, just being authentic will stir up enough trouble in your life.

Authenticity: What about Fortune and Fame?

For me, the most challenging part of Zhuangzi's story has to do with his refusal to be Prime Minister. This tells me that authenticity is not simply about being real in our interactions with others but that it also has to do with the values, decisions, and actions that inform our life. This is where Sartre (see above) and Zhuangzi seem to agree. When offered the position as Prime Minister, Zhuangzi had to understand the situation, make a decision, and take action. In Sartre's words, he could respond either authentically or inauthentically. For example, Zhuangzi could have said to himself, "What a great opportunity! This will give me a platform to influence thousands of people in the ways of spiritual wisdom." In other words, Zhuangzi could have accepted the position and provided himself and others with an excellent rationalization for having done so. But Zhuangzi did not think this way. His values were different. He had no interest in becoming Prime Minister. He was happy just being himself and fishing in the Pu River.

Would I have made the same decision as Zhuangzi? Would you have made the same decision? After all, what's wrong with being Prime Minister? Can't one be oneself and also hold a position of authority and influence? I suspect most of us would have accepted the position and considered it an advancement in our professional careers. But Zhuangzi refused. Is it possible that he knew something we do not? Did he know that if he became Prime Minister, something essential would be lost? Did he know that fortune and fame were not the goals of life? Did he know that the integrity of his own way of being, the very source of his spiritual wisdom, would be tainted and compromised if he became rich and famous?

Zhuangzi's refusal to become Prime Minister is the heart of this story and it raises serious questions about what it means to live an authentic life. The story hits home for us who live in a time when fortune and fame are often the measure of one's success in life. Have we been sold a delusion that fortune and fame will make us happy? Is it possible that fortune and fame are not, after all, the goals of life? What if it really is better to fish in the Pu River and to drag one's tail in the mud than to be Prime Minister? Or to make this more relevant to us and our situation today: what if it's better to live a quiet existence, being true to ourselves and bringing kindness and healing to those around us, than it is to be, for example, a famous scholar teaching at a prestigious university and writing books of philosophical or psychological wisdom? In short, what if we have it all wrong and have no idea what is really required to live an authentic life?

Zhuangzi's story crushes my romantic notions about authenticity and makes me question whether or not I can live an authentic life. I can be real in my interactions with others and I can say what I think and feel. However, if I'm honest, I don't want to spend my life fishing in the Pu River and dragging my tail in the mud. I think being Prime Minister, or its equivalent in my own life, would be pretty nice. I like a little fame. I also like money and what it can buy.

I don't need to have great wealth or be in the "one percent" that the politicians talk about, but I like having enough money to buy whatever I want and to go wherever I want to go. As the saying goes, "I've been rich and I've been poor. Rich is better."

I grew up in the Ozark Mountains of Arkansas. My family was poor. My parents could never get ahead financially, even though they worked hard all of their lives. The best they could do for their three children was to put a roof over our heads, put clothes on our backs, and make sure we had enough to eat. Beyond that, my parents could do no more in terms of material things. However, I remember my parents with great respect. I think Zhuangzi would have liked them. They lived a simple life; they loved their children; they had no "airs" about them; they were honest and good; and in a racist South, they told us kids that everyone was equal in the sight of God and that we should never look down our nose at another human being. I look at my life now, which is so different from theirs, and I wonder if I have really made progress from my Ozark roots or if I have simply fooled myself. I'm a professor; I hold a Ph.D.; I have enough money to take care of my material needs; I can make more money in an hour than my father made in a week. And yet, as I've grown older, I find myself admiring my parents more than I admire myself. Like Zhuangzi, they loved simple things. Dad's greatest joy was to fish in the creek or take a drive through the Ozark countryside. He had no interest in being famous, nor did he want to be wealthy. He wanted to provide for his family, go to church, live a life of integrity, have good friends, and enjoy a few simple pleasures along the way. Mom was devoted to the same simple goals. She was a fountain of love who made sure that my brother, sister, and me felt loved and cared for. My parents would never have used the word "authentic" to describe themselves. That word would have been too "high falutin'" for them. Yet, they were the most authentic people I have known. They were "dirt farmers," a term used in the backwoods of Arkansas to describe poor people who farmed the land. A couple of years ago, I wrote a poem to honor my parents and to remind myself of who I am. The title of the poem is "Dirt."

> I come from dirt
> My daddy came from dirt
> My momma came from dirt
> sister and brother too
> Arkansas dirt, Ozark dirt, sharecropper dirt
> Daddy and Momma buried their dreams
> So I could have mine
> So I could grow up
> Not have to work in dirt
> go to school
> go to college

get a PhD
I came to the graveyard today, just to say
I'm standing on your shoulders, Daddy
I'm standing on your shoulders, Momma
I can see a long ways now, Daddy
I can see things you never saw, Momma
Because I'm standing on your shoulders
Those tired, strong shoulders
Those tired, strong, selfless shoulders
I'll never forget what you did
I'll never forget what you were
I'll never forget who I am
I'm dirt
Arkansas dirt
Ozark dirt
Sharecropper dirt
Beautiful, beautiful dirt.

I have to end this essay now. Zhuangzi is calling me to go fishing with him in the Pu River. It sounds pretty boring and I'd rather be doing something else. But, then, Zhuangzi is a very wise man. Maybe he knows something that I don't.

References

Bugental, J. F. T. (1965). *The search for authenticity: An existential analytic approach to psychotherapy*. Austin, TX: Holt, Rinehart, & Winston.

Kierkegaard, S. (1941). *The sickness unto death*. Princeton, NJ: Princeton University Press.

May, R. (1983). *The discovery of being*. New York, NY: W. W. Norton & Co.

Merton, T. (2010). *The way of Chuang Tzu*. New York, NY: New Directions Publishing Corp.

Rogers, C. R. (1957). The necessary and sufficient conditions of therapeutic personality change. In *Journal of Consulting Psychology, 21*, 95–103.

Sartre, J. P. (1988). *Anti-Semite and Jew*. New York: Schocken.

10

PLOUGH DEEPLY

Cultivating Authentic Living

Jennifer Tam

FIGURE 10.1 Created by Gina Belton

Zhuangzi, who was a philosopher in China during the Warring States Period (475–221 B.C.), wrote about ways of attaining personal freedom and peace of mind. According to Zhuangzi, true freedom comes from within, and making a conscious choice to live it out. He described a state of "carefree wandering" which encouraged individuals to seek inner true freedom rather than be driven by outward worldly standards. The process of change begins with the seeker's readiness to "wander," as illustrated by the following parable:

> Confucius had pottered along for fifty-one years and had never heard anyone speak of the Tao until he went south to Pei and went to see Lao Tzi.
>
> Lao Tzi said, 'So you've come then, Sir? I have heard of you, that you are the wise man of the north. Have you, Sir, followed the Tao?'
>
> 'I have not yet followed it,' replied Confucius.
>
> 'Well, Sir, where have you looked?'
>
> 'I looked for it in what can be measured and regulated, but even after five years I still haven't been able to find it.'
>
> 'So, Sir, what did you do then?' asked Lao Tzi.
>
> 'I looked for it in yin and yang, but ten, twelve years went by and I still couldn't find it.'
>
> 'Obviously!' said Lao Tzi. 'If the Tao could be served up, everyone would serve it up to their lords. If the Tao could be offered, there is no one who would not offer it to their parents. If the Tao could be spoken of, there is no one who would not speak of it to their brothers and sisters. If the Tao could be passed on, there is no one who would not pass it on to their heirs. However, it obviously cannot be so and the reason is as follows.
>
> 'If there is no true centre within to receive it,
> it cannot remain;
> if there is no true direction outside to guide it,
> it cannot be received.
> If the true centre is not brought out
> it cannot receive on the outside.
> The sage cannot draw it forth.
> If what comes in from the outside is not
> welcomed by the true centre,
> then the sage cannot let it go.
>
> (Zhuangzi, 2006, Chapter 14, para. 46)

According to Zhuangzi, the beginning of a transformational journey always starts with a quest for change. It is the same with my personal story.

Beginning of the Wandering

I am very fortunate to call two my favorite cities home: Hong Kong in the East, New York in the West. Although culturally these two cities are very different, they share a lot in common. Both cities are dazzling urban, full of glamor, chic, and design. Everywhere you go, you are surrounded by a sea of information and advertisement consisting of large posters, billboards, and images. Advertisement about everything in daily life, from how to improve your skin and physical image, to diets and supplements, fashion and make up, intellectual enhancement, education, career advancement, investment, capital gain, on and on ad nauseam. The images that I'm bombarded with every single day are very different. But behind those images, no matter what they are trying to "sell," there exists a consistent message: either I do not have enough or there is something missing in my life. Like many others, I believed in these messages which became personal baggage that I've carried for far too long. Some of my baggage involved Chinese cultural values, social, behavioral, and familial patterns which shaped my inner world. I was strongly influenced by the Chinese emphasis on collectivism, compliance, and prescribed social behavior for harmonious relationships. Looking back, I did not feel good about myself since childhood. No matter how hard I tried, I always felt that I was not good enough. I earned my worthiness through proper behavior, performing the right way, following all the right rules and directions. I struggled to be a better person in order to feel worth and acceptance. When I became confused as to who I was and where my direction should be, following the masses was the safest way to go. I traversed the traditional path in order to "fit in."

I kept searching to become someone better than the person I knew myself to be. I led a life driven by the fear of rejection, limited creativity, and risk aversion. Until one day, I stopped and paused. I asked myself "who am I really?" and "what do I really want?" In search of the answers, I made one of the most important decisions in my life. I quit all my work in Hong Kong and decided to go on a journey without a specific plan. This was the beginning of my wanderings according to Zhuangzi. New York was the first place that came to mind because of my love for the arts and theater.

I arrived in New York at end of the summer of the year 2000. Through the help of a friend of a friend, I quickly settled in a small studio on the east side of Lower Manhattan. My first plan was simply to let go of daily planning. For the first couple of weeks, I enjoyed wandering around the city, gazing at the big full moon on those clear dark nights. In the East people used to say that "the moon in the foreign land is more round and full than the one at home." I used to wonder if this was true. But then through lived experience, I realized that perhaps it was. The moon in New York was more full because it captured a big part of my world I left behind in the East.

On one of the subway rides along my wandering, an advertisement about creative arts therapy caught my attention. Because of my theatre background, I decided to sign up for some classes as a way to occupy my leisure time. The first day of class found me sitting with other students and sharing my reasons for enrolling in the class. I shared my desire to take a break in order to restore my peace of mind. Upon hearing this, the lecturer chuckled and responded, "This is interesting. First time I heard of someone coming into the city for rest and peace. We New Yorkers leave the city and look for peace elsewhere."

After fifteen years in New York, I understand what she meant. But at that time, New York gave me a sense of freedom of who I wanted to be. It was a choice that I made to be away from the environment where I was so "boxed" into being someone else. For the first time in my life, those first weeks upon my arrival gave me the chance to enjoy an "unproductive" life style. I did not have to identify with any "fixed role" prescribed by the prevailing social norm. I took the opportunity to explore the possibilities within me. As a result, this short break paved the way for me to pursue my graduate studies the following year in New York, and eventually led me to enter the field of psychology. Looking back, the journey was not initiated with the intent of pursuing a particular academic degree or career. Instead, it was a process of following my heart's desire for self-discovery. I yearned for a deeper knowledge of who I was and where my heart belonged. When I let go of my original prescribed roles and assumptions about the meaning of life, I found another place called home—a home where I felt comfortable enough to pause and reach inward to examine deeply about what mattered to me.

Plough Deeply

In the midst of the turmoil of his era, Zhuangzi encouraged the importance of going inward as a way to achieve peace and harmony. He espoused a lifestyle that pursued the examination of deep personal thoughts and feelings and the expression of authenticity. The following parable is an example of Zhuangzi's teaching on how to "plough deep":

> The border guard at Chang Wu said to Tzi Lao, "The ruler of a state must not be careless, nor should he be careless with the people. Previously when ploughing my fields, I was careless, and the result was a poor crop. When weeding, I was thoughtless, and the result was a diminished harvest. In recent years I changed my ways, I ploughed deep and was careful to bury the seed. My harvests are now plentiful and therefore I have all I need all year round."

Chuang Tzu heard this and said, "People today, when looking after themselves and caring for their hearts, are very much like this border guard's description. They ignore Heaven, wander from their innate nature, dissolve their real being, extinguish their spirit and follow the common herd. So it is that someone who is careless with their innate nature causes evil and hatred to arise, affecting their innate nature like rank weeds and bushes. These weeds and bushes, when they first appear, seem helpful and supportive, but slowly they affect the innate nature. They become like a mass of suppurating sores which break out in scabs and ulcers, oozing pus from this disease. This is how it is."

(Zhuangzi, 2006, Chapter 25, para. 37)

According to Zhuangzi, when people "ignore Heaven, wander from their innate nature, dissolve their real being, extinguish their spirit and follow the common herd," they bring ailment not only to the body, but also to the mind. Most important of all, they lose their authentic self, and vitality for living. Farmers need to plough deeply before planting their seeds. Only in this way will the seeds grow, leading to a plentiful harvest. A process of ploughing deeply that leads to a deep sense of personal fulfillment, or "plentiful harvest" according to Zhuangzi, requiring an act of courage and connectedness with their environment. The following are lessons that are related to my journey of learning what it means to plough deeply.

Courage to Be

I remember vividly what it was like. While I was sitting at my desk working, I felt my heart rate increasing. I had a hard time catching my breath. Seconds later, my heart tightened and I was having chest pains. I thought I was on my way to a heart attack. The palpitations continued. I felt desperate and scared. Many questions arose in my mind: I was diagnosed with a medical condition. I thought that my condition was getting worse. I was also in the middle of starting my private practice. Was it because of stress? Or was this the beginning of a panic attack?

In reality, I had experienced similar episodes multiple times in the past month. I did not pay much attention to them. After the momentary shortness of breath, I moved on when I caught my breath again. The symptoms went away and I moved on with other activities. Instead of confronting my fear of heart problems or fear of other physical symptoms, I chose to ignore, forget, and just walk away. There were times in my life I lived following what Zhuangzi described as "ignore . . . wander . . . dissolve . . . extinguish" as a way of dealing with my existence. I ran away and lived without allowing myself to truly connect with what was important to my body and my mind. It was so easy to find distractions from everyday to-do lists rather than focusing on the present moment.

Zhuangzi reminded us to plant the seed carefully and pay attention to the emergent rather than just simply living. Instead of running away from distressful experiences, he emphasized ongoing engagement with the self and the world. Individuals were encouraged to stay in the present moment and trust in one's inner experience. This practice is an act of courage which is inherent in the state of inner stillness. Consider the following parable by Zhuangzi, where he teaches us about the art of inner stillness:

> When Confucius was traveling in Chu, he passed through a woods and saw there a hunchback catching cicadas at the end of a long, sticky pole as easily as if he were gathering them up with his hands.
> "That's quite a skill you have!" said Confucius. "Is there a special way to do it?"
> "I have a way. For five or six months, I practice balancing two pellets at the end of my pole. When I can keep them from falling down, then I'll only lose a small fraction of the cicadas. When I can balance three balls and keep them from falling down, then I'll only lose one cicada in ten. When I can balance five balls and keep them from falling down, then I can gather up the cicadas as easily as if I were using my hands. I position my body as though it were an erect stump with twisted roots. I hold my arms as though they were the branches of a withered tree. The greatness of heaven and earth and the numerousness of the myriad things notwithstanding, I am aware of only the cicada's wings. I neither turn around nor to the side and wouldn't exchange the wings of a cicada for all the myriad things. How can I not succeed?"
> Confucius turned to his disciples, "In exercising your will, do not let it be diverted; concentrate your spirit. This is the lesson of the hunchback gentleman . . .
> His skill is still the same, but there is something that distracts him and causes him to focus on externals. Whoever focuses on externals will be clumsy inside."[1]
> *(Zhuangzi, 1998, pp. 176–177 [excerpts])*

Zhuangzi encouraged us to appreciate each present moment and let go of rigid thoughts and assumptions, trusting in transience, movement, and growth. This involves the willingness to delve deeply into whatever is in front of us, the courage to experience the unknown, and the readiness to launch into deep inner journeys. These are the pathways to authentic living.

One day, I experienced the heart palpitation again. That time I decided to stop disconnecting from my experience. I listened and paid close attention to my irregular heartbeat. Strangely enough, as I became mindful of every racing heartbeat, surrendering myself to each moment, my thoughts become more focused and clear. The process was much more than attuning to my bodily needs. It was also listening to what really was important to me at that very moment. I became less frightened and scared. As my breathing became easier and calmer, eventually returning to normal, I started resting on the thought that I was still alive. Being grateful. This experience propelled me to contemplate more about the precious moments of being alive, to look at areas where I was afraid, and to learn where I can grow.

I believe the first step in the process of ploughing deeply that lead to a "plentiful harvest" is related to the courage to be. This is similar to the state of Wu Wei, as described by Zhuangzi. To align ourselves with the Tao in each given moment. Wu Wei can be translated as "non-doing," but it does not mean a passive mode of living. Rather, it means non-interference. Instead of resisting what is in front of us, Wu Wei is the surrendering of ourselves to the moment with faith and courage. According to Zhuangzi, Tao is the Way of Nature. He emphasized aligning with the natural way in order to achieve great harmony. By trusting the moment, it helps to unfold gradually the meaning of each given experience. Courage allows our hearts to expand, be ploughed, and examine what matters most to us.

Authentic Self

The catalyst for my personal growth and change often originated from incomprehensible anxieties and a sense of self-alienation. Growing up in the East, I frequently confined myself within Eastern social roles, standards, and values. I was preoccupied by fixed preconceptions of who I was and what I want. I defined myself as the generous friend, enthusiastic helper, responsible teacher, productive artist, caring sister, and loyal daughter. The nice and virtuous persona became all of who I was. There was no room for my shadow. No space for the wild-natured needy child who was also impulsive, self-seeking, innocent, and even wrathful. I made decisions (consciously and unconsciously) to limit my self-concept to that which best endorsed approval and maintained my good image in the eyes of others while repressing the parts of myself which I perceived as vice and socially unacceptable. Such confinement led to anxiety and alienation, which I also chose to hide and ignore. I was overly familiar with Zhuangzi's description of the loss of existence as "dissolving the real being, extinguishing their spirit." Thankfully through the pursuit of my professional development, I finally found the courage to give voice to my fears and struggles.

In the beginning, what I had originally thought would be a professional journey in psychology training turned out to be a much longer odyssey, with a far greater redefining of my own sense of self than I anticipated. At that time, little did I know that in addition to my training, I would also engage in a voyage of self-discovery.

Among all the courses in psychology that I had taken, I was most drawn to the course on Existential-Humanistic Psychology. I was fascinated by the writings that deeply described the human struggles related to emptiness and meaningless. I resonated with the anxiety associated with simply being alive.

Since my youth, I always had the fear of exposing myself in public situations, especially those which I am being evaluated. What if I simply shut down or became inarticulate and handicapped in my communications? I avoided such feared environments. I hid parts of myself because of the fear of rejection. I learned to exhibit only the personality traits and qualities that were socially acceptable. I hid the parts of myself that I perceived as a vice and was socially unacceptable. This reminds me of another story by Zhuangzi: Flight from Shadow:

> There was a man who was so disturbed by the sight of his own shadow and so displeased with his own footsteps that he determined to get rid of both. The method he hit upon was to run away from them.
> So he got up and ran. But every time he put his foot down there was another step, while his shadow kept up with him without the slightest difficulty.
> He attributed his failure to the fact that he was not running fast enough. So he ran faster and faster, without stopping until he finally dropped dead.
> He failed to realize that if he merely stepped into the shade, his shadow would vanish, and if he sat down and stayed still, there would be no more footsteps.
>
> (Merton, 2010, p. 155)

While I learned about the relational approach in Existential-Humanistic Psychology, I became inspired by the importance of living authentically. If I believed that one of the conditions for growth was self-acceptance and honesty, let it begin with me. Then came the day of my class presentation. At the time of the presentation, I had already known my classmates for more than three years but have never revealed my shadow side. But I decided that it was time to stop running away. Instead of hiding my feeling of inferiority, I chose to step out from behind my fear. I stood in front of my classmates and shared that I had social phobia. I was afraid to tell people who I really was. Yet, through this experience, I learned that relationships can heal, and the safety created in therapy brought about healing. That experience gave me hope and courage for self-acceptance.

After my disclosure, I received overwhelming positive support from my classmates. Support that helped me to consolidate a more real and honest self-concept. I do not believe my fellow classmates and instructor realized that they had actually carried me across a difficult threshold of breakthrough . . . a process of being broken and opened. I walked out from a hidden place that I had held on to so tight for so long. Then came a point of great release. I opened up. I felt more connected and receptive to others. Most important of all, I felt alive, being so close to my true self. Zhuangzi discouraged people from following worldly standards as measures for self-acceptance. Genuineness and authenticity are ways of the Tao.

Connectedness

In Zhuangzi's parable urging us to "plough deeply," the border guard at Chang Wu reminded Tzi Lao that a ruler of a state who needs to govern people must not be careless, nor should he be careless with the people. Like a farmer who takes care of the field, a ruler should take his people seriously. Dig deep with the understanding that roots promote growth. Zhuangzi understood individuals as active participants in their existence through the process of seeking their true nature in the context of their ongoing relationships with their environment.

When I began to plough deeply, I realized that relationships are fundamental to shaping my sense of a true self. It matters a great deal to me to engage in meaningful activities with those I care deeply about. On my birthday in 2014, I decided to invite various close friends to visit memorable places of my life with me. I asked different friends to meet up with me at various times and different locations. Each of the locations were filled with personal meaning. I started off in the morning with a visit to the hospital where I was born. A close female friend of more than twenty years met me there. We had morning coffee at the café inside the hospital. We reminisced about our childhood memories over tears of joy and laughter.

My parents were born and raised in a village in mainland China. I was the first generation to be born outside of China. I was also the first to achieve a tertiary education. Bringing pride to my family brings me great satisfaction. The degree was not a personal accomplishment. It was the culmination of all the family's hard work through the difficult times of the 1960s in Hong Kong. Returning to the place of my birth reminded me of the deep gratitude I felt toward my parents. I am glad that they believed in me . . . that I could make a difference in this world. To be able to share this family pride with my good friend brought me great joy.

Following the hospital, I visited my elementary and secondary school, the university that I attended with various groups of friends, as well as the different neighborhoods where I grew up. The visits brought back memories of all the people who came along such as teachers, classmates, friends, mentors, and comrades, who have carried me across difficult thresholds throughout various points of my life. Each of the relationships was instrumental in shaping the person that I am today. Relationships are important to me. They remind me of the life that is worth living.

Open Heart

During a recent retreat which was part of my ongoing educational journey in Existential-Humanistic Psychology, I embarked on an interesting road trip. The retreat was held at Fraser Hills, a mountain retreat center located deep in the beautiful Malaysian forest. I went with a group of five people. We were picked up during rush hour by a van at the city center of Kuala Lumpur. It took us one and a half hours to arrive at the foot of the mountain. And then another one-and-a-half hour drive awaited us up the mountain to the retreat center. The road that led up the mountain was narrow and serpentine, with numerous switchbacks and blind curves. At points along the road, two lanes became one. The sun was setting and there was no street lights along the twisty mountain road. We drove up that mountain in the pitch darkness that was part of the forest.

Everyone in the vehicle fell into a deep silence. Some fell asleep due to fatigue. One became car sick. Yet, I was fully awake sitting at the back corner of the van. I tried to make myself comfortable. I've never been to a tropical forest before. I was transfixed by the large lush leaves hanging from gigantic trees. Simultaneously, I was also highly alert of each turn engaged by the driver. I knew that we were fortunate to have a very experienced driver who had driven the same route before. But this did little to assuage my fear. There were times I could feel the back wheels of the vehicle skid off the pavement. I lost count of how many times I thought the car was about to fall off the side of the road. My senses were heightened and I was scared! While others conversed, I barely uttered a word.

Mid-point during the journey, I decided to focus on my breathing and take notice of the images that fell across my field of vision. I focused on the shadows of the trees and paid attention to the calling of the birds. If this was the end, I wanted to die with something beautiful. Each and every moment that passed, I sought images to remember, to cherish and hold on to, as if each of the moments would be my last. On this unsuspecting long and winding road to my destination, I soon found myself detaching from the fear of the unknown through being mindful and totally absorbed by the greatness of each moment. My sense of danger was remarkably comforted by the power of stillness. That experience helped me to better understand the following parable by Zhuangzi:

> The non-action of the wise man is not inaction.
> It is not studied. It is not shaken by anything.
> The sage is quiet because he is not moved,
> Not because he wills to be quiet.
> Still water is like glass.
> You can look in it and see the bristles on your chin.
> It is a perfect level;
> A carpenter could use it.
> If water is so clear, so level,
> How much more the spirit of man?
> The heart of the wise man is tranquil.
> It is the mirror of heaven and earth
> The glass of everything.
> Emptiness, stillness, tranquility, tastelessness,
> Silence, non-action: this is the level of heaven and earth.
> This is perfect Tao. Wise men find here

Their resting place.
Resting, they are empty.

From emptiness comes the unconditioned.
From this, the conditioned, the individual things.
So from the sage's emptiness, stillness arises:
From stillness, action. From action, attainment.
From their stillness comes their non-action, which is also action
For stillness is joy. Joy is free from care
Fruitful in long years.
Joy does all things without concern:
For emptiness, stillness, tranquility, tastelessness,
Silence, and non-action
Are the root of all things.

(Merton, 2010, pp. 80–81)

Through stillness and non-action, I began to see more clearly that things happen for a reason. That the world is ordered and connected and that there is definitely meaning to my existence.

I eventually arrived safely to the retreat center. Although it was a safe journey, I could not help but reflect upon what made my life worth living. What gives meaning to my life? How close am I to my true being? It was fascinating to me that the difficult times I feared opened me up to "plough deeply" and propelled me to ask such important questions. Zhuangzi's parable about plowing deeply is about such times. He encourages us to overcome fear and seek the reasons for our true living. He encourages us to stay close to our true natures and choose growth over fear as we traverse through the numerous turns of our lives. I wish to continue to step boldly into the fullness of life, with all its dangers and promises. To approach the challenges of life with such openness, faith, authenticity, and honesty. This is the Zhuangzi who I have come to know.

Note

1 Permission to republish granted by University of Hawaii Press. Zhuangzi. (1998). *Wandering on the way: Early Taoist tales and parables of Chuang Tzu*. (V. Mair, Trans.). pp. 176–177. Honolulu, HI: University of Hawaii Press.

References

Merton, T. (2010). *The way of Chuang Tzu*. New York, NY: New Directions Publishing Corp.
Zhuangzi. (1998). *Wandering on the way: Early Taoist tales and parables of Chuang Tzu*. (V. Mair, Trans.). Honolulu, HI: University of Hawaii Press.
Zhuangzi. (2006). *The book of Chuang Tzu*. [Kindle for Android, 4.3.0.204]. (M. Palmer, Trans.). Retrieved from Amazon.com

11

USEFULNESS OF USELESSNESS

Freedom before Death

Zhen Shiyan
Translated by Lihua Yang

FIGURE 11.1 Created by Robin Good

I love Zhuangzi. I often read his writings in my spare time and quote him in my writings. When I was invited to write a chapter in this book, I became quite excited, for I finally had the opportunity to write something about Zhuangzi and existential psychology. However, many days passed and I found myself procrastinating. Procrastination is not a disease. There must be a rationale. One day, I suddenly began suspecting that perhaps my love for Zhuangzi was insincere—I liked his writings but never read him thoroughly. I quoted him often but never in depth. I began to reflect, "What is this source of this insincerity?"

It could be argued that almost all the psychological problems are not completely idiosyncratic. Maybe this insincerity of mine reveals the problem of modern man in that even though Zhuangzi's way of life is quite appealing, it's unrealistic to live life accordingly. Zhuangzi's (1998) dictum that "the ultimate man has no self, the spiritual person has no accomplishments, and the sage has no name" (pp. 5–6) seems highly untenable in our current culture of endless accumulation. According to anthropologist Ernest Becker, all of us have a dream of "greatness" deep inside—all of us strive to accomplish some heroic deeds and be a hero known to all! However, what's the motivation behind this "heroic dream"?

In his book *The Denial of Death*, Becker (1973) offered an outstanding analysis of the hero complex: "The first thing we have to do with heroism is to lay bare its underside, show what gives human heroics its specific nature and impetus. Here we introduce directly one of the great rediscoveries of modern thought: that of all things that move man, one of the principal ones is his terror of death" (p. 11). Death makes everything vanish into nothing. Thus in our lives, we all struggle to leave some imprint behind.

Human beings are fundamentally different from animals because we are self-conscious. For human beings, "death" does not come at the last minute, though it is the end of life. To some degree, human beings know we are going to die. Becker (1973) writes:

> Man is literally spilt in two: he has an awareness of his own splendid uniqueness in that he sticks out of nature with a towering majesty, and yet he goes back into the ground a few feet in order blindly and dumbly to rot and disappear forever. It is a terrifying dilemma to be in and to have to live with. The lower animals are, of course, spared this painful contradiction, as they lack a symbolic identity and self-consciousness that goes with it.
>
> (p. 26)

So animals have a limited awareness of their mortality while human beings are filled with dread.

The eminent existential therapist Irvin Yalom described such dread as "the distant thunder at our picnic" (Yalom & Josselson, 2011, p. 214). We are constantly worried about the approaching storm leaving us unable to enjoy the fancy lunch of the moment. Death and the fear of death play an important role in our lives, as Yalom (1980) described: "The fear of death plays a major role in our internal experience; it haunts as does nothing else; it rumbles continuously under the surface; it is a dark, unsettling presence at the rim of consciousness" (p. 27). In his classical text *Existential Psychotherapy*, Yalom (1980) presented us with four givens or ultimate concerns of existence that all human beings must face: death, freedom, isolation, and meaninglessness. The confrontation with these ultimate concerns presents us with intense psychological conflicts, especially the confrontation with death. Yalom pointed out that we all employ two interdependent defense mechanisms towards death: one is the belief in our specialness or inviolability, which has us believing that death is the business of the others having nothing to do with me; and the other is our belief in an ultimate rescuer, which often takes the form of a "deity" who saves us when we are in dire straits.

According to Yalom, the confrontation with death is extremely terrifying because death means that everything will come to an end. In fact, Yalom wrote a recent book titled *Staring at the Sun* (2008), aimed at teaching people to overcome the fear of death. As the title of the book suggests, confronting death is akin to staring directly at the sun. Both must be done obliquely for a direct confrontation can be devastatingly harmful. At the same time, one wonders are there other possible perspectives when it comes to confronting death?

As we turn back to Zhuangzi, we find that he offers a profound alternate possibility for how to face death. If we are sincere in our efforts to understand his teachings, we will find that death is not so terrifying. Zhuangzi can help us overcome death anxiety and gain unprecedented freedom.

In Chapter 3 of *Zhuangzi*, there is a story about the death of a friend:

> When old Longears died, Idle Intruder went to mourn over him. He wailed three times and left.
> "Weren't you a friend of the master?" a disciple asked him.
> "Yes."
> "Well, is it proper to mourn him like this?
> "Yes. At first, I used to think of him as a man, but now I no longer do. Just now when I went in to mourn him, there were old people crying over him as though they were crying for one of their own sons. There were youngsters crying over him as though they were crying for their own mother. Among those whom he had brought together, surely there were some who wished not to speak but spoke anyway, who wished not to cry but cried anyway. This is to flee from nature while redoubling human emotion, thus forgetting what we have received from nature. This was what the ancients called "the punishment of fleeing from nature." By chance the master's coming was timely, and by chance his going was favorable. One who is situated in timeliness and who dwells in favorableness cannot be affected by joy or sorrow. This is what the ancients called "the emancipation of the gods."[1]
>
> *(Zhuangzi, 1998, p. 28)*

Here, Idle Intruder understood that old Longears's death and life were the same—they both followed nature's rhythms. Therefore, Idle Intruder needn't carry his grief to excess. Of course, he wouldn't be worried about his own death because of this.

In Chapter 18 of *Zhuangzi*, there is another story describing the scene of the death of Zhuangzi's wife:

> Zhuangzi's wife died. When Huizi went to convey his condolences, he found Zhuangzi sitting with his legs sprawled out, pounding on a tub and singing. "You lived with her, she brought up your children and grew old," said Huizi. "It should be enough simply not to weep at her death. But pounding on a tub and singing—this is going too far, isn't it?"
>
> Zhuangzi said, "You're wrong. When she first died, do you think I didn't grieve like anyone else? But I looked back to her beginning and the time before she was born. Not only the time before she was born, but the time before she had a body. Not only the time before she had a body, but the time before she had a spirit. In the midst of the jumble of wonder and mystery, a change took place and she had a spirit. Another change and she had a body. Another change and she was born.
>
> Now there's been another change and she's dead. It's just like the progression of the four seasons: spring, summer, fall, winter. Now she's going to lie down peacefully in a vast room. If I were to follow after her bawling and sobbing, it would show that I don't understand anything about fate. So I stopped."
>
> (Zhuangzi, 2013, Chapter 18, para. 8)

At first glance, this story seemed extremely ridiculous: Zhuangzi's wife died, but he sat on the floor, legs wide apart, singing while beating a pot. This is because Zhuangzi knew that there wasn't something understood as birth, and human being's entire life from birth to death is just like the succession of seasons. Zhuangzi was glad that his wife was in repose as part of nature.

In Chapter 32 of *Zhuangzi*, he showed his positive attitude towards death when he was at the very end of his life:

> When Master Chuang was on the verge of death, his disciples indicated that they wished to give him a sumptuous burial. Master Chuang said, "I shall have heaven and earth for my inner and outer coffins, the sun and the moon for my paired jades, the stars and constellations for my round and irregular pearls, and the myriad things for my mortuary gifts. Won't the preparations for my burial be quite adequate? What could be added to them?"
>
> "We are afraid that the crows and the kites will eat you master," said the disciples.
>
> Master Chuang said, "Above, I'd be eaten by the crows and the kites; below, I'd be eaten by mole crickets and ants. Why show your partiality by snatching me away from those and giving me to these?"

> If you even things out with what is uneven, the evenness that results will be uneven; if you verify things with what is unverified, the verification that results will be unverified. The keen-sighted person is merely employed by others, whereas the person of spirit verifies them. Long has it been that keen sight does not win out against spirit, yet those who are stupid rely on what they see and attribute it to other men. Their achievement being external, is it not sad?[2]
>
> *(Zhuangzi, 1998, p. 332)*

Death anxiety not only shows itself in the way people arrange their lives, but also in the way people arrange their lives after death. Many who are dying want to bring their belongings and lifestyle to the afterworld. This is likely because of their fear of death and consequent desire to extend their lives. However, Zhuangzi understood death and knew that nothing compares with the company of nature.

Through these three stories regarding the death of his friend, his wife, and himself, Zhuangzi expounded his attitudes towards death. They all shared one thing in common. Zhuangzi saw life and death in nature as a whole and rejected a disconnected dualistic view towards death. Zhuangzi saw human beings existing as part of nature, so death was not equated with obliteration but rather a reintegration with nature. Life and death were the same as the succession of the seasons. Zhuangzi went on further to state:

> For life is the disciple of death and death is the beginning of life. Who knows their regulator? Human life is the coalescence of vital breath. When it coalesces there is life; when it dissipates there is death. Since life and death are disciples of each other, how should I be troubled by them?
>
> *(Zhuangzi, 1998, p. 212)*

If in Zhuangzi's acceptance of death, we agree that life and death were both part of nature and death was inherent in life, then Zhuangzi also showed that we could take pleasure in death. In Chapter 6 of *Zhuangzi*, the dialog among Sir Sacrifice, Sir Chariot, Sir Plow, and Sir Come reflected the attitude of "friendly death." Indeed Sir Come stated when he was dying that, "The Great Clod burdens me with form, toils me through life, eases me in old age, rests me in death. Thus, that which makes my life good is also that which makes my death good" (Zhuangzi, 1998, p. 59). Here, death was seen as a rest after a life of labor. If life could be treated in a friendly manner, then we should also treat death the same way. Zhuangzi (1998) said: "Soundly he slept, suddenly he awoke" (p. 59). He meant that death is just like sound sleep, and life is just like waking up with joy.

Furthermore, in Chapter 18 of *Zhuangzi*, through the dialog between Zhuangzi and a skeleton, we see that the acceptance of death advanced another step towards an attitude of "joyful death" when the skeleton did not want to be alive again:

When Master Chuang went to Ch'u, he saw an empty skull. Though brittle, it still retained its shape. Master Chuang tapped the skull with his riding crop and asked, "Did you end up like this because of greed for life and loss of reason? Or was it because you were involved in some treasonous affair and had your head chopped off by an ax? Or was it because you were involved in some unsavory conduct, shamefully disgracing your parents, wife, and children? Or was it because you starved or froze? Or was it simply because your time was up?"

When he had finished with his questions, Master Chuang picked up the skull and used it as a pillow when he went to sleep. At midnight, the skull appeared to him in a dream and said, "Your manner of talking makes you sound like a sophist. I perceive that what you mentioned are all the burdens of the living. When you're dead, there's none of that. Would you like to hear me tell you about death, sir?"

"Yes," said Master Chuang.

"When you're dead," said the skull, "there's no ruler above you and no subjects below you. There are no affairs of the four seasons; instead, time passes leisurely as it does for heaven and earth. Not even the joys of being a south-facing king can surpass those of death."

Not believing the skull, Master Chuang said, "If I were to have the Arbiter of Destiny restore life to your physical form, to give you back your flesh, bones, and skin, to return your parents, wife, children, and village acquaintances, would you like that?"

Frowning in deep consternation, the skull said, "How could I abandon 'the joys of a south-facing king' and return to the toils of mankind?"[3]

(Zhuangzi, 1998, p. 170)

Through the skeleton, we are told that life is suffering and death is joyful, as if death is the real home for human beings. This perspective of "seeing death as going home" influenced later generations, such as Emperor Wen in the Wei Dynasty, when he wrote, "Men's life is like boarding in this world, so why should we worry so much?" (Cao Pi).[4] Li Bai, the great poet in Tang Dynasty also wrote, "The living are transient passengers, and the dead are going home."[5] If we also could adopt this attitude of "looking upon death as going home," then we can also overcome death anxiety, without the need for defense mechanisms.

If we adopt this attitude of "looking upon death as going home," then death can be the ultimate goal of life, instead of the traditional belief of an "abrupt termination" or "complete vanishing." However, adopting such an attitude does not mean living life in a careless or frivolous fashion. Death, not a complete vanishing after all, is another state of life. We should cherish this state when we are alive. Based on such an attitude towards life and death, we can achieve a state of freedom in our lives. In such a state of freedom, we need not be "patients who are obsessive about death," nor "nihilistic about life." Instead, we can live a life filled with numerous possibilities.

In his book *Freedom and Destiny*, Rollo May (1981) defined freedom as:

> The capacity to pause in the midst of stimuli from all directions, and in this pause to throw our weight toward this response rather than that one . . . The significance of the pause is that the rigid chain of cause and effect is broken. The pause momentarily suspends the billiard-ball system of Pavlov. In the person's life, response no longer blindly follows stimulus.
>
> *(p. 163)*

The word "pause" is very meaningful because it represents "no thing" and "nothing" while also containing many things. In this "pause," we no longer follow the role of stimulus-response and do not have to react instantaneously. We don't have to drift with the tide, or follow what others have said. We have a kind of freedom, and we can think, make choices, follow our heart, and be our true selves. Freedom has a lot to do with being oneself. Freedom means an unrestrained state, and becoming oneself. In his book *Man's Search for Himself*, Rollo May (1953) defined freedom as:

> Man's capacity to take a hand in his own development. It is our capacity to mold ourselves. Freedom is the other side of consciousness of self: if we were not able to be aware of ourselves, we would be pushed along by instinct or the automatic march of history, like bees or mastodons.
>
> *(p. 160)*

All in all, if we do not know death, how can we know about life? Once we learn more about death, we can reduce our fear of death and thus live a free and better life. Montaigne, the French essayist, once wrote, "The premeditation of death is the premeditation of liberty; he who has learned to die has unlearned to serve."[6] Understanding death properly will allow us to achieve liberty and freedom. This kind of freedom helps us to discard outer constraints to some extent, and become more authentic. The book *Zhuangzi* contains many instances of this form of freedom as "having a choice." For example, in the Parable of the Marsh Pheasant, the pheasant knew the truth that while it needs to eat in order to live, it may also need to starve in order to truly live. That is, the pheasant would rather live the hard life than lose its freedom due to confinement:

> The marsh pheasant has to take ten steps before it finds something to pick at and has to take a hundred steps before it gets a drink. But the pheasant would prefer not to be raised in a cage where, though you treat it like a king, its spirit would not thrive."[7]
>
> *(Zhuangzi, 1998, p. 27)*

Similarly Zhuangzi also tells the story of a tortoise who would rather be alive and drag its tail through the mud than be dead and have its bones preserved as objects of veneration. Through this story, Zhuangzi expressed that he chooses to live a life dedicated to ideals rather than being confined to a workplace that makes oneself dumb and stilted:

> Master Chuang was fishing in the P'u River. The king of Ch'u dispatched two high-ranking officials to go before him with this message: "I wish to encumber you with the administration of my realm."
>
> Without turning around, Master Chuang just kept holding on to his fishing rod and said, "I have heard that in Ch'u there is a sacred tortoise that has already been dead for three thousand years. The king stores it in his ancestral temple inside of a hamper wrapped with cloth. Do you think this tortoise would rather be dead and have its bones preserved as objects of veneration, or be alive and dragging its tail through the mud?"
>
> "It would rather be alive and dragging its tail through the mud," said the two officials.
>
> "Be gone!" said Master Chuang. "I'd rather be dragging my tail in the mud."[8]
>
> (Zhuangzi, 1998, p. 164)

With bitter sarcasm, Zhuangzi goes on to describe a man who flatters others and sold himself out at work. Zhuangzi warns that when one chases after something desperately, one will surely be in danger of losing something else. Likewise, when one tries too hard to be a "useful" man, one can easily lose himself:

> There was a man of Sung named Ts'ao Shang who was sent by the King of Sung on a mission to Ch-in. For his journey there, he received several carriages from the King of Sung and the King of Ch'in, who was placed with him, added a hundred more carriages. Upon his return to Sung, he saw Master Chuang, to whom he said, "To live in a narrow lane of a poor village, to be so poverty stricken that I have to weave my own sandals, to have a scrawny neck and a sallow complexion—these are what I'm bad at. But immediately to enlighten the ruler of ten thousand carriages, and to be granted a retinue of a hundred carriages, that's what I'm good at."
>
> "When the King of Ch'in is ill," said Master Chuang, "He summons a physician. One who lances an abscess or drains a boil will receive one carriage. One who licks his hemorrhoids will receive five carriages. The lower the treatment, the greater the number of carriages received. Did you treat his hemorrhoids, sir? How did you get so many carriages? Be gone!"[9]
>
> (Zhuangzi, 1998, pp. 327–328)

In similar fashion, Zhuangzi teaches that when an ox desires to be "useful" to society and thus live a life of luxury, it will ultimately regret its decision:

> Some ruler sent gifts to Master Chuang with an invitation to accept office under him. Master Chuang responded to the messenger, "Have you seen a sacrificial ox, sir? It is garbed in patterned embroidery and fed with chopped grass and legumes, but when the time comes for it to be led into the great temple, though it wishes that it could once again be a solitary calf, how could that be?"[10]
>
> *(Zhuangzi, 1998, pp. 331–332)*

By now, you likely have discovered the importance of becoming "useless" if you desire to be free. By "uselessness," we do not mean becoming useless to society. In fact, uselessness is actually quite useful when we have yet to lose our freedom and true selves in blind pursuit of "usefulness." Correspondingly, an important concept in the philosophy of Zhuangzi is "the usefulness of uselessness." He writes:

> The mountain trees plunder themselves, the grease over a fire fries itself. Cinnamon can be eaten, therefore the trees that yield it are chopped down. Varnish can be used, therefore the trees that produce it are hacked. Everybody knows the utility of usefulness, but nobody knows the utility of uselessness.
>
> *(Zhuangzi, 1998, p. 41)*

Indeed uselessness is useful and usefulness may be harmful. If something in nature is useful, it will be exploited vigorously and become exhausted; when someone is useful, he will be occupied by many affairs and risk losing himself.

In Chapter 12 of *Zhuangzi*, he expressed the theme of "gain and loss" even more vividly:

> When the answer they have hit on constrains them, can it be the answer? If so, then the dove or the owl in a cage may also be said to have hit on the answer. Furthermore, preferences and aversions, sounds and colors are like so much firewood piled up within; leather caps and hats with kingfisher feathers, and official tablets inserted in long sashes restrain them from without. Inside, they are stuffed full with barricades of firewood and outside they are bound with layers of rope. Looking around from inside their ropes with a gleam in their eye, they think they have hit on the answer. If that be so, then criminals with their arms tied together and their fingers in a press, and the tiger and the leopard in their sacks or cages may also be said to have hit on the answer.[11]
>
> *(Zhuangzi, 1998, p. 117)*

Often, a change of perspective will reveal something to become quite useful when originally considered useless. For example, in regards to the Parable of the

Large Gourd and Useless Tree discussed in Chapter 1 of this book, it is precisely the large emptiness of the ground that makes it useful as a flotation device even though it has grown beyond usefulness when evaluated according to conventional values. Similarly, the knotted and crooked "useless tree" is not suitable as timber. Therefore, it can be fearless and grow up free to become itself.

As one can see, the usefulness of uselessness is a form of freedom and a means to be oneself. When we overcome the fear of death, let go of defense mechanisms, no longer pursue worldly standards, and live an ideal life, then we are free to develop our potential and become our true selves. In a manner of speaking, a man may be useless when in fact he may be most useful because he makes the most of his life.

Zhuangzi was one who embraced freedom completely and he practiced what he preached. He was once an official at the Lacquer Garden. Being an official meant he received a salary to support his family; he was also sufficiently away from the emperor to be unburdened by complicated rules and ceremonies. For Zhuangzi, this constituted his "freedom from limitations." Nevertheless, Zhuangzi desired complete inner freedom. He understood that "things indeed bring trouble to each other, one creature inviting calamity from another" (Zhuangzi, 1998, p. 196), so he resigned from the job as a directorate and went home, making a living through fishing and weaving straw sandals. All the while, he created precious spiritual resources for later generations.

Such humanistic and existential concepts about how to overcome the fear of death and achieve freedom are remarkably applicable to the practice of psychotherapy. Irvin Yalom valued these concepts very much. He compared them to certain strange but familiar special ingredients in the culinary arts and understood them as the key factors responsible for the success of treatment:

> I believe that the experienced clinician often operates implicitly within an existential framework: "in his bones" he appreciates a patient's concerns and responds accordingly. That response is what I meant earlier by the crucial "throw-ins." A major task of this book is to shift the therapist's focus, to attend carefully to these vital concerns and to the therapeutic transactions that occur on the periphery of formal therapy, and to place them where they belong—in the center of the therapeutic arena.
>
> *(Yalom, 1980, p. 12)*

In *Freedom and Destiny*, Rollo May (1981) pointed out that the aim of psychotherapy was to set people free:

> I propose that the purpose of the psychotherapy is to set people free. Free, as far as possible, from symptoms, whether they be psycho-somatic symptoms like ulcers or psychological symptoms like acute shyness. Free from compulsions, again as far as possible, to be workaholics, compulsions to repeat self-defeating habits they have learned in early childhood, or

compulsions perpetually to choose partners of the opposite sex who cause continual unhappiness and continual punishment.

(p. 19)

In the eyes of May (1981), freedom was to become oneself in the psychotherapy. In the same book, he continued:

> In psychotherapy the closest we can get to discerning freedom in action is when a person experiences "I can" or "I will." When a client in therapy says either of these, I always make sure he knows that I have heard him; for "can" and "will" are statements of personal freedom, even if only in fantasy.
>
> *(p. 53)*

Of course, it is not our wish for man to chase after the usefulness of uselessness blindly, as if it was a hopeless choice in a less-than-ideal society. Instead, our hope is that the freedom of the individual and the needs of society can be integrated. This means, beyond individual freedom, we also desire a greater freedom. Rollo May (1953) wrote about this in his book *Man's Search for Himself*:

> We simply propose that our social and economic ideal be that society which gives the maximum opportunity for each person in it to realize himself, to develop and use his potentialities and to labor as a human being of dignity giving to and receiving from his fellow men. The good society is, thus, the one which gives the greatest freedom to its people—freedom defined not negatively and defensively, but positively, as the opportunity to realize ever greater human values.
>
> *(p. 160)*

Perhaps this is the form of freedom Zhuangzi (1998) meant when he wrote about *carefree wanderings*, the title of the first chapter of his book *Zhuangzi*: "Supposing there were someone who could ride upon the truth of heaven and earth, who could chariot upon the transformations of the six vital breaths and thereby go wandering in infinity, what would he have to rely on" (p. 5). No doubt this is the freedom that we all desire—as long as we can embrace death and are in no hurry to be a hero. This freedom can be ours to be had.

Notes

1 Permission to republish granted by University of Hawaii Press. Zhuangzi. (1998). *Wandering on the Way: Early Taoist Tales and Parables of Chuang Tzu.* (V. Mair, Trans.). p. 28. Honolulu, HI: University of Hawaii Press.
2 Permission to republish granted by University of Hawaii Press. Zhuangzi. (1998). *Wandering on the Way: Early Taoist Tales and Parables of Chuang Tzu.* (V. Mair, Trans.). p. 332. Honolulu, HI: University of Hawaii Press.

3 Permission to republish granted by University of Hawaii Press. Zhuangzi. (1998). *Wandering on the Way: Early Taoist Tales and Parables of Chuang Tzu.* (V. Mair, Trans.). p. 170. Honolulu, HI: University of Hawaii Press.
4 Cao Pi. *Shan Zai Xing(first),* http://baike.baidu.com/subview/130614/9417121.htm.
5 Li Bai. *Ni Gu twelve(ninth),* http://baike.baidu.com/view/3360813.htm.
6 Michel de Montaigne. (1580). *Essays of Montaigne, Vol. 1,* http://oll.libertyfund.org/titles/107.
7 Permission to republish granted by University of Hawaii Press. Zhuangzi. (1998). *Wandering on the Way: Early Taoist Tales and Parables of Chuang Tzu.* (V. Mair, Trans.). p. 27. Honolulu, HI: University of Hawaii Press.
8 Permission to republish granted by University of Hawaii Press. Zhuangzi. (1998). *Wandering on the Way: Early Taoist Tales and Parables of Chuang Tzu.* (V. Mair, Trans.). p. 164. Honolulu, HI: University of Hawaii Press.
9 Permission to republish granted by University of Hawaii Press. Zhuangzi. (1998). *Wandering on the Way: Early Taoist Tales and Parables of Chuang Tzu.* (V. Mair, Trans.). pp. 327–328. Honolulu, HI: University of Hawaii Press.
10 Permission to republish granted by University of Hawaii Press. Zhuangzi. (1998). *Wandering on the Way: Early Taoist Tales and Parables of Chuang Tzu.* (V. Mair, Trans.). pp. 331–332. Honolulu, HI: University of Hawaii Press.
11 Permission to republish granted by University of Hawaii Press. Zhuangzi. (1998). *Wandering on the Way: Early Taoist Tales and Parables of Chuang Tzu.* (V. Mair, Trans.). p. 117. Honolulu, HI: University of Hawaii Press.

References

Bai, L. *Ni Gu Twelve(Ninth).* Retrieved from http://baike.baidu.com/view/3360813.htm
Becker, E. (1973). *The denial of death.* New York, NY: The Free Press, Inc.
May, R. (1953). *Man's search for himself.* New York, NY: W. W. Norton & Co.
May, R. (1981). *Freedom and destiny.* New York, NY: W. W. Norton & Co.
Michel de Montaigne. (1580). *Essays of Montaigne, Vol. 1.* Retrieved from http://oll.libertyfund.org/titles/107
Pi, C. *Shan Zai Xing(first).* Retrieved from http://baike.baidu.com/subview/130614/9417121.htm
Yalom, I. (1980). *Existential psychotherapy.* New York, NY: Basic Books.
Yalom, I. (2008). *Staring at the sun: Overcoming the terror of death.* San Francisco, CA: Jossey-Bass.
Yalom, I., & Josselson, R. (2011). Existential psychotherapy. In R. J. Corsini & D. Wedding (Eds.), *Current psychotherapies* (9th ed.). Belmont, CA: Cengage Learning.
Zhuangzi. (1998). *Wandering on the way: Early Taoist tales and parables of Chuang Tzu.* (V. Mair, Trans.). Honolulu, HI: University of Hawaii Press.
Zhuangzi. (2013). *The complete works of Zhuangzi.* [Kindle for Android, 4.3.0.204]. (B. Watson, Trans.). Retrieved from Amazon.com

PART IV
Autumn Floods

The Autumn Floods

"The Autumn Floods," Chapter 17 of the book *Zhuangzi*, is considered by many to be an excellent summary of many of Zhuangzi's most important ideas. For this reason, three authors chose to write on this seminal chapter. Given its central importance, the first half of this chapter from *Zhuangzi* is included below for the reader's ease of reference (Zhuangzi, 1998, pp. 152–157).

> When the time of the autumn floods arrived, the hundred tributaries poured into the Yellow River. Its onrushing current was so huge that one could not discern an ox or a horse on the opposite side or on the banks of its islets. Thereupon the Earl of the River delightedly congratulated himself at having complete and sole possession of all excellences under heaven. Following along with the current, he went east until he reached the Northern Sea. There he looked eastword but could not see the water's end, whereupon he crestfallenly gazed across the surface of the sea and said with a sign to its overlord, "There is a proverb that says, 'He who has heard the Way a hundred times believes no one may be compared with himself?' This applies to me. Furthermore, when I heard those who belittle the learning of Confucius and disparage the righteousness of Poyi, I did not believe them. But now that I behold your boundlessness, I realize that, had I not come to your gate, I would have been in danger, and would have been ridiculed forever by the practitioner of the great method."
>
> The Overlord of the Northern Sea said, "You can't tell a frog at the bottom of a well about the sea because he's stuck in his little space. You can't tell a summer insect about ice because it is confined by its season.

You can't tell a scholar of distorted views about the Way because he is bound by his doctrine. Now you have ventured forth from your banks to observe the great sea and have recognized your own insignificance, so that you can be told of the great principle.

"Of all the waters under heaven, none is greater than the sea. The myriad rivers return to it ceaselessly but it never fills up; the drain at its bottom endlessly discharges but it never empties. Spring and autumn it never varies, and it knows nothing of flood and drought. Its superiority to such streams as the Yangtze and the Yellow rivers cannot be measured in numbers. Yet the reason I have never made much of myself on this account is because I compare my own form to that of heaven and earth and recall that I receive my vital breath from yin and yang. Amid heaven and earth, I am as a little pebble or tiny tree on a big mountain. Since I perceive of myself as small, how then can I make much of myself? May we not reckon that the four seas in the midst of heaven and earth resemble the cavity in a pile of stones lying in a huge marsh? May we not reckon that the Middle Kingdom in the midst of the sea is like a mustard seed in a huge granary? When we designate the number of things there are in existence, we refer to them in terms of myriads, but man occupies only one place among them. The masses of men occupy the nine regions, but wherever grain grows and wherever boats and carriage reach, the individual occupies only one place among them. In comparison with the myriad things, would he not resemble the tip of a downy hair on a horse's body? The succession of the five emperors, the contention of the three kings, the worries of human men, the labors of the committed scholars, all amount to no more than this. Poyi declined it for the sake of fame. Confucius lectured on it for the sake of his erudition. This is because they made much of themselves. Is it not like you just now making much of yourself because of your flooding waters?"

"This being so," asked the Earl of the River, "may I take heaven and earth as the standard for what is large and the tip of a downy hair as the standard for what is small?

"No," said the Overlord of the Northern Sea. "Things are limitless in their capacities, uncertain in their beginnings and ending. For this reason, great knowledge observes things at a relative distance, hence it does not belittle what is small nor make much of what is big, knowing that their capacities are limitless. It witnesses clearly the past and the present, hence it is not frustrated by what is far off nor attracted by what is close at hand, knowing that their occurrences are incessant. It examines fullness and emptiness, hence it is not pleased when it obtains nor worried when it loses, knowing that their portions are inconstant. It understands the level path, hence it is not enraptured by life nor perturbed by death, knowing that beginnings and endings are uncertain. We may reckon that what man knows is less than what he doesn't know; the time when he is alive is less than the time when he isn't alive. When he seeks to delimit the boundaries of the extremely large with what is extremely small, he becomes disoriented and can't get hold of himself. Viewed from this vantage, how do we know that the tip of a downy hair is adequate to determine the parameters of the extremely small? And how do we know that heaven and earth are adequate to delimit the boundaries of the extremely large?"

"The deliberators of the world," said the Earl of the Yellow River, "all say, 'That which is extremely minute has no form; that which is extremely large cannot be encompassed.' Is this true?"

"If we look at what is large from the viewpoint of what is minuscule," said the Overlord of the Northern Sea, "we won't see the whole. If we look at what is minuscule from the viewpoint of what is large, we won't see the details. Now, that which is minute is the smallest of the small; that which is enormous is the largest of the large. Hence, their differences are suitable and in accord with their circumstances. Yet, the minute and the coarse are both dependent upon their having a form. That which has no form is numerically indivisible; that which cannot be encompassed is numerically undelimitable. That which can be conceived of in thought is the minuteness of things. That which can neither be discussed in words nor conceived of in thoughts is independent of minuteness and coarseness."

"How then," asked the Earl of the Yellow River, "are we to demarcate the value and magnitude of a thing, whether it be intrinsic or extrinsic?"

The Overlord of the Northern Sea said, "Observed in the light of the Way, things are neither prized nor despised; observed in the light of things, they prize themselves and despise others; observed in the light of the common lot, one's values is not determined by oneself. Observed in the light of gradations, if we consider to be large what is larger than something else, then the myriad things are without exception large; if we consider to be small what is smaller than something else, then all the myriad things are without exception small. If we regard heaven and earth as a mustard seed and the tip of a downy hair as a mountain, we can perceive the numerousness of their relative gradations. Observed in the light of merit, if we grant whatever merit they have, then the myriad things without exception have merit; if we point to whatever merit they lack, then the myriad things lack merit. If we recognize that east and west, though opposites, cannot be without each other, their shared merit will be fixed. Observed in the light of inclination, if we approve whatever they approve, then the myriad things without exception may be approved; if we condemn what they condemn, then the myriad things without exception may be condemned. If we recognize that Yao and Chieh approved of themselves but condemn each other, we can perceive their controlling inclinations.

"Long ago, Yao yielded his throne to Shun and the latter became emperor, but when K'uai yielded his throne to Tzu Chih, they were both cut down. T'ang and Wu became kings through contention, but the Duke of Po contended and was destroyed. Viewed in this light, the etiquette of contending and yielding, the conduct of Yao and Chieh, may be either prized or despised in accord with the times, but may not be taken as constants. A beam or a ridge-pole may be used to breach a city wall, but it cannot be used to plug a hole, which is to say that implements have specific purposes. A Ch'ichi or a Hualiu may gallop a thousand tricents in a day, but for catching rats they're not good as a wild cat or a weasel, which is to say that creatures have different skills. An owl can catch fleas at night and can discern the tip of a downy hair, but when it comes out during the day it stares blankly and can't even see a hill or mountain, which is to say that beings have different natures. Therefore, when it is said, 'Make right your teacher, not wrong; make good government your teacher, not disorder,' this is to misunderstand the principle of heaven and earth and attributes of the myriad things. It would be like making heaven your teacher and ignoring earth, like making yin your teacher and ignoring yang. The unworkability of this is clear. Still if one goes on talking like this and does not give it up, one is either being stupid or deceptive. The emperors and kings of old had different modes of abdication, and the rulers of the three dynasties had different modes of succession. He who acts contrary to the times and contravenes custom is called a usurper; he who accords with the times and conforms to custom is called a disciple of righteousness. Keep silent, oh Earl of the Yellow River! How could you know about the gate of honor and baseness and about the practitioners of small and large?"

"Then what am I to do?" asked the Earl of the Yellow River, "and what am I not to do? With regard to rejecting and accepting, taking and giving, how should I behave?"[1]

Note

1 Permission to republish granted by University of Hawaii Press. Zhuangzi. (1998). *Wandering on the way: Early Taoist tales and parables of Chuang Tzu.* (V. Mair, Trans.). pp. 152–157. Honolulu, HI: University of Hawaii Press.

Reference

Zhuangzi. (1998). *Wandering on the way: Early Taoist tales and parables of Chuang Tzu.* (V. Mair, Trans.). Honolulu, HI: University of Hawaii Press.

12

ALONG THE WAY TO SPIRITUAL FREEDOM

From Rivers to Seas and Heaven to Tao

Yang Shaogang and Li Yun

FIGURE 12.1 Created by Lisa Vallejos

I have humbly chosen to base my chapter on the first section of Zhuangzi's seventeenth chapter, titled "The Autumn Floods," because of the fine and flowing nature of Zhuangzi's prose. The dialogue between the Earl of the Yellow River and Overlord of the Northern Sea serves as an excellent analogy for illuminating Chinese Taoist principles found in Existential-Humanistic Psychology.

Broadening One's Horizon in Search of the Meaning of Existence

Zhuangzi (1998) was purposeful in employing the Autumn Floods as an analogy for existence at the outset because people were familiar with its common occurrence:

> When the time of the autumn floods arrived, the hundred tributaries poured into the Yellow River. Its onrushing current was so huge that one could not discern an ox or a horse on the opposite side or on the banks of its islets. Thereupon the Earl of the River delightedly congratulated himself at having complete and sole possession of all excellences under heaven.[1]
>
> *(p. 152)*

One could argue that the Earl's joy was arrogant and shortsighted (for believing that he alone possessed all the beauty under heaven) but understandable given his geographical constraints. Indeed arrogance and shortsightedness are natural and common characteristics of man. The arrogance of the Earl embodied the essential features of self-experience in one's sense of being raised by Rollo May. May, Angell, and Allenberg (1958) proposed that the core process of psychotherapy is to "help a patient recognize and experience his existence" (p. 77); that is, discover one's sense of being guided by the following three possible principles: (1) freedom as a foundation of one's existence and therefore "a quality of one's whole existence." (p. 57); (2) a sense of religious morality as a dynamic factor to guarantee an individual's existence and to facilitate his personality becoming complete; and (3) a healthy self-expression. Guided by these principles, the self-consciousness or the sense of being of the Earl can be described as complacent. Complacency is characterized by stagnation, the refusal to grow, and the possession of an inflated self-worth or false pride. Conversely, one's sense of being can also be characterized by freedom with a healthy degree of self-consciousness. Indeed, the greater one's self-consciousness, the wider one's range of free choice. Consequently, one is more likely to engage in self-exploration and be more proficient, creative, and responsible in determining one's own fate. To be fair, a certain degree of self-worth and self-consciousness is necessary in order for the Earl to achieve a sense of freedom. Indeed expanding one's consciousness of existence is the beginning of growth and development. The question becomes how can the Earl overcome and expand his limited awareness of existence and self-consciousness?

The Earl failed to understand how ridiculous his complacency was until he flowed down to the sea and saw the broad and vast landscape. To his credit, the Earl retained sufficient humility to engage in some serious soul-searching after his vision and horizon had been expanded. Humbly the Earl proclaims, "There is a proverb that says, 'He who has heard the Way a hundred times believes no one may be compared with himself?' This applies to me" (Zhuangzi, 1998, p. 152). This was the obvious beginning of the Earl's awakening and search for the meaning of human existence. As Victor Frankl (2003) said, "The true meaning of life should be found in the world, rather than in one's heart, neither in a closed system, which is considered to be his spirit" (p. 204). It is through the search for the meaning of existence that the Earl began to accept his deficiency. To the Overlord, he said remorsefully: "But now that I behold your boundlessness, I realize that, had I not come to your gate, I would have been in danger, and would have been ridiculed forever by the practitioner of the great method" (Zhuangzi, 1998, p. 153).

Having heard this, the Overlord inspired him to transcend his limitations a step at a time:

> You can't tell a frog at the bottom of a well about the sea because he's stuck in his little space. You can't tell a summer insect about ice because it is confined by its season. You can't tell a scholar of distorted views about the Way because he is bound by his doctrine.[2]
>
> *(Zhuangzi, 1998, p. 153)*

These three analogies share a similar meaning but each is chosen to emphasize a different limitation to the understanding of the Tao. In life, each of us cannot hear the great Tao because of various constraints. So much so that even when we have a chance to hear the Tao, we would probably put it away. As Lao Tzi (1997), the founder of Taoism, said:

> When the man of highest capacities hears Tao, he does his best to put it into practice; when the man of middling capacity hears Tao, he is in two minds about it; and when the man of low capacity hears Tao, He laughs loudly at it.
>
> *(p. 89)*

If a person has too much worldly prejudice, he/she cannot really understand the meaning of human existence. You are wasting your breath if you discuss the philosophy of life with such a person. You may even be ridiculed and reviled. And so even the sage can only say that: "As to what lies beyond the six realms of Heaven and Earth, East and West, North and South, the sages set aside without discussion. As to what lies within the six realms, the sages discuss without comments" (Wang, 1999, p. 31). From here we can see that even sages too must maintain humility and know their limitations. Us common people should be modest as well so that we too can grow with such attitude.

The point in which the Earl became self-critical, which is the first step to self-awareness, is similar to the awakening of a client in Existential-Humanistic Psychotherapy. Although he was scolded severely by the Overlord, it was done in the spirit of care. Are you complacent? In order to promote introspection, I must first broaden your outlook and reveal your limitations. When you eliminate your arrogance, I will tell you the truth. Thus the Overlord suddenly changed the topic and said: "Now you have ventured forth from your banks to observe the great sea and have recognized your own insignificance, so that you can be told of the great principle" (Zhuangzi, 1998, p. 153). One is worthy to be taught when one is willing to correct one's mistakes upon awareness. Only when one has recognized one's limits, admitted one's fragility, can one transcend limitations and strive for greatness. Existential philosophy attaches great importance to death, pain, anxiety, and limitation, emphasizing one's potential for growth in the face of human limitations (May et al., 1958; Burston, 2003). The dialogue between the Overlord and the Earl analogously embodies the necessary path of awaking the client's mind. Such is the wisdom of the Chinese Taoist's existential-psychological values over two thousand years ago.

What sort of life philosophy will the Overlord narrate to the Earl next?

> Of all the waters under heaven, none is greater than the sea. The myriad rivers return to it ceaselessly but it never fills up; the drain at its bottom endlessly discharges but it never empties. Spring and autumn it never varies, and it knows nothing of flood and drought.[3]
>
> *(Zhuangzi, 1998, p. 153)*

How could this be? Some may point out that it's simply because of the enormous capacity of the ocean. Furthermore, the Overlord is hypocritically criticizing the Earl about his complacency and committing the same mistake by tooting his own horn. But in fact, this is just the prologue of the Overlord's understanding of his own sense of being. The sentences that follow show the Overlord's clear sense of self-awareness:

> Yet the reason I have never made much of myself on this account" is because I understand profoundly that amid heaven and earth, I am as a little pebble or tiny tree on a big mountain. Since I perceive of myself as small, how then can I make much of myself? May we not reckon that the four seas in the midst of heaven and earth resemble the cavity in a pile of stones lying in a huge marsh? May we not reckon that the Middle Kingdom in the midst of the sea is like a mustard seed in a huge granary?[4]
>
> *(Zhuangzi, 1998, p. 153)*

The Overlord used the grains of millet in a large granary to inspire the Earl to broadly expand his mind. Only in this way can the Earl appreciate the greatness of all existence. The recognition that there are mountains beyond mountains, and heavens beyond heavens is precisely the existential pursuit of human nature, and descriptive of the Overlord's developmental process of self-perception and self-fulfillment. The analogies employed by the Overlord reveal the developmental process of the self in an existential-humanistic psychotherapist.

Arriving at the Realm of Tao through Governing by Non-Interference

In comparison with the vast cosmos, the Middle Kingdom is akin to a small grain in a large granary, and the whole earth is nothing but a small ping-pong ball. At the same time, of the vast universe, what modern science could interpret is nothing but a drop in the ocean. From this perspective, we can appreciate the broadness of Zhuangzi's outlook with which one can appreciate the significance of human existence.

The Earl, out of his understanding and appreciation for the teachings of the Overlord inquired, "This being so, may I take heaven and earth as the standard for what is large and the tip of a downy hair as the standard for what is small" (Zhuangzi, 1998, p. 154)? Exasperated, the Overlord replied, "I have just praised you, how could you be confused again now? While I've told you the truth, I haven't discussed The Tao with you. Viewed from this vantage, how do we know that the tip of a downy hair is adequate to determine the parameters of the extremely small? And how do we know that heaven and earth are adequate to delimit the boundaries of the extremely large" (Zhuangzi, 1998, p. 154)? Similarly from the perspective of modern science: is the atom the smallest indivisible particle of matter? No, there are many other particles smaller than an atom, such as a proton, neutron, electron, quark, and so on. Is the Milky Way galaxy the largest universe at the grandest scale? No, there are hyper galaxies which are much larger. On the macro level, the hyper galaxy is as small as an atom. From the micro level, an atom can be considered a hyper galaxy within which are many smaller particles. All in all, a psychotherapist informed by the Taoist principles within the existential-humanistic approach can thus include the macro and micro into his/her spiritual world in the search for spiritual freedom and surpass the limitations of heaven and earth and arrive at the realm of the Tao.

What then is Tao? It cannot be defined within the existential philosophy of Zhuangzi. Tao is both big and small, both good and evil, both stable and changing, both positive and negative, both outside and inside. It transcends everything and includes and connects all:

> As Tao cannot be heard, what can be heard is not Tao. As Tao cannot be seen, what can be seen is not Tao. As Tao cannot be spoken, what can be

spoken is not Tao. Do you know that what creates the form is formless? Tao should not be given a name.

(Wang, 1999, pp. 377–379)

Having encountered the wonderful Tao, one can know clearly that every single thing in the universe has its own value of existence ontologically, and possesses all its magical effect in accordance with the Tao of existence. Heaven and earth are indeed vast, great, and wonderful, but aren't all the worldly objects similarly vast, wonderful, and great? "Observed in the light of the Way, things are neither prized nor despised; observed in the light of things, they prize themselves and despise others" (Wang, 1999, p. 155). Everything in the world has its own reasons for existence. Therefore human beings, as mere drops in a huge ocean, should naturally obey the rule of existence. Only when one casts away worldly honor and disgrace can one rid oneself of the secular prejudice of material desires and experience the true happiness of life in a state of Tao.

Individuals living in this world have to face the following facts: the world is uncertain and life is incomplete. These two facts tell us that both life and the world are limited in their nature and therefore leave people in a perpetual state of unease. For example, a neurotic with obsessive-compulsive disorder can be understood as being consistently in conflict with the fact that the world is uncertain and people are incomplete. This causes profound distress within the depth of his/her mind. Thus he/she is always searching for perfection and absolutes, for these are the conditions which helps him/her to feel safe. In essence, such a neurotic symptom is evident in the mind of the Earl, who was initially safe in his limitations but shortsighted and arrogant. Yet, his distress increased when he flowed down to the Northern Sea and became aware of his limitations. Thanks to the interpretation of the Overlord, whose role is akin to a psychotherapist, the Earl gradually understood that his neurosis originated from the narrowness of his mind. The Overlord helped the Earl to awaken to existence, broaden his perspective/mind, and thus accept and eventually transform his limitations.

Zhuangzi inherited Lao Tzi's philosophy or attitude of letting it be as it is, and consequently raised a state of Tao that transcended limits and self. Through the conversation between the Earl and Overlord, he drew forth the differentiation between big and small, right and wrong, high and low, honor and disgrace, which can be understood as illusions led by deliberate effort. People could break through the infinite and burst from boundaries ultimately only by doing things without any interference. Through Zhuangzi's beautiful chapter "The Autumn Floods," we are taken along the way from river to sea, to heaven and earth, and finally to the realm of the Tao, guiding our thoughts gradually to an increasingly broader and beautiful realm of spirituality. This is a profound reflection of Zhuangzi's existential and philosophical psychology for the meaning of human existence. The Western practice of existential-humanistic psychotherapy is analogous to the dialogue between the Earl and the Overlord. It invites the client to understand the wide-ranging expansive world through self-recognition via the relational dialogue between the therapist and client. If a psychotherapist can read this book in a peaceful mind and encounter the Tao, I believe he or she will be mentally communing with not only Zhuangzi but the rest of humanity and all that is under the universe. Such way of being can be understood as the carefree wondering in absolute freedom espoused by Zhuangzi by which one could attain the true great *libre*[5] of human existence.

Notes

1 Permission to republish granted by University of Hawaii Press. Zhuangzi. (1998). *Wandering on the way: Early Taoist tales and parables of Chuang Tzu.* (V. Mair, Trans.). p. 152. Honolulu, HI: University of Hawaii Press.
2 Permission to republish granted by University of Hawaii Press. Zhuangzi. (1998). *Wandering on the way: Early Taoist tales and parables of Chuang Tzu.* (V. Mair, Trans.). p. 153. Honolulu, HI: University of Hawaii Press.
3 Permission to republish granted by University of Hawaii Press. Zhuangzi. (1998). *Wandering on the way: Early Taoist tales and parables of Chuang Tzu.* (V. Mair, Trans.). p. 153. Honolulu, HI: University of Hawaii Press.
4 Permission to republish granted by University of Hawaii Press. Zhuangzi. (1998). *Wandering on the way: Early Taoist tales and parables of Chuang Tzu.* (V. Mair, Trans.). p. 153. Honolulu, HI: University of Hawaii Press.
5 Latin *libre* means free. In Roman religion and mythology, Libre means "the free one."

References

Burston, D. (2003). Existentialism, humanism and psychotherapy. In *Existential Analysis: Journal of the Society for Existential Analysis, 14*(2), 309.

Frankl, V. (2003). *Man's search for meaning.* (He Zhongqiang & Yang Fengchi, Trans.). Beijing, China: Xinhua Press.

Lao Tzi. (1997). *Tao Te Ching.* (A. Waley, Trans.). Hertfordshire: Wordsworth Editions Limited.

May, R., Angell, E., & Allenberg, H. E. (Eds.). (1958). *Existence: A new dimension in psychology and psychiatry.* New York, NY: Basic Books.

Wang, R. P. (1999). *Qi Wu Lun.* Hunan, China: Hunan's People's Publishing House.

Zhuangzi. (1998). *Wandering on the way: Early Taoist tales and parables of Chuang Tzu.* (V. Mair, Trans.). Honolulu, HI: University of Hawaii Press.

13

THE ENLIGHTENMENT OF AUTUMN FLOODS

Wu Fei
Translated by Doreen Xuekang Deng

FIGURE 13.1 Created by Mona Elsayed

In Chinese culture, a variety of revelations are derived from water. For example, "the best of man is like water" (Chapter 8, *Tao Te Ching*, by Lao Tzi). This means that ultimate morality has the quality of water, which nourishes all things but never competes with them. Or, "the virtuous delights in mountains and the wise delights in water" (The Analects 6:23). In other words, the virtuous is as solid and generous as the mountains and the wise is as lively and flexible as water. Similarly, Zhuangzi passed down the wisdom of human existence to his followers through an essay on water. The essay "The Autumn Floods," Chapter 17 in the book *Zhuangzi* (1998), is titled after the first two Chinese characters of the chapter. Through the allegory of the annual Autumn Floods, Zhuangzi delivers his unique lively and flexible wisdom which echoes numerous central tenets of existential-humanistic psychology.

The setting of the Autumn Floods is significant. During the seasonal floods, the Yellow River swells extensively before emptying into the North Sea (北海). Along its topography is Pu Lake, where Zhuangzi fished peacefully when he firmly rejected the envoy of the State of Chu who came to invite him to serve the state. Further along its path is the bridge over Hao Lake where Zhuangzi and Hui Tzu debated the Joy of The Fishes, another famous Taoist Parable attributed to Zhuangzi.

Through the various allegorical imagery of water, Zhuangzi expounded upon human being's limitations and dialectics, one's accordance with nature, and the pursuit of inner freedom, harmony and ease while rejecting fame and wealth.

Part 1: The Limited Mind of the Earl of the Yellow River as Related to the Vast and Extensive Swelling of the River During Flood Season

The Autumn Floods arrive during the fall season when thousands of tributaries pour into the Yellow River, swelling it to the point of submerging a number of small islands along the way. The river becomes so broad that it was impossible to tell a cow from a horse on the opposite bank. Due to the enormous swelling, the Earl of the Yellow River became joyful and haughty. That is until he encountered the vastness of the Sea. After seven conversations with the Overlord of the Northern Sea, the Earl progressively awakened to the relative diminutive dimensions of the rivers and lakes compared to the sea and the universe. The Earl's mind was broadened and he finally recognized human limitation and the infiniteness of the universe (Zhuangzi, 1998).

The Earl acquired a different perspective and broadened his mind after he saw the sea and realized the difference and his limitation. He learned from the Overlord that "you can't tell a frog at the bottom of a well about the sea because he's stuck in his little space. You can't tell a summer insect about ice because it is confined by its season. You can't tell a scholar of distorted views about the Way because he is bound by his doctrine" (Zhuangzi, 1998, p. 153).

The well-frog is limited by its environment; the summer insect with a life span of one summer is limited by the season; a scholar from the rural countryside is limited by his education. Zhuangzi suggests that everything has its limitations just as human knowledge is limited by such objective conditions as environment, season, and education because "what man knows is less than what he doesn't know; the time when he is alive is less than the time when he isn't alive" (Zhuangzi, 1998, p. 154).

"I know not the truth of Lu Mountain because I am inside it" (不識廬山真面目，只緣身在此山中，宋蘇軾《題西林壁》). Poem on the wall of Xilin Temple, Sushi, Song Dynasty). One cannot overcome one's limitation unless one comes to know it clearly. Thus, taking a distant outsider's perspective, it is only possible for the therapist to achieve breakthroughs through ongoing learning and exploration. Hence protecting him from being trapped or strung along by the client. A therapist can only help his client to encounter the "vastness of the sea" and the "truth of Lu Mountain" by stepping outside of himself and enlarging his own perspective. The following are examples where clients are entrapped by their own narrow perspectives and living within a confined space: depressed clients focusing on the negative and seldom appreciating the kindness of others; parents troubled by their children's failure to adapt to school yet failing to see their own problems; frustrated students attributing their poor performance to being not smart enough or the incompetence of their teachers or school; couples in marriage crisis failing to recognize their own shortcomings and locating the problem in their partners. "The insider is lost while the outsider knows everything clearly" (當局者迷，旁觀者清, Chinese idiom). Therapists need to help their clients broaden their minds so that they can view things from different perspectives and change their cognition of the world. If clients repetitively complain, "Why am I always like this?" they are in fact limited by their "perspectives" and "experiences." Therapists should help their clients see this clearly and understand their situations in a broader context. For example, when told that "many people are like this and it is normal," part of the anxiety has already been reduced. Hence, we lead our clients to more open spaces liberating them from their traps.

If the therapist himself has never encountered the sea, it is difficult to imagine how he can help his client. The therapist must be wise enough to make it clear that he is only in the position of helping the client help himself. In practice, it's impossible for the therapist to grasp all the techniques and approaches of the different schools of psychotherapy or to solve all the client's problems. The goal of psychotherapy is to grasp the human condition or the fundamental givens of life and help the client to find their inner potential resources so that the client can be motivated to find the meaning of life. "Haughtiness invites loss while modesty brings benefit" (宋歐陽修《五代史伶官傳序》, Ouyang Xiu, Song Dynasty). Therapists should be careful not to be as haughty as the Earl who knew nothing about the Sea. In order to be able to thoroughly contain their clients, therapists must purify themselves and broaden their minds so as to embody Zhuangzi's approach of "being void and peaceful." There is no end to learning. Life is enriched through continuous study. For both therapists and clients, the possibility of infinite growth comes from the facing of limitations. For therapists, the "way to the sea" comprises cultivating one's mind, facing ever-increasing challenges, overcoming one's restraints and limitations, and expanding one's boundaries (境界), thereby transforming oneself.

New discoveries will appear upon expanding one's perspective. More freedom can be obtained if one can clearly assess, master, and thus overcome one's limitations. A painting is constrained by the frame; a poem is structured by its rhythm; an article is limited by its length; and a song is restricted by its tone. The creation of a painting, poem, article, and song is all made possible due to its restrictions. Restrictions in a certain extent are crucial in manifesting the intrinsic character and nature of things, bring about a stronger artistic appeal, and allow for the emergence of beauty in a more concentrated form. For example, the creation of Chinese characters based on pictograms is the process of simplification through the elimination of complicated parts. There are six forms of character creation. All six forms derive the characters' abstract meanings from the comprehensiveness of natural and social event and evidence the brilliance of creating the infinite from finiteness. Such a realm (境界) of creative freedom can be achieved in therapy if one recognizes one's limitations.

Once the mind is opened, experience will be enriched. The Earl came to a broader understanding of the world and expanded his perspective after encountering the Overlord. Paradoxically, awakening to his own frivolousness and nothingness is the beginning of the Earl finding a way out of his own limited existence. Accepting his limitation initiated the Earl's apprehension of the personal meaning of his existence in the universe. The Earl's sense of his own value and existence is gradually increased with the unfolding of his conversation with the Overlord.

Part 2: The Yellow River and the North Sea. Dialogue between the River and the Sea—the Relativity of Existence and Dialectic of Things

When asked how long one minute is by the teacher, a four-year-old boy answered that one minute feels short when I am playing with Legos and becomes much longer when sitting on the hot seat.

The dialogue between the Earl and the Overlord is similar to the relative experience of this four-year-old boy. The boy's subjective feeling varies according to the situation encountered. Similarly, the Earl understands the relative dimension of things. The teaching of the Overlord involves all aspects of the universe. Their discussions involve the relativity of things and extend to the law of the unity of opposites inherent in relativity. In "The Autumn Floods," Zhuangzi expounds upon the relativity of things through the words of the Overlord:

> Amid heaven and earth, I am as a little pebble or tiny tree on a big mountain. Since I perceive of myself as small, how then can I make much of myself? May we not reckon that the four seas in the midst of heaven and earth resemble the cavity in a pile of stones lying in a huge marsh? May we not reckon that the Middle Kingdom in the midst of the sea is like a mustard seed in a huge granary? When we designate the number of things there are in existence, we refer to them in terms of myriads, but man occupies only one place among them. The masses of men occupy the nine regions, but wherever grain grows and wherever boats and carriage reach, the individual occupies only one place among them. In comparison with the myriad things, would he not resemble the tip of a downy hair on a horse's body?[1]
>
> *(Zhuangzi, 1998, pp. 153–154)*

The dimension of things is not only relative but also interdependent. Zhuangzi wrote, "If we recognize that east and west, though opposites, cannot be without each other, their shared merit will be fixed" (Zhuangzi, 1998, p. 155). The Overlord warns us not to adhere to any single aspect of things. Even in the narrative structure of the essay, Zhuangzi's theme of the dialectic is expressed through the relative and interdependent relationship between the Earl and the Overlord and the river and the sea. They are simultaneously opposing and unitary. Zhuangzi has the Earl play devil's advocate while representing his own thinking through the Overlord. They each help to highlight the opposite characteristic in the other. They represent two different perspectives and two levels of the spiritual realm. As expressed in the poem (西風頌) by Percy Bysshe Shelley (1993), "If winter comes, can spring be far behind" (p. 76)? The law of interdependence and mutual transformation is universal. The red forest flowers fade in the spring so as to produce autumn; the warm sunshine of spring originates from the winter cold.

"The life of things is like the cantering and galloping of a horse—they are transformed with each movement. They change with each moment (物之生也，若驟若馳，無動而不變，無時而不移)" (Zhuangzi, 1998, p. 158). In the twenty-second chapter of *Zhuangzi*, titled "Journey to the North" (知北遊), it says "human life between Heaven and Earth is like a white colt glimpsed through a crack in the wall, quickly past (人生天地間，若白駒過隙，忽然而已)" (Zhuangzi, 2013, Chapter 22, para. 37). Life passes in the twinkle of an eye and everything is inseparable from the unity of opposites; life and death, existence and non-existence, the positive and negative. Such state of change means that human existence is completed through the change and equilibration of life and death. Living with paradox maintains the tension between the infinite and finite.

In *The Lecture on Life of Huainan Zi* (西漢劉安《淮南子》), it is written that "a tree's roots will be damaged if it is to produce a second round of fruit within a year" (再實之木根必傷). The metaphor warns that being overly lucky will lead to disaster. This is the equivalent of "overdoing is just like not doing enough" (過猶不及, Chinese idiom). What is needed is a form of dynamic equilibrium. Not being absolute or extreme, letting things flow naturally without reluctance or excess. Therein lies the enchantment of dialectic unity and counterbalanced transformation.

An interdependent relationship can be transformed through comparison. Through dialectic thinking, a therapist could help her client see the other side of things including vitality from crisis, light within darkness, hope from adversity, and positive meaning from negative affect. Therapy endeavors to help clients recognize unpleasant experiences as opportunities for self-growth. Therapists help clients learn to handle troubles dialectically. To comprehend through reflection the meaning of life brought on by frustrations, and to gain life wisdom through the transformation of mental "rubbish" into life resources, thereby offering a brighter future. This requires life experience, philosophical thinking, and the accumulation of life wisdom that is the result of dialectical thinking as a habit. The dialectic unity thinking of Laozi and Zhuangzi lays the Chinese cultural foundations of opposites symbolized by the Yin and Yang. It helps the Chinese transform disaster into luck and balance their internal worlds when confronted with honor and humiliation, gain and loss. The following common Chinese idiom reveals the wisdom of dialectic unity: "no matter how big a thing is today, it will be tiny tomorrow; no matter how big the thing this year, it will only be a story next year; and no matter how big the thing this life is, will be no more than a folklore in the next life" (今天再大的事，到了明天就是小事；今年再大的事，到了明年就是故事；今生再大的事，到了來世就是傳說).

Dialectic unity is abundant in Chinese idioms. For example, "a foot has its disadvantages while an inch has its advantages" (尺有所短，寸有所長); "how do you know it's not luck when Uncle Sai lost his horse" (塞翁失馬，焉知非福); "a pot will spill over when filled with too much water and a piggy bank will survive only when it's empty" (欹器以滿覆，撲滿以空全); "disaster and luck are interdependent" (禍福相依); "Yin and Yang accompanies" (陰陽相隨); "Yin and Yang balances" (陰陽平衡); "Yin and Yang compensates" (陰陽互補), etc.

Some Chinese characters such as "above and under, left and right, root and top" can demonstrate dialectic unity directly through its structure—the opposing meanings can be read directly from their ideograms. For example, 𠃌 𠂆 represents above and under, 屮 𡳿 stand for left hand and right hand, 凹 refers to the root of the tree while 凸 refers to the top of the tree. Ancient Chinese characters embody dialectic unity through its structure. The graphic Chinese ideograms 凹 (*au—concave*) and 凸 (*tu—convex*) are very vivid. There are a number of other terms which are made up of words with opposite meanings. For example, 動mobile and 靜quiet, 攻attack and 守defend, 強strong and 弱

weak, 男male and 女female, 生life and 死death, 高high and 矮short, 胖fat and 瘦thin, 興thrive and 廢decay, 內inner and 外outer, 得get and 失lose, 榮honor and 辱humiliation, 盈wax and 虧wane, etc. To integrate dialectics is to allow opposing parties to transform and co-exist, improving the capability to tolerate all things and contain all things.

If we examine the ancient Chinese character 爰 (modern Chinese font is 受, shòu, meaning to receive or accept), we can see two different intersecting hands passing through an object in the middle. This is symbolic of the idea of give and take. On one hand, one gives (給予) to others; at the same time, one receives (接受) for oneself. Thus, this ancient Chinese character for receiving embodies the idea that giving and receiving are two sides of the same coin, as espoused by the teachings on happiness by Harvard Professor Tal Ben-Shahar.[2] In other words, helping others is helping ourselves while helping ourselves will indirectly be of benefit to others.

Client lives will be activated and their thoughts will be more flexible and vigilant if therapists can be guided to think and view things more dialectically. Unlimited energy for life growth can be unlocked if the value and positive meanings behind misery, poverty, adversity, and sadness can be explored. Clients will acquire more freedom for their own existence if they can integrate the meaning of opposites. This is another enlightened gift Zhuangzi bestowed to us through the words of the Overlord in "The Autumn Floods."

Part 3: The Surging Yellow River Flows Eastwards— Let it Be and Fascinating Things Will Happen Naturally

In the fifth conversation between the Earl and the Overlord, through the words of the Overlord, Zhuangzi encouraged readers to step outside of their subjective limitations, accord themselves with the nature of things, and change in accordance with the natural law.

In the sixth conversation, the idea of knowing the natural laws, being in accordance with the nature of things, examining the basis of all change, and acquiring freedom is expressed through the relationship between human beings and nature. The theme of the "Tao taking nature as its law" is also stated in Chapter 25 of the *Tao Te Ching* by Lao Tzi.

The seventh conversation took place when the Yellow River met the sea. The flood season comes in autumn with the surging of the branches of the Yellow River. The geography of the Yellow River is such that west is elevated above the east. The Yellow River, with its origin from the Qinghai-Tibetan Plateau, runs east until it reaches the sea. This "running eastwards" of the Yellow River is simply a natural flow in accordance with nature without any external force.

Everything operates according to natural law. Everything can be mastered and freedom, according to Zhuangzi, can be achieved once this law is recognized and respected. Therefore, if a therapist can respect and believe in the client's inherent resilience and innate potential for growth, neither intervening nor over-imposing, staying with the client with a loving heart and allowing everything to happen in accordance with the natural law, a realm of freedom will very likely be achieved. Zhuangzi reminds us to accord with the changes of all things, set aside utilitarianism, and wait for the flowers to bloom quietly in therapy.

"To respect the destiny of a tree so that it fulfills its own nature" (順木之天, 以致其性). This is the secret of growing a tree as recorded in *The Story of Guo Tuotuo, Planter of Trees* (種樹郭橐駝傳) by Liu Zhongyuan from the Tang Dynasty (柳宗元, 773–819). Respecting the tree's natural law of growth and permitting it to "do its own thing" is the only way to "allow its full given nature to blossom forth" and maintain its unique identity as that particular tree. By fully respecting that each form of matter has its own propensities, and trusting that every seed and every sprout has the potential for its own reaching for the sky, we can then let the tree pursue its destiny naturally. Only through this non-interference can we allow for the unseen essence to avail itself of the freedom to flourish naturally. Liu Zhongyuan continues to quote Quo Tuotuo: "Therefore, all I have done is not impede its growth. I do not have the ability to accelerate its growth and production. I have only not wasted its fruit. I have not the ability for making it reproduce any faster" (故吾不害其長而已, 非有能碩茂也; 不抑耗其實而已, 非有能早而蕃之也).[3] By not violating the laws of its natural course, the tree can then be allowed to follow its inherent nature and mature spontaneously.

How does this apply to psychotherapy? To honor a person means to honor and accept the client as he is; to help an individual is to assist him to follow his own tempo and propensity for maturation. Continuously fostering new perspectives and encouraging progress is to assist the recovery of the client's own initiative and uncorrupted original nature. As noted earlier, the natural practice of psychotherapy is a state of "live and let live," without excessive intentionality and deliberations. Therefore, the therapist's life experience, vicissitudes, cultural background, professional skills, cumulative knowledge can all be part of the process—all of which serves to enhance therapeutic movement and is spontaneously elicited as needed.

The ability to accompany a child is essential to motherhood. In order to meet the needs of the child's continuous growth, the mother comes to understand and create coping strategies and skills. The mother must focus on the child's every behavior with unconditional love and comprehend his changing needs during the process of accompanying the child. The mother provides varying support and coping skills during different stages based upon the child's developmental needs. Thus the mother and child must jointly develop a developmental path that is individually tailored to the child. Therapists must accomplish the same with their clients.

Conversely, Zhuangzi wrote an outrageously mocking story about how a benefactor was repaid for his kindness by the drilling of seven holes in his body because everyone else had seven orifices for seeing, hearing, eating, and breathing. Of course the benefactor died in the end (Zhuangzi, 1998, p. xxxix). The story reminds us to respect the difference and uniqueness among individuals and not to judge others according to our own cultural norms or to replace others' experiences with our own. Everybody is unique and so are their experiences. The moral of the story is that if we "view the world of others through our own lenses" (以己心度人意, Chinese adage) and impose our own needs without being aware of our own prejudices, we may cost them their lives. Therefore, accordance with natural law includes respecting individual differences and needs along with the value of life (和个体差异、个别需求). Otherwise, it is impossible to make others happy.

In order to accompany Zhuangzi into a grand and pure spiritual realm, one is bound to view life from a different perspective, respect nature, and gain trust in the existence of a natural law that integrates everything harmoniously. Conversely, even kind intentions will end up badly if we breach natural law and impose our personal experience or the ways of existence of others onto our clients.

Part 4: Watching Fish and Fishing on the Hao River and the Pu River (Contentment自得、Adaptation自適、Freedom自由、Freedom to Be自在)

> Zhuangzi and Huizi were strolling along the dam of the Hao River when Zhuangzi said, "See how the minnows come out and dart around where they please! That's what fish really enjoy!"
> Huizi said, "You're not a fish—how do you know what fish enjoy?"
> Zhuangzi said, "You're not I, so how do you know that I don't know what fish enjoy?
> Huizi said, "I'm not you, so I certainly don't know what you know. On the other hand, you're certainly not a fish—so that still proves that you don't know what fish enjoy!"
> Zhuangzi said, "Let's go back to your original question, please. You asked me how I know what fish enjoy—so you already knew that I knew it when you asked the question. I know it by standing here beside the Hao."
> (Zhuangzi, 2006, Chapter 17, para. 51)

Zhuangzi's joy as he watched the fish is a construct of his inner world which is unencumbered by others. Such internal happiness exists in the subjective realm. Hence different individuals will feel differently about the same thing. Their happiness will be experienced differently. Therapists must consider and understand such subjectivity in order to help their clients explore their inner worlds and construct more positive thoughts through self-awareness. Huizi's challenge to Zhuangzi in this passage can enlighten us to Zhuangzi's wisdom in understanding the subjective. However, let us put aside this argument about subjectivity and "other minds" and focus on Zhuangzi's pursuit of natural freedom. This alone can be beneficial to therapists.

Zhuangzi's observation of the joy of the fish is in fact the outward manifestation of his own internal joy. One's subjective consciousness can enter into nature to create an I-Object spiritual realm of oneness. This bright and optimistic mental state, containing the life experience of Vipassana[4] and the joy of self-satisfaction, results from the extension of the mind and is full of inspiration. The actualization of this mental state cannot be achieved without a peaceful, easy, and unrestricted mind.

To feel the joy of the fishes as Zhuangzi does requires the ability to "remain calm in the face of disaster and let go of honor and humiliation" (處變不驚, 寵辱皆忘); "watch the blooming and fading of the flowers with a light heart; and fold and unfold leisurely with the clouds at the edge of the sky" (閑看庭前花開花落，漫隨天際雲卷雲舒 Chinese idiom). The poem, "any observation of nature comes from one's own peaceful mind; any change in one's mind is as natural as the changing of the four seasons" (萬物靜觀皆自得，四時佳興與人同) describes the realm beyond the material. Hence Zhuangzi is able to be "carefree whereever he travels" (我心處處自優遊).[5]

This pursuit of freedom is better demonstrated in the tale of Zhuangzi (1998) fishing by the Pu River found in Chapter 17. Zhuangzi was fishing by the Pu River when a messenger sent by the Emperor of Chu comes to invite him to join the civil administration. In response, Zhuangzi told the messenger the story of a sacred tortoise who is worshipped with the highest ceremony of the state three thousand years after his death. Then he asked the messenger rhetorically, if he was a tortoise, would he rather die and be worshipped or live and wag his tail in the mud? Zhuangzi makes his own choice clearly between an honorable death versus an unrestricted life. Zhuangzi's life goal is to repudiate any utilitarian aims and obligations in order to enjoy full freedom outside of the material world. Zhuangzi chose to be a tortoise wagging its tail in the mud, fishing by the Pu River, focusing on inner ease and freedom, rather than pursue the temptation of wealth and fame.[6]

Adhere to the inner world, unbound by external materials. "The heart is not driven by the physical body" (心不為形役, Tao Yuanming, Jin Dynasty), return to one's true self. In reality "whether the crowd comes or goes, they are motivated by profit" (天下熙熙，皆為利來；天下攘攘，皆為利往, Si'ma Qian, "史記"). One cannot acquire freedom unless he/she is not lured by profit but instead remains true to his/her spiritual pursuit. Such is Zhuangzi's influence upon the Chinese people and culture. The poem titled "Drinking" by Tao Yuanming states that "when clouds no longer float in from behind the mountain, the weary bird knows to return home" (雲無心以出岫，鳥倦飛而知還, 歸去來辭). This poem describes the unity with nature that occurs when one takes off one's uniform and returns home so that one can "pick chrysanthemum under the fence to the east and gaze leisurely upon the Southern mountain" (采菊東籬下，悠然見南山). Only a free mind can ensure living the aesthetic attitude of the arts. Such an attitude means to live an easy, carefree, and unrestricted life, pursuing freedom and transcending utilitarianism.

Some clients suffering from anxiety or obsession are in reality bothered by wealth and fame. Those with anxiety disorders fear loss and are unable to make any decisions. Such clients lack an unrestricted and carefree spirit. Therapists must help these individuals improve or cultivate their appreciation for the aesthetics that implicitly affect the client's character and value systems in all of their interactions.

As a master of parables, Zhuangzi serves as an excellent model for both therapists and clients. We must listen to every client and believe their life stories to be immortal legends if we desire to enter into our clients' inner worlds. Gaining a sense of curiosity from each of Zhuangzi's parables, and striving to understand each client's destiny, we can dance with and encounter our clients in the depth of their hearts.

Furthermore, Zhuangzi can also serve as a model for clients to achieve growth through the process of creating their own metaphors, analogies, and parables. Metaphors can help clients recall their past experiences and facilitate free association or further elaborations. They also help us to respect the client's own ability to problem solve, explore inner resources, and make changes based upon their own abilities and experiences. In many occasions, clients' own narratives boost self-esteem while reducing blame and defensiveness. In the space between parable and "reality," responsibility, choice, and self-efficacy are readily enhanced.

Zhuangzi has long been part of the original cultural spirit and personality of the Chinese intellect. Currently as I approach Zhuangzi again, a movement of standardization and normalization is progressing furiously, causing me significant enduring mental and physical stress. Under such circumstance, I spare my weekends writing about Zhuangzi. This conversation with Zhuangzi is for me a return to the enjoyment of spiritual freedom. My response to Zhuangzi's original intent of awakening people lost to reality is to shake off my shackles and return to nature, dispel my troubles and depression, pursue the authentic and joyful life, and swim in the unrestricted spiritual realm. Through the unrestrained nature of Zhuangzi's writings, the enormous and ambitious vision of the Autumn Floods reverberates through the mind of all mankind. To think as Zhuangzi thinks elicits happiness and detachment, leading to a life with rich aesthetics—this is what reviewing Zhuangzi brings to me today.

Notes

1 Permission to republish granted by University of Hawaii Press. Zhuangzi. (1998). *Wandering on the way: Early Taoist tales and parables of Chuang Tzu*. (V. Mair, Trans.). p. 153. Honolulu, HI: University of Hawaii Press.
2 http://www.prweb.com/releases/Tal_Ben-Shahar/positive_psychology/prweb1638824.htm
3 From the Chinese Article: 種樹郭橐駝傳
4 Vipassana meditation is an ancient practice taught by Buddha in which the mindfulness of breathing and of thoughts, feelings, and actions are being used to gain insight in the true nature of reality.

5 From the Chinese Poem: 宋代程灝《秋日偶成》
6 A short explication of this Parable of the Tortoise in the Mud can also be found in the chapter titled "Usefulness of Uselessness: Freedom before Death" in this book.

References

Shelley, P. B. (1993). *Selected poems of Percy Bysshe Shelley*. (Liangsheng Zha, Trans.). Beijing: People's Literature Publishing House.

Zhuangzi. (1998). *Wandering on the way: Early Taoist tales and parables of Chuang Tzu*. (V. Mair, Trans.). Honolulu, HI: University of Hawaii Press.

Zhuangzi. (2006). *The book of Chuang Tzu*. [Kindle for Android, 4.3.0.204]. (M. Palmer, Trans.). Retrieved from Amazon.com

Zhuangzi. (2013). *The complete works of Zhuangzi*. [Kindle for Android, 4.3.0.204]. (B. Watson, Trans.). Retrieved from Amazon.com

14

CAN YOU TELL A DRAGON FLY ABOUT ICE?

Implications of Zhuangzi's "Relative Gradations" for Therapeutic Care

Todd DuBose

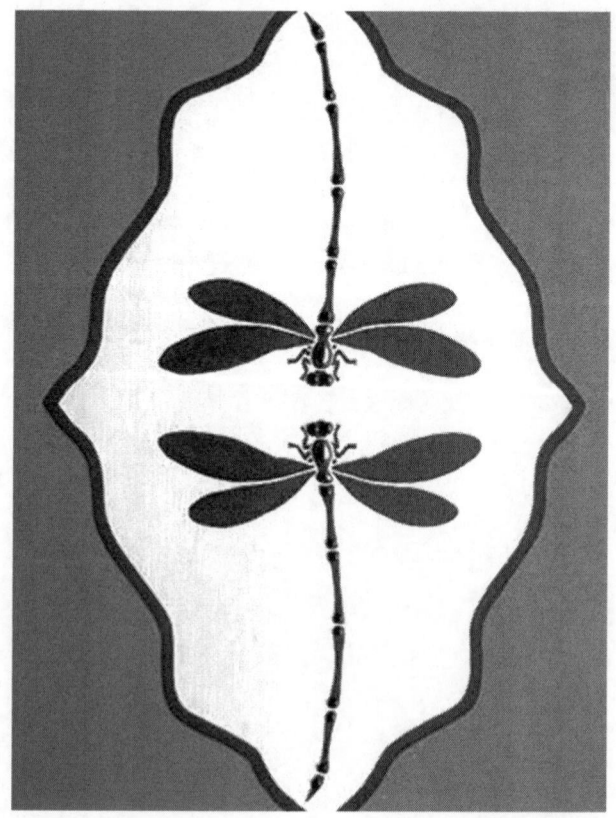

FIGURE 14.1 Created by Jimmy Hernandez

Embosom all the myriad of things, taking each one under your protective wings. . . . there being no long or short among them. The Way has neither beginning nor end, but things have life and death.[1]

Zhuangzi (1998, p. 157)

Introduction

Competently practicing psychology necessitates a transformation of traditionally held presumptions regarding persons, suffering, therapeutic care, and the good life through Eastern-Western dialogue. We are called to do more than just converse and share intrigue, but to be and practice differently—if we are serious about mutual respect across the seas. If we claim to be multiculturally sensitive, it follows that Western psyches and essentialist, absolute hierarchies of Truth can no longer hold hegemonic dominance in the field of psychology; in fact, one wonders whether we can even continue to call this field "psych"-ology (rather than *Tao*-ology, *Dasein*-ology, or *Existenz*-ology).[2]

I experienced this challenge most vividly during a recent trip to China, where I found many unexpected points of conversation between Taoism, existential-hermeneutical-phenomenological practices of care, and spirituality as lived meaning. What held the most valiance for me is the seeming exquisite compatibility between phenomenological bracketing, horizontalization, hermeneutical contextualization,[3] and the relative and radical validation of any way of being in the world on one hand, and the Taoist Zhuangzi's (350–300 B.C.E.) principles of "relative gradation" and the "equalization of all things" on the other.

Both traditions are getting at a particular heart-felt way of caring for others that: a) does not assume how someone is in the world, particularly in terms of how we would like that person to be; b) treats all expressions of meaning respectfully and equally important; and c) understands anything only in its particular context. Rather than discerning a dragonfly by the privileged qualities of an icy winter or the size of a whale, a dragonfly is understood only in the web of meaning in which its flight is given birth: summertime, among the family of insects that fly, who are predators of smaller insects while being prey to larger animals, whose lifespan is limited, and whose beauty is beyond measure. All of life follows suit: each aspect understood and experienced in its own way, with equal appreciation and awe.

This chapter focuses on the relationship between these traditions and their radical implications for contemporary psychology, existential or otherwise, East or West. More specifically, I will focus on the concept of "relative gradation," which implies the "equalization of all things," as discussed in the text "The Autumn Floods," and its implications for therapeutic care. "The Autumn Floods" is one of the outer chapters of *Zhuangzi*, which refers to not only the author himself, also known as Chuang Tzu, but also to the classical, foundational Taoist text itself.

The text is made of fables, or more accurately, parables, in "inner" and "outer" chapters. The parabolic nature of a parable opens up worlds if not inverts them in surprising and transformative ways. Although the parabolic themes in the chapters imply and build on each other, each chapter focuses on a particular point of wisdom in the foundation of classical Taoism. Also noted above, I will be referring to "The Autumn Floods", which is Chapter 17 of the outer chapters and focuses on "relative gradation," a concept with powerful implications for both Eastern and Western psychological thought and practice. Some scholars debate the authorship of the later chapters, but most agree that Master Zhuang did exist, and "The Autumn Floods" is quite congruent with the wisdom of the inner chapters.

I also find Zhuangzi's emphasis on relative gradations a possible forgotten antecedent to later Continental philosophy in the West, particularly Nietzsche's development of the "transvaluation of values" and his "perspectivism," as well as much in existential-hermeneutical-phenomenological thought that subsequently developed. Zhuangzi's thoughts on context and relative gradation read like much postmodern thought, and written from the fourth century nonetheless.[4] I write that these connections and influences are "possible," as, viewing historicity in metabletic ways—that is, as discontinuous and contextualized by a myriad of simultaneously converging happenings—I do not believe one can isolate unilateral influence of one person's thought on another in pure and clean ways without forcing connections and reading back into traditions lines of thought that are redactions rather than origins. Nevertheless, the similarities are uncanny and other scholars have explored these relationships in detail (Parkes, 1987, 1991, 1996; Guying, 1996; Nelson, 2004; Craig, 2007; Hoffman, Yang, Kaklauskas, & Chan, 2009). At the very least, the points of dialogue are vast, and the implications for therapeutic care more so. At most, which is my interest, the lineage and generation of these ideas provide bonding between divergent traditions in the service of a particular way of caring for others.

What Is "Relative Gradation"?

Before explicating the principle of relative gradation and its implications, I will quote heavily from Zhuangzi's own words to open our conversation. The first half of "The Autumn Floods" is listed in the beginning of this last section of the book. Throughout these reflections, I will be using Burton Watson's classic translation of Zhuangzi's work, which uses the name Chuang Tzu when citing him (Chuang Tzu, 1968/2014, Online Edition).

> Jo of the North Sea said, You can't discuss the ocean with a well frog—he's limited by the space he lives in. You can't discuss ice with a dragonfly—he's bound to a single season. You can't discuss the Way with a cramped scholar—he's shackled by his doctrines. Now you have come out beyond

your banks and borders and have seen the great sea—so you realize your own pettiness. From now on it will be possible to talk to you about the Great Principle.

(Chuang Tzu, 2014, p. 32)

Here Zhuangzi introduces us to the relativity of situations, not only regarding our created natures, but also our participation and freedom in co-creating our lived situations.

For instance, a cramped scholar, as Zhuangzi puts it, is not cramped solely due to genetics, nor is being shackled by his doctrines a situation that is beyond his control. We choose to be cramped by our doctrines, even though we often face realities of imposed beliefs, policies, or practices. Even then, though, we are free to be burdened, rebellious, or creative in response to such situations. What "is," therefore, is how we live these situations as there are no situations, no natures that are not at the same time co-created by what meaning they hold for us. A classroom is a real, physical space in an educational institution, but its meaning may be a place of inspiration or shame or boredom, as something desired or feared, as a classical non-negotiable, physical space, or an archaic relic in an age of online education. There is no "classroom" as such; only this or that classroom as meaningful for this or that person. Such is every aspect of life.[5]

Our possibilities are conditioned by our limitations in our "situated freedom," which is very compatible with an existential understanding of finitude. Situated freedom means that we are both limited by contingencies and resources in situations we find ourselves in, but are free to act or attitudinally shift how such situations matter to us; neither freedom nor limitation are absolute or without the other in some form or another. Notice, though, that as a Taoist, Zhuangzi recognizes that all nature has both limits and possibilities beyond the typical human-centric speciesism endemic to existential thought.

Vastness and smallness are common themes in Zhuangzi's work as well, primarily used to invite humility and displace the centricity from which we view nature. Putting it simply, Zhuangzi is reminding us that nature and life do not exist solely for us, is not measured only by what is near or far, large or small as we see it, and, bluntly, does not revolve around us. To me a dragonfly is small, but not to an ant. My understanding of strength may be measured in how much weight I can lift, until I come across an elephant clearing a pathway of trees in the jungle. This point is well put in the quote below:

Compare the area within the four seas with all that is between heaven and earth—is it not like one little anthill in a vast marsh? . . . When we refer to the things of creation, we speak of them as numbering ten thousand—and man is only one of them. . . . is he not like one little hair on the body of a horse? . . . From the point of view of differences, if we regard a thing as big because there is a certain bigness to it, then among all the ten thousand things there are none that are not big. If we regard a thing as small because there is a certain smallness to it, then among the ten thousand things there are none that are not small. If we know that heaven and earth are tiny grains and the tip of a hair is a range of mountains, then we have perceived the law of difference.

(Chuang Tzu, 2014, pp. 32–33)

Perceiving the law of difference means realizing that whatever indexical category we apply to existence, the same can be applied to anything else. Everything is large and everything is small, according to relative situations. This idea seems counter-intuitive as a flea is not as large as an elephant, but it is like an elephant in relation to a microscopic cell or an atom. An elephant is small in relation to a train, as a train is small in relation to an ocean. Things are not just *perceived* as relatively large or small, but "are" naturally both large *and* small; and, for that matter, good and bad, near and far, right and wrong, according to *lived* perspective.

Zhuangzi shows us that function is relative as well: "From the point of view of function, if we regard a thing as useful because there is a certain usefulness to it, then among all the ten thousand things there are none that are not useful" (Chuang Tzu, 2014, p. 33). The theme of useful- and uselessness is discussed at length in the introductory chapter of this book. *What* we are is *how* we are in situations, as things or persons. Purposefulness is situated:

A beam or pillar can be used to batter down a city wall, but it is no good for stopping up a little hole—this refers to a difference in function. Thoroughbreds like Ch'i-chi and Hua-liu could gallop a thousand li in one day, but when it came to catching rats they were no match for the wildcat or the weasel—this refers to a difference in skill. The horned owl catches fleas at night and can spot the tip of a hair, but when daylight comes, no matter how wide it opens its eyes, it cannot see a mound or a hill—this refers to a difference in nature.

(Chuang Tzu, 2014, p. 34)

Much like Martin Heidegger's (1962) understanding of something as "ready-to-hand," a thing is what it is according to its function, such as when a hammer hammers, rather than drills. But for a relative gradist, even a hammer may function differently in a relatively different situation.

It does not make sense for the owl to assess its "owl-ness" by a criteria of what it means to be a horse or a wildcat. Its nocturnal prowess is neither better or worse than the skills of a day hunter, just different. Difference neither means deficient nor exemplary, but simply "is." Which is the better fruit, an apple or an orange? From a relatively graded position, the answer is: it depends on preference, by this or that person, in this or that circumstance. The rightness or wrongness of what "is" depends on preference and how it serves (or not) a particular goal:

> From the point of view of preference, if we regard a thing as right because there is a certain right to it, then among the ten thousand things there are none that are not right. If we regard a thing as wrong because there is a certain wrong to it, then among the ten thousand things there are none that are not wrong.
>
> *(Chuang Tzu, 2014, pp. 33–34)*

Relative gradation is not suspended when it comes to moral decision-making. What is right and what is wrong are relative to various situations, and according to the lived values and purposes of such situations.

Therefore, Zhuangzi's unfolding of the principle of relative gradation in this fabled dialogue between The Lord of the River and Jo of the North Sea emphasizes the relativity of measurement, knowing, and life itself. The equalization of all things is possible based on relative gradations such that any indexical conclusion regarding proximity, amount, function, or meaning is relative to context and may very well change given a different positioning, project, or purpose. Typically, measurement presumes an essentialist norm from which something can be compared, such as intelligence, distance, heaviness, success, or a delicious meal. What Zhuangzi notes is that such essentialist, immutable norms are themselves relative to situation and perspective.

Moreover, nothing is forever; what "is" is constituted by its situation, and changes when the situation changes. In one moment I am the one who teaches, until I research and learn from others. I cannot say that I am a teacher in an essentialist, absolute way, nor that I am a learner in an absolute way. I am both in different circumstances, neither one trumping the other in significance. No indexical conclusion about measurement or function is absolute. Wisdom is the ability to recognize not only the relativity of each experience, but also the relativity of permanence and impermanence. Whatever one's experience, the next moment co-constructs it and brings its transformation.

> There is no end to the weighing of things, no stop to time, no constancy to the division of lots, no fixed rule to beginning and end. Therefore great wisdom observes both far and near, and for that reason recognizes small without considering it paltry, recognizes large without considering it unwieldy, for it knows that there is no end to the weighing of things. . . . The Way is without beginning or end, but things have their life and death—you cannot rely upon their fulfillment. One moment empty, the next moment full—you cannot depend upon their form.
>
> *(Chuang Tzu, 2014, pp. 32, 34)*

Zhuangzi invites us to consider that any conclusion about any of these indexical measurements can be applied to any and everything. To us, the tip of a horse's hair seems miniscule, but not to a flea. The planet seems enormous, until we see it in relation to the Milky Way. In turn, the Milky Way is miniscule when placed in relation to other galaxies. Chicago to London seems far until I travel from Chicago to Hong Kong. My coffee cup functions quite well in holding my coffee, but not as a tool to trim the bushes.

A fulfilling life is lived in accordance with the Way, which also means in accordance with the naturalism of relative gradation. Working against how things are in existence self-frustrates. Relative gradations are a part of what we know, how nature is, and how we practically live out our daily activities. Needing something to be otherwise than what it is, is a life lived in opposition with the Tao.

> It has a clear understanding of past and present, and for that reason it spends a long time without finding it tedious, a short time without fretting at its shortness. . . it does not delight if it acquires something nor worry if it loses it, for it knows that there is no constancy to the division of lots. It comprehends the Level Road, and for that reason it does not rejoice in life nor look on death as a calamity, for it knows that no fixed rule can be assigned to beginning and end.
>
> *(Chuang Tzu, 2014, p. 32)*

In sum, Zhuangzi's "Level Road," or "equalization of all things," recognizes that all sentient being is relative to goal, situation, and function. No absolute or permanent conclusion in measurement of significance is in accordance with the Way. The naturalness of the Way equalizes us all and is taken up in incomparable ways within incomparable contexts.

Implications of Relative Gradation for Therapeutic Care

Rather than any particular prescriptive approach to therapeutic care, the congruence of this East-West practice lies in its ability to clarify the possibilities particular to a person and situation within what is non-negotiable about that situation's limitations; its ability to disclose how meaning is discerned through relative contextualization; and its capacity to radically bracket what "should be" the case in order to allow "what is" to show itself in its own way, relative to its situated context, and to remain horizontal in seeing meaning in any and every moment. Creating this kind of space for others in therapeutic care allows for transformation to occur, but a transformation that does not instigate, coerce, or manipulate change, particularly change that has as its purpose "getting" someone from a deficient place to a "better," corrected way of being based on a hegemonic norm of the appropriate way of being in the world. The alignment with the ancient principle of Wu Wei is obvious.

Therapeutic care that practices from this perspective demands much from us, though; it calls us to attend to our absolutism, which is most often flushed out when we get "tight" in encounters with what we index as "other" or "different," especially when we begin to classify such disturbing experiences in pathologizing ways. We are called to release allegiances, absolutes, and essentials for relative, situated variance and mutability of who a person is, how he or she suffers, how to care, and what is considered a "good" outcome. As our perspective is limited in what we can know, how well bracketed, relative, and horizontal we are depends on the situation in which we find ourselves and what meaning we give to it. It is easier to embrace a radical respect and understanding of something in its own way when we like or agree with its presence; the challenge comes when what confronts us is at odds with our deeply held convictions. We may not even know how deep our convictions may be until we find ourselves defensive, wanting to change the other, not giving a hearing to an alternative view of matters. This information is helpful, though, as it signals a departure from a stance of relative gradation.

I remember working with a man in therapeutic care who was in a terrible dilemma of this sort. He saw his duty as a husband and father to be the family's spiritual leader and teacher. His wife and daughter, however, were seeking a more egalitarian family way of relating and did not want to be taught by him. I was initially able to clear space in an equalizing and horizontal way, respecting the relative gradation of how this person's values were operating in another way than my own inclusive, egalitarian preferences in family life. As time went on, though, my capacities to stay bracketed in a relatively graded place began to wobble. My collapse from this stance came one night when I felt frustrated he would not "be taught" by me that there are other ways to be faithful and stay married. He wouldn't listen to me, and I pointed out my frustration at not being "received" much like his wife and daughter were experienced by him as not "receiving" him. I thought it was a great moment to show a parallel process occurring for experiential "growth." I am not sure how he resolved his dilemma, as he never returned to talk with me about it, nor returned my calls.

It would be simple to either pathologize him or me for the breach of empathy. We could say that he wasn't open to growing, or that I was imposing inclusive egalitarian values on him. Either conclusion, though, privileges one value as "better than" another, collapsing a relatively graded stance. Both hierarchy and egalitarian structures have their merit and meaning. The therapist's task is to create an atmosphere of relative gradation for exploration. Comporting oneself in this way may come across as not caring for "the right way" to live, but in actuality may offer deeper compassion and flexibility to explore any way of be-ing in the world. Life, the Way, not therapists, confronts us and our contingent choices.

The question remains, though, as to why, if existence is relatively graded, do we shy away from living congruently with this awareness. There are a myriad of answers to this question, but at least part of the answer is that we are called to recognize the humility of our perspective, to let go of controlling how others should live their lives, and open ourselves to be changed by a radical respect for divergent ways of living from our own. Not living congruently with the Way will naturally leave us with the consequences of the non-negotiables in life. For instance, as embodied beings, we need to rest at some point, even if in excellent shape with extensive capacity for endurance. If an Olympic athlete does not rest, she can find her immune system compromised and become ill. As a lover of cakes, pies, and the sweetness of the culinary arts, I can eat all I want, but the natural contingencies of my choice will lead to excessive weight gain. Staying horizontal, gaining weight, and enjoying delicious cuisine is neither better nor worse than staying thin and eating low-calorie meals, just different, each with different consequences, each pathway available for choice.

Not only are we embodied beings, but also beings that live in relationship, that are limited by our perspectives, live in space and time, are mortal, have choice, are never out of a situation of some sort or another, and are embedded in the webs of meaning our languages provide. No matter how free we are, these non-negotiables of existence will not go away. The Taoist knows this tacitly, and works with these aspects of nature. The existential therapist, likewise, clarifies how we are attuning to our ways of living in the world in concern with (or at odds with) our existence.

For instance, eagerly waiting to board a delayed plane for a much-anticipated vacation may experience the given of temporality quite differently than waiting for a boring lecture to end, or for painful neuropathy to end, or when waiting for the test results of a possible terminal illness. Temporality is the common given while how we take it up is relative. Hence, there is no essential "time." The therapeutic task is not to privilege one way of taking up one's ontological giveness over others; such reactions make sense as each and every reaction calls for respect in the equalization of all things. Relative gradation is the reality of a myriad of realities. But it is important to realize that this myriad of ten thousand experiences occur in the context of a shared Way, or a shared existential condition.

Clinical discussions are common about the nature of reality and who gets to determine it are nearly ubiquitous in each session of therapeutic care. This dilemma is concentrated among couples who "see it differently" and see this situation as a failure of relating, simply due to presumptions about needing to be on the "same page." They are on the same page as human beings participating in the non-negotiable given of co-existence, but relative gradation shows that such co-existence is taken up from the values embedded in different life stories. Rather than forcing a homogeneity, which may be pleasurable for the time being, the relatively graded therapist is aware that existence is radically incomparable and relative and, instead, walks with couples to find win/win resolutions of their divergently lived experiences.

A father may not want his daughter to date a particular person, while her mother gives permission. Rather than see this as a no-win situation, or appealing to a hierarchical/compliance resolution, a win/win can occur if both stances are heard and horizontally validated in their significance. The father's prohibition may serve his concern to protect his daughter from being hurt, while the mother's permission serves her desire to see her daughter make good choices and to support the delight of love in her eyes. Both stances have merit. Both require realizing that non-negotiable limits are present as well as choices within those limits: the father cannot be with his daughter at all times no matter how much he wants to protect her, nor can he control how the world will respond; the mother cannot control whether or not her daughter will be happy or make good decisions and very well may view a "good" decision differently than her daughter. But parenting their daughter with protection, belief in her growth, and a desire for her joy can be done in a myriad of ways—all equally valuable.

Facts do occur, but are nonetheless weighted differently according to what valiance and meaning something holds for someone. For instance, in addressing relational conflict, one partner will talk of feeling intimidated by another's yelling, while the accused one will insist he isn't yelling. In light of relative gradations, a physical measure of amplitude (of sound loudness) often does not resolve this issue.

Amplitude may indeed be very low relative to the noise in a rock concert or a football stadium. But the stern facial expressions, the steeled tone of voice, the grit teeth, the context of relational politics, and resource security all contribute to the experience of "yelling." An event is occurring, and thus not imagined. But "yelling" may be named as being passionate or intense, even though experienced by the recipient as frightening and distancing. A relatively graded view recognizes both stances, while privileging neither one.

Part of the relative gradation of such experiences has to do with the project that is operative. Inviting couples to not only consider the possibility that there is no Truth (capital "T") and that each truth has lived meaning to understand, but also to discern what their goal is with each other, often deconstructs opposition as irreconcilable (which itself is predicated on a non-negotiable norm established by one in power) to an opposition that co-constitutes.

What is "right" has to do with whether they want to win an argument or relate as partners in collaboration. Here the functional gradation varies according to task. If one wants to intimidate or shame, then yell. If one wants to be heard by a particular person who recoils from yelling, then yelling does not fit the function of being heard. Again, the task is not to judge yelling as good or bad, but to explore how it functions relative to one's desired goal.

The principle of relative gradation is also part of the practice of hermeneutical reframe in therapeutic care. Reframing, or punctuating significance differently, is made possible by relative gradation. A troubled parent comes to therapy to address persistent sadness and malaise since the departure of her last adult child for college. Time cannot be reversed and she missed him as the child he used to be. Yet, the beauty of becoming a man and thriving in a new chapter of life holds promise and beauty in another kind of way for her, if she can relatively be open to seeing it otherwise. Neither perspective is granted primacy, as any and all moments are meaningful in the equalization of all things. What is important, though, is whether or not she is aware of life's relative gradation and its promise of variation, perspective, and function without shaming herself or her son for not doing it the "right" way. Talk of the "right" way raises another troubling dilemma common to therapeutic practice and to which relative gradation offers a challenge.

Rank-ordered scales of measurement may grant markings of progress, such as losing weight or increasing one's semester grade. But rank-ordered scales of measurement can also be very oppressive when one negatively measures oneself in light of an essentialist and absolute norm, which blatantly inattends to the principle of relative gradation. Concerns about how one measures up to another's expectations, particularly when privileging the other's values over one's own values, invite a sacrifice of integrity and often much shame regarding one's adequacy, relevance, and loveability.

The oppression of rank-ordered scales of measurement is present when we compare each other's ways of being as somehow better or worse than ourselves, while ignoring the uniqueness of each way of being in the world as valuable and meaningful. As Zhuangzi pointed out, "the K'uei envies the millipede, the millipede envies the snake, the snake envies the wind, the wind envies the eye, and the eye envies the mind" (Chuang Tzu, 2014, p. 35). Each moment, each thought, each action, each situation has its say and is no better or worse than anything else. Envy forgets that what one seeks is itself relative.

The seduction of perfection, betterment, growth, on which therapeutic care often capitalizes, is powerfully attractive only if the goal is seen as without comparison—a false dream predicated on the presumption of a non-relative, non-contextual, immutable resting place. Essentialist norms are chosen ways of privileging one value over others, in spite of the relativity of ontology and epistemological perspectivism. One "is" where one "is" at any given time, neither good nor bad, and any and all moments are transitory. "From the point of view of the Way, things have no nobility or meanness" (Chuang Tzu, 2014, p. 33).

Being with others in such a radically validating way requires the ability to release allegiances, drop essentials, and open ourselves to meaning of any and every moment. "Be broad and expansive. . . . Embrace the ten thousand things universally—how could there be one you should give special support to? This is called being without bent" (Chuang Tzu, 2014, p. 34). The myriad of things in life have their place, but nothing too much; a great man or woman understands that *each experience is unique to itself, but no experience reigns.* This "lived relativity" is not an apathetic nonchalance, but a compassionate equalization, horizontaliza-tion, validation of all moments. A relatively graded therapist lives these values, and thus becomes relatively graded him or herself; the therapist becomes the myriad of things. In doing so, there is a place for anyone in any situation.

Radical Implications of Relative Gradation for East and West: Critiques and Challenges

As everything has its place, so do critiques and challenges of a relativist position. In spite of the massive implications for political structures and ethical positions in both the East and the West of the principle of relative gradation, given the limits of this discussion, I will keep my comments to therapeutic practice. Thera-peutic care, though, discloses both political and ethical convictions nonetheless. A stance of relative gradation is most challenging in therapeutic care when considering how relative we can be without having to draw absolutist, non-negotiable lines, as well as when addressing the implications this stance has for multicultural dialogue.

Zhuangzi's relative gradations, like other relativist positions, welcome an often uninvited guest to the table: the threat of nihilism. Relative equalizations and multi-partiality tend to invite the question: "If there is no Absolute Truth, then anything goes, and if anything goes, does anything matter?" If one truly is radi-cally validating of the horizontalization beyond a mere romanticism of this way of living, then one also sees the beautiful in the ugly, or the ugly as beautiful, as in the case of Zhuangzi's parable of the useless tree, to recall Nietzsche's emphasis on *amor fati*, including validation of the revolting, the horrifying, and the destructive (Nietzsche, 1967, p. 714).

If everything has its place, though, and if there is no absolute "right" and "wrong," how do we take up child abuse, spousal battering, rape, assassinations for profit, a child's blood on the streets as an artifact of unrelenting, retaliative gang violence, and other events? When these examples show up in consideration of a relativist position, discussants typically reach for absolutes. If there are abso-lutes regarding certain behaviors that are unethical regardless of the situation, then a relativist position can only go so far. Mandated reporting, child protection, and a duty to warn others who are targets of harm are examples of lines drawn by our professional codes of responsibility that limit a relativist stance. But wouldn't a relatively graded stance still call for situational discernment in any of these responsibilities?

What may be helpful in addressing this dilemma is that understanding and collusion are not identical. One need not share the lived values of another person one is trying to understand. Too often when more disturbing ways of relating come across our pathway, we cease wanting to understand and reach to patholo-gize. The very act of pathologizing another's thoughts, feelings, or actions returns to a privileged norm from which to denote deviance. The principle of relative gradation need not be ignored, though, when we come across what is disturbing for us. When counseling someone who has raped or killed, radical validation pursues an understanding of the project rape or killing seeks to serve. The rightness or wrongness of these acts are understood in light of the intended purpose. Such as act may be "right" in the use of power and control to exact revenge or enforce response, but "wrong" in the project of respecting the integrity and the preservation of life. A sniper with 160 confirmed kills may be seen as a serial killer by one standard and as a hero by another. A pedophile's project of grooming children serves the project of securing uncomplicated sex with others who are easily controlled, while violating the projects of developmental differentiation and the protection of children. The relativity rests in the various criteria that contextualize one's comportment in the world.

As uncomfortable as this discussion may feel, the therapist who practices from a relatively graded stance does not privilege in the therapy one way of being over others, in spite of personal convictions one way or another. The therapist presumes significance in any and all situations, and provides space for clarification of a person's ontic ways of living out the human condition, or the Way, knowing all too well that destructive ways of living out the Way merit a hearing as well. Paradoxically, often the hearing of what no one wants to hear without agendas to fix, cure, or alter provides transformative possibilities of alternative ways of being non-destructive with others. Our level of discomfort in discussions of this nature light up the limits of openness to diversity.

Most of us consider ourselves open and receptive of diverse ways of being in the world, that is until we come up on an "otherness" that is disturbing for us. We tend to then pathologize in order to justify or handle our own discomfort of what is uncanny, revolting, or horrifying. Examples abound: "Well, she is borderline and you know how they relate," or "To kill all those people, he must be crazy," or "He must be struggling with something much deeper to act that way." For that matter, I cannot think of anything, any action, thought, or feeling, that cannot be pathologized in one way or another if we wanted to do so. Taking too much time to complete a task can be seen as careful patience or as obsessive-compulsive delay. Wanting to be alone can be understood as enjoying solitude or as unhealthily withdrawing. Eating too much can be seen as gluttony or as the ability to enjoy sensuous celebration. Killing can be seen as necessary to protect others' lives or as the breaking of a most universal commandment regarding the preservation of life.

What I have called "radical validation" elsewhere (DuBose, 2014) rests well in the heritage of relative gradation of Zhuangzi. All is sunshine and giggles as long as we are in agreement with what we are trying to understand, and if the lived values we encounter are similar to ours. Dialogue becomes difficult when we are disturbed by an experience, in response to which we then evoke demarcating categorization such as "different" or "other" in devaluing ways. Being open to diversity means also being open to understanding what disturbs us, and to understanding how "being disturbed" discloses a return to essentialist norms and an immigration from relative gradation. In doing so, we posit an essentialist stance, which is typically our own, as normal, healthy, or "right," from which we designate "other" and "different." I consider this move to be a "segregation of diversity." This is the paradox of subjects such as "diversity studies." What would be considered a "non-diversity" study? From the stance of relative gradation, there is no norm from which to designate an absolute "other" or "different" from one stance alone. Is there a moment that does not exhibit uniqueness, as well as otherness and difference, according to perspective and stance?

If it is the case that every experience, every way of being in the world, has its own story, its own way of ontically taking up ontological throwness and possibility, then there is no same to an-other, no likeness to difference that is static and one way. The Way is, as Zhuangzi knew, a *myriad* of things. Moreover, my difference and otherness to you, or yours to me, are not generic, but particular.

This is what is problematic about "case presentations." More often than not when a "case" is presented, a computed list of essentialist data is reported regarding indexed identity predicates when presenting a "case" rather than describing and bringing to life a person in his or her relative and radically incomparable uniqueness and significance. Someone is not a 45–year-old, divorced, Asian mother of three children. How does she feel about being 45? What is her experience of being Asian? Female? Divorced? How is it parenting these children? What is each relationship with each child like? What is it like when they are together? When do they laugh, cry? What is their favorite time together? Do her friends understand her in pain and celebration? Does this friend understand certain things that another friend does not? The questions literally are infinite, if we take relative gradation to its logical conclusion.

Lastly, diagnostic language, whether from the DSM or from the family table, whether "narcissistic" or "lazy," is indexed against a back-dropped norm of deficit correction, aiming at how things should be in relation to a certain norm. Relative gradation does not grade ice as greater or lesser than a dragonfly. It simply understands the beauty of each in its own way. The relatively graded therapist is called to do the same.

Conclusion or Continuation? Where to Go from Here?

I wanted to end these reflections with some suggested directions to explore in light of Zhuangzi's relative gradation in and beyond therapeutic care and psychology. I am not sure how the East has addressed the pressure of proving that one's way of care is an empirical, evidence-based best practice. What is problematic from the perspective of relative gradation about this designation is continually overlooked, or ignored, in much of the West. What is empirical, evidential, and "best," from a relatively graded stance is, of course, relative. The science of psychology remains obstinate in privileging logical positivist, experimental values as the norm for discerning this designation, a blatant violation of relative gradation. As I opened our discussion with the point that true dialogue between the East and the West requires more than the sharing of ethnic differences, an authentic openness to such dialogue also means a horizontalization and a relative grading of what is considered data, truth, science, evidence, and outcome (DuBose, 2013, 2014). Zhuangzi did not include quantitative stats or scatter graphs in his writings, but how dare we say this fourth-century sage was devoid of "evidence" of the Way?

Another next step in practicing a relatively graded-based psychology is to explore the implications for assessment. No longer can we appeal to a substantial, essentialist self. Consistent with the existential stance that who we are is how we are in situations, assessment summaries can no longer be absolute, nor pertain to an isolated individual that is de-contextualized and a/situational. A relatively graded assessment would assess situations of beings in the world. It would assess situations rather than persons. The situational assessments, or the assessment of lived events, is itself relative. Someone who is anxious, distractible, or withdrawn is so in situations, at certain times, and may very well be different in the same situation at a different time and place. This is also what is problematic about standardized testing based on a comparative norm.

Likewise, how we suffer is relative and horizontal. There is no need for a hierarchy of who suffers more, or whether one kind of suffering needs attention over others. A small child's mourning over the loss of a stuffed animal is no less or more significant than the loss of a child. The level of suffering, how one suffers, whether it is inherent or ameliorated is relative to each person, situation, and perspective.

A final challenge to address in future explorations of the implications of relative gradation is in discerning how to live together in a relative world. Would such a world be an anarchic one, and would an anarchic world necessarily be chaotic and destructive? We are all a part of a shared Way and shared ontological givens. We all radically take up this shared condition in unique, relative ways. A relatively graded society would be such that a collective cannot be a homogenization nor can a system based on individualism ignore the co-constituted situated freedom that creates such individuals. What we share provides the basis for empathy and compassion, while how we radically and incomparably take up our shared giveness respects the relative gradation of a myriad of existences. But this challenge, as the other ones before it, merit much thought and conversation beyond the parameters of these reflections and of my ability to resolve these dilemmas.

Hence, a life of relative gradation is never completed. Radical validation of the unique, though co-constituted, moment in all its relative, incarnate glory merits further study. Our challenges will continue in learning how to be resolute without being hegemonic, how to be egalitarian without being amorphous, how to value without rank-ordering, and how to accept whatever is the case, including the moments when we are unaccepting. Can you tell a dragonfly about ice? As I continue to ponder a lifetime of wisdom in this query, I wonder if there has ever been an event where a dragonfly has been encased in ice . . . or, at least, such a thing as an icy dragonfly? I bet Zhuangzi would know where to find one. Whatever end or conclusion we find to this question, it is temporary. There is no end. Where we stand has its merit and "thisness" that has its integrity, but only in its place, and only as transitory. Practicing this way requires tolerance, nay, an *embrace* of relative mutability, but being in motion keeps us humble, and hence, caring well.

Notes

1 Permission to republish granted by University of Hawaii Press. Zhuangzi. (1998). *Wandering on the way: Early Taoist tales and parables of Chuang Tzu*. (V. Mair, Trans.). p. 157. Honolulu, HI: University of Hawaii Press.
2 Essentialism and hegemony are words often used in this paper to describe an enforced attempt in thinking and practice to take what is unique and particular to one experience, thing, or person and apply it generically across all circumstances. Doing so nullifies the radical incomparability of each situation, thing, or person in its own character and nature. I have discussed this point more extensively in DuBose, T. (2012). Essentialism. In Leeming, D. (Ed.), *Encyclopedia of critical psychology*. Norwell, MA: Springer Science and Business Media, 599–604.
3 Bracketing, horizontalization, and hermeneutical contextualization, so central to the traditions of phenomenology and hermeneutics, mean respectively, *bracketing*: keeping one's biases from clouding one's understanding of an experience as it is and showing itself rather than as we would like it to be; *horizontalization*: privileging all experiences as meaningful, and meaningful in equal ways; and *hermeneutical contextualization*: understanding any one particular word, feeling, thought, experience, or event in light of a larger context, or larger/whole story, from where it gets its meaning.
4 Christina Gschwandtner (2012) has synopsized that postmodernism "challenges the idea that there is one overall coherent version of the Truth . . . (or) that it is possible to get to some objective position from which to see the world in a neutral fashion . . . (and emphasizes) that we always speak from within a particular . . . context and that truth is thus always embodied and particular (p. 11)." Zhuangzi's writings on relative gradation and the centrality of perspectivism and context, in my reading of them, would concur with most or much of postmodernism on the point of relativity.
5 Contemporary Continental philosophy in the West is not seeing a challenge to the age-old phenomenological ideas of correlationalism, or the idea that reality cannot be understood outside of what it means to a person; that is to say, there is no reality beyond or behind how it is experienced. The long-standing debate that has not resurfaced between phenomenologists and speculative realists is interesting in that Zhuangzi's understanding of both the epistemology and ontology of the Way, in my opinion, offers a win/win resolution to this debate. If interested in the intricate philosophical debate, see Sparrow (2014).

References

Chuang Tzu. (2014). Autumn floods. In B. Watson (Trans.), *The complete works of Chuang Tzu* (pp. 31–38). Terebess Asia Online (TAO). Retrieved from http://terebess.hu/english/chuangtzu.html Chapter 17.

Craig, E. (2007). Tao psychotherapy: Introducing a new approach to humanistic practice. In *Humanist Psychologist, 35*, 109–133.

DuBose, T. (2012). Essentialism. In D. Leeming (Ed.), *Encyclopedia of critical psychology* (pp. 599–604). Norwell, MA: Springer Science and Business Media.

DuBose, T. (2013). Let the Kierkegaardian comedy resume: Faith-phobia and faithful leaping in evidence-based criteria for therapeutic care. In *Existential Analysis, 24*(1), 70–81.

DuBose, T. (2014). Engaged understanding for lived meaning. In *Journal of Contemporary Psychotherapy, 44*(3), Published Online First: DOI 10.1007/s10879-014-9276-x.

Gschwandtner, C. (2012). *Postmodern apologetics? Arguments for God in contemporary philosophy*. New York: Fordham University Press.

Guying, C. (1996). Zhuang Zi and Nietzsche: Plays of perspectives. In J. Sellmann (Trans.), G. Parkes (Ed.), *Nietzsche and Asian thought* (pp. 115–129). Chicago: The University of Chicago Press.

Heidegger, M. (1962). *Being and time*. (J. Macquarrie & E. Robinson, Trans.). New York: Harper & Row.

Hoffman, Yang, & Kaklauskas, Chan (Eds.). (2009). *Existential psychology East-West*. Colorado Springs: University of the Rockies Press.

Nelson, E. (2004). Responding to heaven and earth: Daoism, Heidegger and ecology. In *Environmental Philosophy, 1*(2), 65–74.

Nietzsche, F. (1967). *Basic writings of Nietzsche*. (W. Kaufmann, Ed. and Trans.). New York, NY: Penguin.

Parkes, G. (1987). *Heidegger and Asian thought*. Honolulu, HI: University of Hawaii Press.

Parkes, G. (1991). *Nietzsche and Asian thought*. Chicago: The University of Chicago Press.

Parkes, G. (1996). *Heidegger's hidden sources: East Asian influences on Heidegger's work*. London: Routledge.

Sparrow, T. (2014). *The end of phenomenology: Metaphysics and the new realism*. Edinburgh: Edinburgh University Press.

Zhuangzi. (1998). *Wandering on the way: Early Taoist tales and parables of Chuang Tzu*. (V. Mair, Trans.). Honolulu, HI: University of Hawaii Press.

INDEX